YOGA SADHANA PANORAMA

VOLUME THREE

With kind regards, ॐ and prem

Swami Niranjan

YOGA SADHANA PANORAMA

VOLUME THREE

Swami Niranjanananda Saraswati

*Lectures and satsangs given in 1997
in Mumbai, India, in Aix-les-Bains and
Aube, France, and in Slovenia.*

Yoga Publications Trust, Munger, Bihar, India

Published by Yoga Publications Trust
    First edition 2005

ISBN: 81-86336-34-6

Publisher and distributor: Yoga Publications Trust, Ganga Darshan, Munger, Bihar, India.

Website: www.yogavision.net

Printed at Thomson Press (India) Limited, New Delhi, 110001

SWAMI SIVANANDA SARASWATI

Swami Sivananda was born at Pattamadai, Tamil Nadu, in 1887. After serving as a medical doctor in Malaya, he renounced his practice, went to Rishikesh and was initiated into Dashnami sannyasa in 1924 by Swami Vishwananda Saraswati. He toured extensively throughout India, inspiring people to practise yoga and lead a divine life. He founded the Divine Life Society at Rishikesh in 1936, the Sivananda Ayurvedic Pharmacy in 1945, the Yoga Vedanta Forest Academy in 1948 and the Sivananda Eye Hospital in 1957. During his lifetime Swami Sivananda guided thousands of disciples and aspirants all over the world and authored over 200 books.

SWAMI SATYANANDA SARASWATI

Swami Satyananda was born at Almora, Uttar Pradesh, in 1923. In 1943 he met Swami Sivananda in Rishikesh and adopted the Dashnami sannyasa way of life. In 1955 he left his guru's ashram to live as a wandering mendicant and later founded the International Yoga Fellowship in 1956 and the Bihar School of Yoga in 1963. Over the next 20 years Swami Satyananda toured internationally and authored over 80 books. In 1987 he founded Sivananda Math, a charitable institution for aiding rural development, and the Yoga Research Foundation. In 1988 he renounced his mission, adopting kshetra sannyasa, and now lives as a paramahamsa sannyasin.

SWAMI NIRANJANANANDA SARASWATI

Swami Niranjanananda was born in Madhya Pradesh in 1960. At the age of four he joined the Bihar School of Yoga and was initiated into Dashnami sannyasa at the age of ten. From 1971 he travelled overseas and toured many countries for the next 11 years. In 1983 he was recalled to India and appointed President of Bihar School of Yoga. Since then he has guided the development of Ganga Darshan, Sivananda Math, Yoga Publications Trust and the Yoga Research Foundation. In 1990 he was initiated as a paramahamsa and in 1993 anointed preceptor in succession to Swami Satyananda. Bihar Yoga Bharati was founded under his direction in 1994. He has authored over 20 books and guides national and international yoga programs.

SWAMI SATYASANGANANDA SARASWATI

Swami Satyasangananda (Satsangi) was born on 24th March 1953, in Chandorenagore, West Bengal. From the age of 22 she experienced a series of inner awakenings which led her to her guru, Swami Satyananda. From 1981 she travelled ceaselessly with her guru in India and overseas and developed into a scholar with deep insight into the yogic and tantric traditions as well as modern sciences and philosophies. She is an efficient channel for the transmission of her guru's teachings. The establishment of Sivananda Math in Rikhia is her creation and mission, and she guides all its activities there, working tirelessly to uplift the weaker and underprivileged areas. She embodies compassion with clear reason and is the foundation of her guru's vision.

Contents

Exploring the
Potential of the Mind

Mumbai, India, 16–22 January 1997

Mind Potential

Imagine there is a printout of a computer image on the ground. An ant wanders onto the paper and walks around it. If you were to ask the tiny ant what it could see, it would reply, "I see a white field with black spots, circles of different shapes and sizes, on it." That is the only description the ant would be able to give you. If you were to ask the ant if it could see anything else, it would say, "No, just a white area with black polka dots." If you were then to ask the ant to climb onto your finger and you lifted it up and asked what it could see, the ant would reply, "Now I see an image, a picture."

What was it that perceived the picture as a white field with black spots initially and what was it that perceived the picture as an image? The events that happen around us and the experiences we have are only a recognition of existing situations and events, but we only encounter these events at specific times in our lives. Therefore, it is said that there is nothing new under the sun. Everything that you have experienced has existed before in the form of an object, in the form of an event in time and in space. Sometimes we are able to recognize and rationalize it, and then we say we have had an experience. Prior to that, the experience was non-existent.

Life goes on. Creation and destruction happen all the time in nature, that is the cosmic law. Creation, everything you perceive, is nothing but an expression of life. Even what you perceive in an inanimate object is life. Life is not confined to movement, motion and the senses. Life is the recognition of an event as and when it happens. Life is the realization of where one is at a particular time, in a particular space.

Each experience is a combination of many images and impressions. When I perceive a rose through my eyes, I see the form and the colour; through my nose, I smell the fragrance; through my touch, I feel the texture. All these different experiences combined create an image of the rose and an association and appreciation of the rose in my mind. But if I see the rose without smelling its fragrance, it will not be the same experience. If I smell the fragrance of the rose without its actual form being present, it is a different experience. If I simply feel the texture of the petals without seeing or smelling the rose, it is a different experience; and if I do not perceive a rose at all, still I cannot deny its existence.

The human mind understands combinations and collections of images, events and objects as one experience. Joy is a feeling, but at the same time it is a collection of many other experiences. Suffering is an experience, a feeling, but it is also a collection of many things. Anger, anxiety, hatred, compassion, jealousy and affection are all different experiences and expressions of human nature which have arisen as a result of a collection of many different factors. All these impressions, images or events which we realize, understand, experience and experiment with emanate from a deeper source within our personality. Yogis have called that layer of personality *mahat*, the greater mind.

Manas, buddhi, chitta and ahamkara

Mahat is a collection of four different states of realization. The first state is manas, rationality. The word *manas*, which is generally translated as mind, is derived from the Sanskrit root *manana*, meaning to reflect, to analyze, to understand, to process. It is this aspect of manas which sees the world in its various forms and colours, and which eventually combines

4

all the little impressions together and gives them a body. What we see with our eyes has no meaning unless it goes through manas, the process of reflection, analysis and rationalization.

Once a picture is complete in the realm of manas the file is transferred to *buddhi*, which in English is translated as intellect. Buddhi classifies a particular experience or impression as being either good or bad, positive or negative, rajasic, tamasic or sattwic, and so on. Buddhi either accepts or rejects it. After analyzing the impressions, images and experiences that it has received from manas, buddhi then transfers that entire file to chitta.

In *chitta*, which in English may be translated as memory, it is stored as an impression known as a *pratyaya*. Whenever a similar event is observed, buddhi immediately brings out the old file from its memory bank, chitta, compares it, and then files away the previous impression along with the new impression. This sequence is a very beautiful system of office filing.

Buddhi is also the aspect which, after composing, analyzing, observing, classifying and deciding, interacts with *ahamkara*, the self, the individual identity, the knowledge of 'I am', and influences ahamkara to react in a certain way. When I see a person coming towards me with a stick in his hand, it is only a dead image. But when all my impressions of that person – the expression in his eyes and on his face, his body language, the stick in his hand, his arms raised – are assembled and processed by buddhi, instantaneously they are compared with the impressions from the memory banks of chitta, and then I realize that he is going to hit me. Immediately the message, "What do I do now?" goes to ahamkara, and ahamkara tells buddhi, "Fight or run away!"

Ahamkara is also a peculiar concept because it is a stage of self-recognition in which you are at one level and the things that happen around you do so either above or below you. When they happen below you, there is no threat to your self-identity and you are ready to face that situation. If I see a child running after me with a stick in his hand, I will stop and laugh and say, "What can the child do to me?" because I know I can pick him up with one hand. But if I see someone twice my size coming towards me with a fierce facial expression, my ahamkara immediately says, "This is a threat to your prestige, your self-esteem and your body. You are going to get hurt if you resist this person. Better adopt a different attitude. Don't confront him, it is better if you run away." If you ignore that warning from ahamkara, you can guess what the result will be.

So, in yoga these four aspects of mind are known as mahat, the greater mind. Manas is the gross mind, buddhi is the subtle mind, chitta is the mind which deals with impressions, and ahamkara is the causal mind.

Interaction with the senses

When we consider these four aspects of our nature in relation to our day-to-day activities and the senses which are interacting within the world of name, form and idea, then a different level or dimension of experience takes place in our personality. We have five senses, but each sense has two aspects: eyes and sight, ears and hearing, tongue and taste, nose and smell, skin and touch. These are the five senses with which we work and relate to the outer and inner worlds.

The absence of any one of these senses gives birth to a different kind of understanding and realization, a different kind of inner appreciation, because the energy in our body and personality, the shakti component, is equally distributed to all the senses. If one sense is missing, that shakti works in a subtle way so that we do not feel any deficiency from the absence of that particular sense. So we are talking of two aspects here: the physical level and the mental level. We are all endowed with these two aspects so that we can live, thrive, grow and survive in this cosmic play of creation.

Shakti, prakriti and maya

In this cosmic play three aspects of shakti are active. The first aspect is known as pure shakti. Shakti is the inherent

6

potential. When you tune the other factors that come into play, shakti manifests: energy, motion and action become visible. That shakti is then given the name prakriti, meaning an activity which is now being perceived or experienced by the greater mind.

It is like a sprout germinating from a seed. The growth potential is seen in the form of a tiny beautiful sprout. Once you see the sprout you know that the potency of the seed is now manifesting. That inherent energy, shakti, is now manifesting and has taken a form. There are an infinite number of possibilities for the growth of that particular force in the form of prakriti. Later, this little sprout slowly grows and becomes a tree. Once it has become a tree with its own branches and leaves and is laden with flowers and fruit, then the pleasure you derive from the manifestation of that tree, and the use you can make of the things it has given you, is the third aspect of shakti, which is known as maya.

Maya is translated in English as illusion, the illusory or transitory force. In maya you desire to enjoy your achievements, you desire pleasure, happiness and satisfaction from whatever you do. But that satisfaction is never permanent. When you are thirsty you drink water, but when the water has been eliminated from the system you feel thirsty again. When you are hungry you eat, but when the food has been eliminated from the system you are hungry again. When you are tired you rest, and after resting again you become tired. This is known as maya, something which is transient, impermanent, but which is the result of your interaction with prakriti.

These are the three forms of manifestation, of creation, of the combination of consciousness and energy. When consciousness responds to the stimulation of energy, when the greater mind responds to the experiences of energy in the manifest world, then the experiences or understanding that you gain define you as a human being. Something which you recognize as real, which you can accept as existing now, is your awareness of an interaction between consciousness and energy.

Nature of stress

This is where we are at present. All the other things that happen in life are peripheral expressions of pain and pleasure, contentment and dissatisfaction, motivation and holding back, of willpower, the drive to attain something, and lethargy, not worrying about anything, feeling and awakening positive qualities or expressing negative ones, fighting with some-body, loving somebody, working for money, for family, for society, for the nation while, at the same time, having our personal aspirations, ambitions and desires, expressing our strengths while being limited by our weaknesses, and wanting to fulfil our needs but being unable to differentiate between our need and our ambition, suffering or enjoyment. These are the peripheral expressions that you become aware of at the time of the interaction between consciousness and energy. But the pull, the gravity, of these peripheral experiences is so great that you lose contact with your source and the stress suddenly becomes distress.

One must have stress. Without stress we would not be alive. In the absence of stress there is no life, no movement, no motion. Take the example of a bow. In order to string a bow, you have to bend it. The bow remains in a state of tension, but there is no distress. The tension represents the state of readiness and alertness. If you remove the string from the bow, the bow has no meaning; you cannot shoot your arrows, you cannot hit the target. Just as the bow and string together create the possibility of a motion and a force, in the same way, consciousness, in the form of the greater mind, and energy, in the form of the outer experiences, create an opportunity for your growth or destruction. It depends on how you wish to use that force. Only when the bow is strung can you fit an arrow and release it.

When you are pulling the arrow towards you, you are creating more stress, but in that stress you are also creating a force. If you simply keep on pulling the string, either the string or the bow will break. That breaking is known as distress. After distress you lose control of yourself, you cannot balance or harmonize yourself, and again you fall

8

into anxiety and depression. We are all in a state of readiness and alertness. We have our aspirations and aims which we want to pursue and achieve in order to experience wholeness and completeness. But in the process, when we are not aware of how much we can handle, we become distressed. The danger lies in distress, not in stress.

How can we balance this aspect of stress and distress so that we can excel in whatever we do? As a sannyasin, I have to harmonize and balance any stress and distress and use the force of stress to discover myself. As an artist, you have to use your stress to create a beautiful picture. As a business person, you have to use your stress to excel in whatever you are doing. We all have to work with our stress. This stress is the result of an interaction between the mind, the senses and what we wish to achieve, our aim in life.

Discovering the inherent potential of the greater mind

In order to harmonize the inner experiences and expressions of the personality and the self, we need to train and educate our inner being. Just as we have educated ourselves in all the necessary skills, training and background to excel in society, we also need to educate ourselves in order to energize and discover the potential of the greater mind.

Yoga has called this potential kundalini. But what is kundalini? What is the potential of the mind? Is it creativity? Is it the ability to relax and let go? Is it acquiring *siddhis*, psychic powers? No, all these are the outcome of an active and dynamic mind which is fully awake. Right now the mind is neither active nor dynamic. Maybe in the business sense you are active and dynamic, but not when you have to relate the mind to yourself. Rather, the mind is in a state of tamas, lethargy and stagnation. Why? Because we fear change, we fear transformation. We desire it, but we do not want it. We desire peace, but when we begin to experience peace it unbalances us completely. We think, "What is this state which is totally alien to my nature?" We desire happiness, but when we experience even a tiny bit of happiness, we are afraid of it. We have an unconscious fear of change which is reflected in our beliefs, our behaviour and in the closed nature of our mind.

If you can recognize this particular aspect of yourself, progress is sure. You want to attain the moon, but you do not want to leave this planet. You want to have your cake and eat it at the same time, and that is not possible. Either eat the cake and be happy that you have eaten it, or save it and be happy that you have saved it. If you keep it, do not desire to eat it, and if you have eaten it, do not desire to have it.

In the same way, in this journey of life, if you desire excellence you have to sacrifice something, if you desire happiness you have to sacrifice something and if you desire peace you have to sacrifice something. You will definitely lose something, but the attainment will always be greater than the loss; that is the consolation. However, our nature and our life remain static, tamasic and stagnating. There is no scope for creativity because we are working only within the confines of the parameters that we have set for ourselves.

Becoming a warrior

Human creativity manifests when we discover, realize or venture into something unique. Usually, however, we are not able to go inside and discover the nature, quality and potential of our mind, nor are we able to experience the nature of our subconscious or unconscious. Therefore, yoga has been very clear that one has to have the attitude of a sadhaka, an aspirant, an adventurer, a warrior. Tantra has also been very clear about this. Tantra says that initially we are all animals, *pashus*. We have the attitude of an animal, *pashu bhava*. We only react, we never act. If you can learn how to act and to stop just reacting to situations, events, people and circumstances, then you come out from that reactive instinct and become a warrior. You develop the aspect of a warrior, *veerya bhava*, within you. Only when you become a warrior and are not afraid of confronting yourself will you eventually attain *divya bhava*, the experience of transcendental reality. If you are not willing to be a warrior,

10

then do not talk about having the experience of transcendental reality, because you are duping yourself.

Therefore, we need to go through certain transformations and changes in our beliefs, attitudes and ideas, in our performance and in our relationship with our environment, our family and other people. These transformations begin with an understanding and appreciation of the people with whom we interact. The greatest quality in life is understanding. Through understanding, many other good things come into your life naturally, but if you lack understanding you can never achieve anything.

Kundalini – the dormant potential to be awakened

According to yoga, the definition of mind potential is kundalini. What is kundalini? Throughout the ages, kundalini has always represented power and wisdom. The image of the serpent has represented power and wisdom. In the Bible, the snake gave the fruit of life to Adam and Eve, and as a result they were thrown out of paradise, Eden. What is the symbology behind it? What does it actually mean? The same symbology is used in yoga. The serpent, representing power and wisdom, gives a fruit, and the fruit is the outcome of a process.

To divert for a moment: What is evolution? Evolution is not an ongoing process. Real evolution is walking continuously for long distances and coming back full circle. What is the evolution of a seed? The final outcome of a seed is not the tree, it is a seed inside the fruit, which is replanted and again grows into a tree. Evolution takes a seed through various stages and it is the seed inside the fruit which is the outcome of manifest creation, the ultimate glory, where there is again the possibility of another creation. So, evolution is from seed to seed, not from seed to tree, or seed to flower, or seed to fruit.

The symbology of the serpent as power and wisdom is found in the tantric and yogic tradition as well as in the Christian tradition. When the serpent, wisdom and power combined, gave the fruit of life to Adam and Eve, it actually

11

gave them a boon: "I am giving you the seed which is the source of everything. That seed is surrounded by a fruit which is the outcome of that seed. Realize that this is life, this is nature, this is divinity, this is birth and this is death." But when Adam and Eve ate the fruit of life, the first thing they felt and expressed was guilt in the form of their nakedness.

This has been explained in very beautiful terms in the *Ishavasya Upanishad*, where it says that wisdom leads to enlightenment, but that wisdom can also be the cause of one's downfall. Aurobindo has said, "Initially rationality was my friend. Now rationality is the barrier. Therefore, in order to evolve one has to transcend rationality." It can become the cause of your downfall. So the mistake or fault did not lie with the serpent, but with the recipients who were unable to handle the wisdom, the power which came with the ultimate realization of seed and fruit.

In the same way, in kundalini yoga the serpent symbolizes that wisdom or power which is dormant at present. Once that serpent, in the form of kundalini, awakens, it transforms one's whole life. It is also known as the philosopher's stone, or *paras mani*, which can transmute metal into gold. You need to realize that you have that potential within you. With the concept of yoga you can experience and awaken that energy and make it a sublime force.

Influence of the gunas

The greater mind, mahat, is also subject to the influence of the gunas, the cosmic nature. The gunas have been recognized as three: tamas, rajas and sattwa. When we are talking to each other we use the word guna freely: "This person is rajasic, that person is tamasic, this person is sattwic." But this use of the word guna in normal language does not really indicate the actual nature of our personality. It does not determine or define the lifestyle, mentality, attitude or behaviour of an individual. The gunas are the actual transformations that happen naturally within us. Just as we grow from childhood to adulthood, then mature and grow old, in the same way there is a growth of consciousness indicated by the gunas.

At present we are in a tamasic state. This tamasic state of the greater mind now has to transform and become rajasic where, let us say, prakriti, motion, activity and dynamism is again felt and experienced. When we achieve that, the rajasic nature has to transform into a sattwic state where we experience only the light. That sattwic nature of consciousness is represented in the awakening of human potential, the kundalini shakti. Therefore, when we speak of mind in the yogic context, we cannot speak of it as a single entity. We have to bring in the concept of kundalini too, because the greater mind, mahat, and kundalini, mind potential, are linked.

States of the greater mind
The concept of mahat is different to the concept of the conscious, subconscious and unconscious mind. The conscious mind which interacts with the world and our environment is only a state of the greater mind. The subconscious mind which psychoanalysis and psychology have talked about is only a state of the greater mind. The unconscious mind is also only a state of the greater mind. From the yogic viewpoint, *jagrit* (wakefulness), *swapna* (dream), *nidra* (sleep) and *turiya* (superconsciousness) are only states of the greater mind, because the greater mind in itself contains all these wide varieties of experiences in different forms of anxiety and happiness.

For example, you go through your daily routine and become happy or sad due to an interaction with somebody or something. That happens at the conscious level. Then you go to sleep. In sleep you see dreams. In dreams you experience happiness, suppression, rejection, fear. What you are experiencing in dreams is definitely not conscious, but at the same time it is as real as the conscious experience. Often when we have nightmares we wake up sweating and suddenly realize, "Oh, it was only a dream, thank God!" When we have good dreams and somebody wakes us up, we get angry.

13

Now what is real and what is unreal? We cannot answer this question because there are certain mysteries in the world which should always remain mysteries. God, death, birth and karma cannot be defined. You can search the whole of creation, travel light years, but you will never see the face of God. No matter how hard you try, you will never know the mystery beyond death, or the mystery before birth, or the reality behind karma. You can speculate, but your speculations will never be the final answer. Therefore, mysteries should remain mysteries. What is real and what is unreal is a mystery. What is dream and what is the wakeful state is also a mystery. But certain answers can be given with which we can understand our nature and then make an attempt to sublimate it.

Through yoga we attempt to become human beings. The aim of yoga is not samadhi or realization. The aim of life is harmony, and through harmony we become human beings. In the absence of harmony we are only reacting and when we react we are animals. Therefore, remember that life has much more wealth to give you than you now possess. The wealth of a human being is not a good bank balance, financial security or property. The wealth of a human being is to be a human being, and this is what yoga attempts. The beginning of yoga is learning how to manage your mind. It begins with the first sutra of Patanjali: *Atha yoga anushasanam*. Through discipline, awareness, recognition and understanding yourself, you can manage, channel, direct and harmonize your mind. You can awaken the mind potential, which is kundalini.

Kundalini Shakti

Yoga sees the activity that goes on continually, day in and day out, in the realm of time, space and object, where there is a subtle interaction of consciousness with the senses and the objects of the world, as happening through the agency of mahat, the greater mind. However, the role of mahat is not only to interact with the manifest world, but also to provide an opportunity for each one of us to discover the shakti, the transcendental, cosmic, universal energy. This is where yoga plays an important role. If there were no possibility of the mind interacting with the cosmos and its higher nature, practices such as yoga, meditation or mantra would not have been devised. It was only because the thinkers believed and realized that it is possible to awaken the higher nature that they devised techniques to give each individual the opportunity to discover the source of shakti within.

Outward movement of kundalini energy
This cosmic, transcendental energy, force or power is called shakti, but when that same power begins to take a shape, an identity, a form, a name and has its own attributes, then it is known as prakriti. When, as human beings, we interact with the realm of prakriti and its products, then that interaction is known as maya. It is a transitory interaction, not a

permanent interaction. Yogis have given the name kundalini to this cosmic energy which can be experienced by the mind. The name kundalini is symbolic. It has two meanings. One definition is the energy that is contained in the deepest recesses of our personality, of our nature, the *kunda*, the most subtle plane which cannot be perceived with the normal frame of mind or through the senses. This energy is the shakti known as kundalini. The other definition is from *kundala*, a field, a vortex in which there is ongoing motion, no beginning and no end.

Yogis have also envisioned that this activity of energy in the realm of the manifest nature is influenced by the three gunas: sattwa, rajas and tamas. Therefore, they said that this energy is in three coils. It has also been given the form of a serpent because traditionally the snake has always represented wisdom and power.

Consciousness and energy complement each other, they are not two different things. Energy, the creative force, is an extension of the rational force, consciousness. This concept has been described in tantra through the image of *ardhanarishwara*, the half male and half female bodies merging together, half Shiva and half Shakti. This image clearly indicates that each aspect, whether consciousness or energy, although they may have different roles to play in this cosmic plan, are still one body, one entity.

In this context we need to understand kundalini yoga in relation to our greater mind. When we talk of energy, the shakti, manifesting in the form of prakriti and being experienced as maya, we are speaking of outward evolution, the outward movement of energy from its primal form. As it has gone from one level of evolution to the next, it has established itself as a particular centre of experience in human consciousness. In yogic terminology these centres of experience have been defined as chakras. Chakras are centres of consciousness, dimensions of experience and realization in consciousness, in the greater mind. Chakras are not situated in the spinal passage, but they have been represented in the body because the body is not only material

16

or physical but composed of five different kinds of experience, known as koshas.

The five koshas
The physical body is *annamaya kosha*, the body of matter: bones, muscles, marrow, blood, internal organs, which are all inanimate organs. What makes them move? They are made active and dynamic by a second layer, known as *pranamaya kosha*. When annamaya and pranamaya koshas come together there is motion in an inanimate object, but there is no mind, no rationality, no thinking, no consciousness. So there is a third layer of experience, of existence, known as *manomaya kosha*, the mental body. Manomaya kosha interacts with the world of the senses, prakriti. At present we are all interacting with these three bodies, physical, pranic and mental. The entire world around us simply moves with the force of these three bodies that are active at present.

There are two more bodies, layers, dimensions or sheaths, which are more subtle. The fourth layer is known as *vijnanamaya kosha*, higher intelligence. When this layer of the mind interacts and throbs at higher frequencies, it connects with and begins to realize the cosmic consciousness flowing into this limited structure of individuality. That connection is known as the vijnanamaya connection. When we become continually aware of that connection which exists all the time, and begin to live that higher reality in our day to day life, then the fifth layer or dimension is experienced. This is called *anandamaya kosha*, the body of joy, fulfilment, contentment, completeness and bliss.

The two final koshas or layers of personality, vijnanamaya and anandamaya, are subtle, and the first three, annamaya, pranamaya and manomaya, are gross. The entire learning process takes place at the level of the first three koshas only. We feel the vibrations of people without speaking. We communicate with people with our senses, speech, eyes and movements. Each of these represents something to this mind because we understand the meaning of movement,

17

vision, speech or the written word. We also understand feelings, which are not written. We understand anger, frustration, compassion, jealousy, hatred, love and many others in the form of feelings.

According to yoga, feeling is what happens when manomaya and pranamaya koshas come together. When prana and mind merge, feelings arise. Linear, sequential logic is simply an activity of manomaya kosha, but feelings and emotions are the outcome of the faculties of manomaya and pranamaya koshas. These two experiences of mind and prana express themselves through the body. This is what we experience from birth to death, in sickness and in health, in suffering and in happiness, in isolation or in communion with people, at home or at work. Externally, when we imbibe the written or spoken understanding, we are activating the faculties of manas and buddhi. We put the jigsaw puzzle together and form a rational picture which we can understand and which is stored in chitta, in the form of memory, an archetype, a pratyaya, an impression.

This flow of energy and consciousness is outward, and the more you flow out into the realm of prakriti, the further away you become from the source, the centre of your being. The more you flow out, the more dilution there is. The more you come towards yourself, the more purity there is. If you stretch a rubber band beyond its capacity, it will snap. The same thing happens to us in times of distress. We snap when we suffer, when we have no control or direction with which to guide ourselves. When we snap, we experience psychological problems and difficulties, mentally and emotionally. Yoga says, don't allow yourself to snap. Manage your distress, maintain your clarity and remain balanced.

Yoga also says that even though you have some understanding of the first three dimensions of your body, in order to evolve as a human being you also have to be aware of vijnanamaya kosha and anandamaya kosha. The initial practices defined in yoga for realizing how one functions at the physical, pranic and mental levels fall into the category of pratyahara. To understand the totality of vijnanamaya

18

kosha the method is dhyana, meditation. As we progress from pratyahara to dharana to dhyana, we are not only dealing with our mind but also interacting with and awakening the energy. When the final awakening of energy takes place, we call it the awakening of kundalini.

The tattwas

As kundalini extends from the unmanifest to the manifest, it gradually adopts a manifest form where it is recognized as a *tattwa*, an element. As that element becomes denser, it is identified as another tattwa, and that tattwa becomes even denser and in turn is recognized as another element. The five tattwas are ether or space, air, fire, water and earth or matter. Matter is the manifest form of shakti, not the pure form. The first manifest form of shakti is space, vastness, which contains everything. Space is a very important element. The Upanishads have said that space is Brahman, *Kham Brahman*. Space is the basis of every other element. If you remove space, all the other elements will cease to exist. Matter is contained in space. Our body grows in space. This building exists in space. Air, fire, water and earth are also contained in space. Space is the most subtle form of shakti. The infiniteness of Shakti, energy, and Shiva, consciousness, is space. These different elements of space, air, fire, water and earth are the transformation of shakti in the form of prakriti. When we begin to enjoy the fruits in the realm of matter, that is maya.

Transforming the gunas

In the realm of matter, the three gunas or attributes of nature become most active and dominant. Tamas is the first attribute or guna of matter, rajas is the second and sattwa is the third. Tamas represents the static nature, the nature which has taken a form or shape, and in order to change that form you have to destroy it. Tamas is a fixed, unchanging identity. Our body is tamasic because it is a recognized shape. Buildings and trees are tamasic because they are fixed. Tamas means a form which is fixed for a certain amount of time, whether cosmic years or human years, months or minutes. It is a state in which there is a fixed understanding.

Tamas is not to be taken in a negative way. It indicates a state of existence, it indicates stability in life. It is not negative in itself; it only becomes negative when we become so fixed that we do not wish to change into something new, something beautiful, something more useful for our development. Then tamas becomes stagnation, and stagnation is definitely negative.

The energy which has manifested in the form of matter is also in a state of tamas. Through meditation, through activating the pranas, through stimulating certain centres in the brain and mind, we can create a metamorphosis in the nature of matter. Then tamas changes into rajas. Rajas means activity, dynamism, movement, flow, change, transformation. It is not a negative quality. Rajas is known as *kriya*, activity, and tamas is known as *sthiti*, stability. This kriya continues and becomes more intense, energy is moved and transformed. You begin to pull the energy from outside back into yourself again. This is known as the rajasic process. When you become established in the purity of your nature, in your own being, that is known as sattwa. We can say that movement from sattwa to tamas, and from tamas back to sattwa is the entire area of rajas.

The chakras

Kundalini, the energy which has manifested in the form of matter, is also at present in a state of tamas, which has been defined as mooladhara. *Mool* means base and *adhara* means support. Mooladhara is considered to be the base of the body. The different chakras or states of human experience have been assigned a special symbolic place in the body, but at the same time they have a connection with our higher nature.

You may wonder why in yogic symbology all the chakras have been explained in relation to the spinal passage. The reason is that in our body there are *nadis* or conductors of

20

prana shakti. Just as veins and arteries in the physical body are responsible for the flow of blood, in the same way the nadis in our subtle body are responsible for the flow of energy or prana shakti. These flows can be experienced in the form of subtle electrical currents. Acupuncture or any other system that deals with energy will tell you that energy always moves through a specific channel or pathway, and if you can tap into these channels you can direct the flow of energy.

Yogis have said the same thing. In the spinal cord all these channels, the physical nerves connected to the *karmendriyas*, the organs of action, and the *jnanendriyas,* the organs of sense perception, as well as the psychic nerves or nadis related to the pranic body, come together in the form of a bunch. At each level of the spinal cord, these nerves give birth to a different awareness as the pranas begin to move, alter and flow. When prana begins to flow in the lower part of the pranic nerves, which we call the mooladhara area, that activity will create a corresponding reaction in the brain and also in the mind. When pranic activity takes places in the region of swadhisthana chakra, it will create a corresponding reaction in the brain and mind. It is the same with manipura, anahata, vishuddhi and ajna. Therefore, in the initial stages of the kundalini yoga practices, in order to awaken kundalini, yoga instructs you to concentrate on the physical location of the chakras, not on the psychic location.

Chakras are actually dimensions of experience, of transformation in the realm of consciousness, but in the physical body they correspond to changes in the pranic level. This relates to the transformation of energy from gross to subtle, to more and more subtle until it becomes pure, undiluted by the gunas. For example, in mooladhara the tamasic quality is eighty percent, rajas ten percent and sattwa ten percent. In ajna, the sattwic quality is eighty percent, rajas ten percent and tamas ten percent. In manipura, the solar plexus, the seat of energy, the rajasic quality is eighty percent, tamas ten percent and sattwa ten percent. In this way each chakra has a particular combination

21

of gunas. As we evolve through meditation, as we move from one chakra experience to another, there is also a change in our mind, in our thinking, attitude and behaviour.

If you are a practitioner of kundalini yoga, you will know that sometimes in a practice a change occurs. We become nervous and tense and feel many different things happening in our body. We become fearful, we become active at different levels of our instincts. Then we say that our mooladhara or swadhisthana or manipura has become active. What does this really mean? It means that our perspective, our vision has changed and now we are having this particular experience. Whether it is fear or happiness, with each experience our mind has changed, the understanding, the realization, the vision has changed.

People who have been exposed to kundalini yoga or techniques to awaken the chakras, or who have practised kriya or kundalini yoga meditations, will know that although they concentrate on different areas of the body, the actual change happens, not in that area, but in the realm of consciousness. Although we may concentrate at mooladhara, the base of the spine, or at anahata, the heart centre, or at manipura, the solar centre, or at ajna, the eyebrow centre, through concentration and activation of energy in these different areas we are stimulating and awakening the corresponding area in our consciousness.

A new door is being opened in the realm of our consciousness and when we peep inside that door we have a vision of something different. Sometimes we become happy, sometimes we become afraid, but whatever we feel is part of our manifest gross nature as well as our cosmic nature. Therefore, kundalini is the final outcome or experience of a mind which is becoming awake. When we say we practise yoga to awaken the mind, expand the consciousness and liberate the energy, we are referring to a very simple concept. Right now you are involved in the experience of annamaya, manomaya and pranamaya koshas, but awakening refers to vijnanamaya and anandamaya koshas.

Pratyahara

Pratyahara is the fifth stage of yoga according to the *Yoga Sutras* of Patanjali. The techniques of pratyahara help us to become aware of the activity of annamaya, pranamaya and manomaya koshas – the physical body and senses, the pranic body and energy, and the mental body and inner senses. We begin with asana and pranayama, which are best suited to this age. When the *Yoga Sutras* were written about two thousand five hundred years ago, the mentality, samskaras, environment and culture were different. At that time people were generally healthy and did not suffer from cancer, HIV/AIDS, asthma or diabetes. In those days awareness and the practice of dharma were more important.

In order to become established in the concept of dharma, righteousness and justice, Maharishi Patanjali advocated the practice of yama and niyama first, and gave second place to asana and pranayama for the health and harmony of the physical body, for the maintenance and nourishment of annamaya kosha. Then comes pratyahara for the maintenance and sustenance of manomaya kosha. After that dharana is important because there is a flowering, an opening up of the mind, which can then imbibe the dharmic concepts. At that time the yamas and niyamas become natural and spontaneous. When these disciplines are not imposed upon you, and you begin to live the dharma in

23

absolute harmony, meditation becomes natural and spontaneous.

Pratyahara is a process through which we learn to become aware of the senses, which are physical, subtle and mental in nature, and to develop our awareness. The ability to relax and let go develops after awareness. After relaxation and concentration comes the ability to guide the flow of prana shakti, by willpower, thus managing the movement of prana in the body and harmonizing the mind with prana. That is why pratyahara has to be perfected. To experience pratyahara properly, you have to adopt the practice as a sadhana, not just as a passing experiment, and perfect it. The entire process of yoga is based on sadhana, experience, understanding and perfection of a technique. So, as the first step, make a resolve to perfect pratyahara in your life.

Stages of pratyahara

What are the stages of pratyahara? First we become aware of the different aspects of our mind: manas, buddhi, chitta and ahamkara. The practice of yoga nidra is a very good example of pratyahara. When you are asked to visualize the body, you see your body, but you are not sharply aware of the different parts. The next stage in yoga nidra is rotation of the attention from one part of the body to the next, identifying all the different parts of the body, acknowledging that they exist and becoming aware of the experiences happening in different areas of the body. After that, when you are told to become aware of your body, the quality of your awareness will be different. It will not just be a general perception, but an awareness of the body from the top of the head to the tips of the toes, and you will see the image of your body. That is pratyahara.

In relation to the mind, you are instructed to become aware of yourself, to observe your mind or nature. At that time you simply observe the activity that is most dynamic and taking place in the uppermost surface of your consciousness. If you are thinking, you become aware of thoughts. If you are agitated, you become aware of that agitation. If you are

24

distracted, you become aware of that dissipation. You can only observe that part of your nature or mind which is dynamic at present, and has hold of your personality.

In antar mouna an attempt is made first to extend the awareness into all the senses, and to see how each sensory organ and sense perception is interacting with the mind and emotions. Then we stop that interaction. So, in the first stage of pratyahara there is expansion of consciousness into the world, not withdrawal of consciousness. After we have extended ourselves fully into the world, into our senses and experiences, then, one by one, we begin to withdraw that awareness and contain it within ourselves.

If you are asked to experience yourself at that time, the experience will be in the form of darshan. Darshan means to see a rose inside as if it were real. It is not the same as imagination, where you are only putting pieces together, but the rose inside you is not vibrant or alive. When the rose becomes alive inside, when you see it inside exactly as you see it with the eyes open, it is known as darshan. *Drishya* is what is seen outside, *drashta* is the one who sees, and *darshan* is the exact replica. This is what we attempt to achieve through the practice of pratyahara.

The following pratyahara practice is a simple and basic one of recognizing experiences that we receive through the senses of sight, taste, smell, hearing and touch. It demonstrates what pratyahara tries to achieve by extending the awareness into the senses and releasing the impressions and memories that are contained in the mind in relation to the sensory experiences.

PRATYAHARA PRACTICE

Preparation

Sit in any comfortable position. Have the body upright and straight, hands either on the knees or in the lap, whichever is comfortable. Gently close your eyes.

Check your body and make sure that you can sit quietly for at least ten minutes without any physical movement. If there is anything tight on the body, remove or loosen it. If your body is tense, try to release the tension. Become comfortable, firm and steady.

Slowly bring your awareness to the eyebrow centre, and with your attention fixed there minimize all activity and movement.

Sight

Now become aware of what you are seeing internally with the eyes closed. Visualize a red rose. You have seen a red rose many times. Visualize it in your mind. In front of the closed eyes, in chidakasha, recreate the image, the form of a red rose . . . a candle flame . . . the rising sun . . . the setting sun . . . a flock of birds flying in the sky . . . a beautiful crystal clear lake . . . rocky mountains . . . snow-capped mountains . . . a forest . . . yourself. As if you are looking at yourself in a mirror, mentally try to see your whole body from outside. Just as I see you, try to see yourself from outside. Try to see yourself seated. What is the position of your hands and legs, spine, neck and head, eyes, lips?

Smell

Now become aware of different smells. We are going to try to smell different things. You have the memory of all these smells deep within the mind. Try to activate those memories. The smell of incense, rose incense, the soft fragrance of roses . . . the smell of a forest after rain . . . the smell of musk . . . the smell of camphor . . . the smell of body sweat . . . the smell of wet earth . . . the smell of clean fresh air . . . the smell of the ocean.

Taste

Now bring your awareness to the sense of taste. All these impressions are in your memory bank. Bring them out. The taste of lemon . . . the taste of milk . . . the taste of pizza, a beautiful steaming hot pizza . . . the taste of an onion . . . the taste of chocolate . . . the taste of sugar . . . the taste of water.

Touch

Now focus on the sensation of touch. The touch of a soft rose petal . . . the touch of sandpaper . . . silk . . . cotton cloth . . . metal . . . smooth wood furniture . . . the texture of a leaf . . . the texture of an orange . . . the feel of an apple.

Hearing

Now come to hearing. The cars on the road . . . the horns of the cars . . . the sound of a flute . . . the sound of raindrops falling on a tiled roof . . . the sound of a gong . . . the sound of tiny little bells.

Inner stillness

Now focus at the region of the eyebrow centre and visualize a flame there. With the attention fixed on the image of the flame become aware of the silence and stillness in your body. Become aware of silence and stillness in your mind. Go deep into the experience of silence and stillness which is both physical and mental. For a few moments do not identify with your body, with the experiences of the body. Do not identify with the mind, its fluctuations, movements and experiences. Just observe the state of stillness, motionless, stability and silence within you. Experience space within.

Ending the practice

Now become aware of the movement of the breath.
Slowly take a deep breath in and chant the mantra Om three times.
Slowly move your body and gently open your eyes.

Hari Om Tat Sat

Pratyahara in Relation to Annamaya, Pranamaya and Manomaya Koshas

The topic is pratyahara in relation to annamaya kosha, the physical body and the senses; pranamaya kosha, the pranic body, the energy; and manomaya kosha, the mental body and the inner senses. One of the basic principles of pratyahara is the extension of awareness into the outer world. Generally, it is said that pratyahara is a system for withdrawal of the senses, but this refers to the final stage. You cannot reach that final stage without initially becoming aware of what is transpiring between you and the world of objects. Therefore, common sense says that first you have to extend your awareness into the senses and tune into what those senses are feeling, and how that particular sense organ, or *indriya*, is connected to your physical body. This extension of awareness into the senses is known as *pratyahara*, from *prati* and *ahara*, meaning to feed the senses. It does not mean withdrawing the senses, but feeding the senses. That is one definition of pratyahara. Another definition of pratyahara is in relation to *pratyaya*, meaning impressions, archetypes, seeds or memories.

Vrittis

In the *Yoga Sutras*, Patanjali speaks of vrittis as modifications, movements, experiences and attractions of the mind. The vrittis are areas of mental involvement, interaction and expression. Patanjali also acknowledges that the five vrittis are both pleasant and unpleasant – *Vrittayah panchatayyah klishta aklishta* (1:5). Vrittis become pleasant when the areas of mental functioning are balanced and harmonized, concentrated and focused. But the same vrittis become unpleasant when there is distraction and dissatisfaction in the mental field, in the sensory field of the indriyas.

When we begin to perfect the aspects of pratyahara, although we close our eyes and it seems we are meditating, we are not. Rather we are more mentally active and dynamic; we are making our consciousness recognize wilfully and forcefully, not only the gross but also the subtle and causal impressions of the world stored in our mind. Therefore, pratyahara is not meditation, nor a part of meditation; rather it is controlled mental activity, guided mental perception which increases mental awareness.

Memory

One of the five vrittis defined by Patanjali is memory, *smriti*. Memory is the aspect or area of our mind where everything that is experienced and recognized by the senses is stored in the form of photographic images in our consciousness. The things that we see are stored in the form of photographic images. Even smell has an image which is eventually filed in our memory. Sound, touch and taste each have an image or a symbol, all of which are stored in our memory.

It is very difficult to bring these subtle images and symbols to the surface of our mind consciously. The mind is an entity which recognizes symbols. The alphabet is a series of symbols which the mind has been trained to recognize in a particular order. We can read English because we know the characters and words, but we cannot recognize Spanish or Latin, although the script is the same. We recognize the characters as being Roman script, but our mind has not been trained to recognize these particular combinations.

We recognize an image, a picture, a form or name. Sometimes that recognition is conscious and sometimes it is unconscious. However, whether it is conscious or unconscious, those symbols or images are stored in the memory in the form of pratyaya. It is like compressing the hard disc of a computer. In the same way, with our mind too we can compress all the bits of information and store them, but we are not able to retrieve them consciously. When these images, symbols or impressions come out, especially if they are unconscious memories, we are unable to recognize them.

Many times we recognize the conscious symbols because in the wakeful state of our mind there has been a conscious recognition. But when the same memory comes from the unconscious it becomes difficult because there is no conscious knowledge that we have seen or experienced it. Memory has been described as a vritti for this specific reason, that when these impressions come out they can create either a very pleasant or a very unpleasant state of being, *klishta* or *aklishta*.

In the initial stage of pratyahara we become aware of the symbols and images that the senses have created. These symbols are conscious symbols because the senses work at the conscious level most of the time. The faculty of vision is more active when we are conscious, as are the faculties of smell, taste, hearing and touch. These different faculties relate to our wakeful state of mind and, therefore, when we close our eyes in pratyahara, the first thing we do is stimulate or bring to the surface the symbols that we have received and understood through the senses.

In the next stage of pratyahara we become aware of the unconscious impressions in relation to the senses. What are these unconscious impressions? Images and symbols will suddenly appear whenever we close our eyes, in the form of a dream or a fantasy or a vision – a geometrical figure, yantra, mandala or object. We tend to ignore the things that we see because we are too caught up in our thoughts. Whenever we close our eyes we see many things in chidakasha, but because our attention is not there we are unable to recognize those symbols, impressions and images.

In order to recognize the unconscious symbols, first you have to become aware and identify with that awareness.

30

Becoming aware is one process, one state of your dynamic, active mind, and identifying with awareness is another state of the dynamic mind. At present you are aware that you are sitting here. You are also aware of the sound of the crows outside, but you have not identified yet with the sound. You have not identified yet with awareness of the senses or of your mind. While I am speaking, you are thinking, trying to understand and analyze the meaning of the words and concepts, but right now it is coming to you only in the form of spoken sentences. However, there is an awareness which can be identified with in relation to speech and sound, in relation to what is happening internally. So, awakening the faculty of awareness and identifying with the faculty of awareness are two distinct processes.

By observing the sensory experiences first, as one does in the first stage of pratyahara, we are making an attempt not only to release, understand and observe the impressions which have gone in, but at the same time to sensitize our awareness and identify with the experience much more deeply, not just superficially as we usually do. So, one aspect of pratyahara sadhana is to become conscious, to know. The process of knowing is a conscious one, conscious knowledge. It is not a passing, transitory understanding of a situation, rather it is absolute knowledge.

Unconscious memory

Then we go into the unconscious memory, *achetana smriti*. Even in the unconscious memory one finds many symbols related to the sensory experience. Once we have gone beyond the senses, the physical, the gross, and we have understood how the senses interact with the world and with other people, we move on to pranamaya and experience, *pranic smriti*, pranic memory. Pranic memory is observation of the emotions and feelings. Whenever we come into contact with anything in the world, there is an association of feelings and emotions with thoughts and rationality or intellect. Everything we are able to comprehend contains a feeling. When you look at a flower or a person, there will be a feeling for the flower or

31

person, and that feeling determines your relationship with the person or object. You look at a person and suddenly find that you love them. The feeling was there before you become aware of that love, but only later on was it identified as love. You experience affection, but that emotion existed before you identified it as affection. We only become aware of that feeling when it blooms fully; we are not aware of the existence of that subtle energy when it is not in full bloom. Love, affection, compassion, anger, hatred and jealousy, for example, are emotions that are in full bloom.

Extension of awareness

Yoga psychology says to try and recognize your experiences before they take a final shape, so that you can maintain your equilibrium and not get caught in the effect of *raga*, attraction, and *dwesha*, repulsion. Attraction gives you the feeling of pleasure or *sukha*, and repulsion, aversion, rejection gives you the feeling of suffering or *dukha*. If you can analyze, understand and observe the subtle experiences before they take the final form, you will be free from sukha and dukha, and maintain your equanimity. This is also one of the messages of the *Bhagavad Gita*. Only when you remain balanced, equipoised and harmonious does the inner nature flower.

We have been taught these things as philosophical concepts, and not as something that can be lived in our lives. Therefore, in spite of our rich heritage we are still caught up in a web of conflict, because we have been unable to understand what these principles stand for. The formula is very simple, and in the course of time it happens naturally. Initially you have to train yourself, by sitting down, observing and then stopping the motion, the activity, in order to become aware. But once you become aware, once the process of observation begins, you don't have to sit down, you can be aware from moment to moment, every second of the day.

This is the final awareness that the yogis inspire everyone to achieve. They say to live in the present, experience and understand the present, perfect the present in whatever you do and think. Whatever happens in your mind, in your interactions, actions, attitudes and behaviour, observe them and live in the present. Why? So that you develop your own awareness of the situation, of the environment, of your state of being. Without awareness, and identification with awareness, pratyahara can never be perfected. Become aware of the feeling before it is given an identity, a shape, and before you recognize it as an expression of your preconceived thoughts and ideas. It sounds difficult, but it is not. Become aware of pranamaya kosha through observation of your feelings and emotions. After that, become aware of manomaya kosha through observation and awareness of your thoughts, rationality, intellect and intelligence. Only when you have gone through these three different stages can you move on to the next stage of dharana.

In the teachings of yoga, a lot of importance is given to the mind, because the yogic traditions have spoken about the mind as being crucial for our growth and development. In the practice of pratyahara we try to deal with our mind directly. For example, in the practice of antar mouna we try to observe our thoughts, to see where they are coming from, what their source is. We try to see the ideas which are conveyed in a thought. We try to develop the ability to stop the thoughts at will. When the chattering of thoughts stops, then one experiences inner silence, and that is the practice of antar mouna.

Witnessing prana

However, here we are working with the third level of our personality and we have ignored the second. In order to work with pranamaya kosha you need to practise antar darshan so that you can be a witness, a *drashta,* of the prana which is interacting with the outer world in the form of feeling, emotion and desire. It is the prana, not the mind, which takes the form of a desire. Desires have very intense emotions attached to them. Desires are not free from emotion. When we desire something we have a very intense feeling and emotion associated with that desire. Of course, we tend to rationalize it, but in their pure form desires, emotions and feelings are prana. Recognition of emotion, feeling and desire takes place in the practice of antar darshan.

After you have recognized how your prana or energy, the subtle life force, interacts externally, you have to observe the same activity happening inside yourself. You have to awaken the subtle prana inside, which happens through the practices of prana vidya. Antar darshan is a technique of pratyahara for recognizing the interactions of prana externally. Prana vidya is for recognizing the existence, role and nature of prana within our subtle body.

In the following meditation practice we will combine the different aspects of pratyahara in relation to annamaya, pranamaya and manomaya koshas. Perfecting this leads to purity and harmony of prana with body, prana with mind, and mind with body. This purity and harmony results in the state of relaxation, or vishram. The word *vishram* means the absence of *shram*, activity or movement, the cessation of activity or movement. That is yogic relaxation.

Relaxation – focused awareness

Relaxation and yogic relaxation are two different things. We relax, but in our relaxation there is no awareness, there is dissipation of energy and awareness. In yogic relaxation there is focusing of energy and awareness. A great example of yogic relaxation is yoga nidra. You are not stopping the mental processes when you practise yoga nidra, rather you are encouraging the movement of awareness and attention. By encouraging that movement, awareness increases and you experience relaxation, because in the process of yogic relaxation, by making the awareness dynamic, you are focusing it where you want it to go. Dissipation becomes focused into concentration. In the normal state of relaxation there is dissipation of energy and awareness. In yogic relaxation there is focusing of energy and awareness. When you focus your energy and awareness properly and sequentially, the entire personality becomes focused.

Therefore, it has been said that if you are able to perfect yoga nidra, you can experience the benefit of twelve hours sleep in only four hours. One hour of yoga nidra equals three to four hours of normal sleep, provided you can perfect it. You have to be persistent. Relaxation is the first symptom of awareness. By developing focused awareness, by developing focused, channelled energy, you attain a state of relaxation and balance. So first comes achieving the state of relaxation through developing or extending your awareness. This state of relaxation and balance leads to the experience of concentration, or dharana.

Sanyam

It is said in the *Yoga Sutras* that pratyahara, dharana and dhyana together are known as sanyam. *Sam* plus *yama* means a balanced expansion of consciousness, absolute control over the movement of consciousness, to be contained in the self. So we can also say that perfection of pratyahara leads to initial sanyam, and that sanyam is important for the experience of meditation. Perfection in dharana leads to sanyam, and that is also important for meditation. What happens in dharana? In pratyahara there is discovery, in dharana there is fixation. In pratyahara there is a process of observation, in dharana there is a process of containment. According to the *Yoga Sutras* that is the next step towards mind management.

PRATYAHARA PRACTICE

Awareness of the body

Sit in any comfortable meditation asana. Make yourself comfortable and close your eyes. Move your mind from one part of the body to the next, making sure there is no tightness or tension.

Be totally aware of the body as it is right now. Try to see yourself fixed in your asana. Develop internal awareness of the body: how you are seated, whether there is discomfort or comfort, relaxation or tension. Make sure that you are absolutely at ease with yourself, with your body. If you need to move and alter your posture, you can do so now. Then, once you have become steady, stable and comfortable, try to minimize all physical movement.

Complete awareness of the whole body. Be a witness to your physical experiences. At first you were feeling, observing, identifying with the body. Now become a witness to the experiences of the physical body.

Say to yourself mentally, "I am not this physical body, nor am I the experiences associated with the physical body."

Just observe yourself as if you are somebody else, the little 'I' sitting inside and observing you and your body.

As you observe the body, become aware of the space inside the body. Feel the body to be like an empty shell containing space.

Become aware of the space inside the body, the space which extends from the head into the trunk . . . into the arms . . . into the fingers . . . into the feet . . . and into the toes. Become aware of the physical inner space.

As you observe the inner space, you begin to experience immobility and silence. In the state of physical immobility, you can also experience silence.

You are aware, as a witness of nothing else but the feeling of space within yourself, the existence of space within yourself. That space contains awareness. The space within you is the conscious space, the space within you is awareness, pervading the entire body from top to toe.

Awareness of sensory impressions

Use this awareness which pervades your entire being to experience, acknowledge and know the different sensorial impressions that are contained within you. Use the awareness to acknowledge the sensory impressions.

Become aware of the images that come naturally and spontaneously in front of your closed eyes: streaks of light, combinations of colours, maybe a defined and clear image of something. What is being generated spontaneously inside you? Maybe a symbol, maybe a yantra, maybe an image, a figure, a shape, a mandala, or nothing – just blank space, with some coloured dots and streaks of light.

36

Now observe the auditory awareness, sounds that you hear, sounds that come from outside into your ears. Acknowledge them. Identify with each one for just a few moments, then become aware of another sound impression.

Now observe the olfactory experiences, the smells that you can become aware of. Observe the smell that you are aware of right now. Acknowledge this and try to discover the next one. Acknowledge each one and try to discover the next.

Move your awareness to the sense of taste. Observe the existing sensation of taste.

Then come to touch. Become aware of the physical sensation of touch: the touch of the skin, of the palms of the hands, the lips touching, where the body is touching the floor, the touch of the clothes on the body, the air.

Once again identify with the stillness of the body, with the inner space and silence, internal silence.

Awareness of thoughts

Now become aware of the thought which is dominant in your mind. No matter what kind of thought it is, the most absurd one, the most logical one or the most negative one, just become aware of the thoughts. Observe the thoughts. There is not a moment when you do not think. You are never thoughtless, but sometimes there is no awareness of the thoughts. Try to develop awareness of the present thought in your mind.

Try also to find out what kind of different thoughts arise in your conscious mind. Go into the realm of thoughts. First see all of them, as and when they come to the surface of your conscious mind.

Now pick one thought. If you cannot pick out one thought, then create one and hold it in your mind. Look at it again. What meaning is conveyed by the thought?

What is the feeling conveyed by the thought?

Is there an emotion attached to the thought? Find out.

What kind of thought is it? An inquiring thought? A thought related to somebody, a close one, a near one or somebody whom you do not know or who is not present?

An intellectual thought, an absurd thought? Related to what? Related to whom?

Just as you peel the skin of an onion, layer by layer, in the same way peel the layers of the thought which you are at present holding in your mind. Try to know the different components of the thought. Try to know everything possible about it. Try to see what kind of feeling or emotion it creates within you. Try to know what kind of attention or stress or understanding that thought is creating inside you.

Try to know if there is any feeling associated with the thought, any aspiration, any desire or emotion associated with the thought.

Now stop the practice. Let the thoughts go free. Just relax.

Awareness of emotions

Now become aware of a feeling, an emotion. Is there any dominant feeling or emotion in you right now? Find out. If there is not, generate one, whichever one is easiest, something which is natural and spontaneous to you. It could be an emotion of affection, respect, compassion or love, a sattwic emotion. It could also be rajasic, something which is bothering you, like anxiety or anger. It could be a tamasic emotion too, like jealousy or frustration. Do not try to change the nature of the emotion, of the feeling, but observe it like a witness. Be a drashta.

Try to know the nature of the emotion, of the feeling.

And let it go.

Ending the practice

Again focus yourself within yourself and experience stillness and silence.

Now become aware of the breath, become aware of the movement of the breath.

Slowly take a deep breath in and chant Om three times.

Slowly and gently move the body.

Open your eyes gently whenever you are ready.

Hari Om Tat Sat

38

Dharana and
Vijnanamaya Kosha

Our subject is the relationship of the dharana practices with the awakening and experience of vijnanamaya kosha. It is clear that in the initial practice of concentration, which is pratyahara, we try to become aware of the different experiences of annamaya, manomaya and pranamaya koshas. This extension of awareness is in the realm of the active or jagrit mind, the awakened senses. It is in the realm of smriti, memory, the fourth chitta vritti. However, when we speak of dharana we imply, not extension of awareness, but focus of awareness within the subtle realm of consciousness.

Before defining dharana, we need to understand vijnanamaya kosha, and to see how humanity has progressed from primitive times to the present age. In the early stages of humanity, people were more aware of their environment because the world they lived in was hostile and wild. At that time their instincts were fully functional; they lived according to their instincts. There was less rationality because of the untamed nature of the environment and its inhabitants. In order to cope with the wilderness of nature, they devised two methods. One method was confronting a situation and fighting with it, the other was running away from it. This is now known as the 'flight or fight syndrome', which is inherent in every human being.

As time progressed, primitive people adapted their lives to the laws of nature and made nature useful and compatible with their aspirations. Slowly, humanity developed a linear, sequential, logical way of thinking and looking at things, of behaving, acting and feeling. It is that linear aspect of our consciousness which has brought us to our present state of being. However, at the same time, there were people who felt that this linear, logical evolution was limited and only suited to material growth and existence. They felt there was another possibility – developing an intuitive, creative, artistic nature, which is also inherent in every human being. When they started to look into the intuitive, creative and artistic abilities, and into which centres in the mind deal with these subtle expressions, they discovered vijnanamaya kosha. Until then people had only been aware of manomaya kosha.

Vijnanamaya kosha is the source, the centre from which such faculties evolve and take control of human life. It does not deal only with the manifest intellect, buddhi or manas, but with deeper aspects of chitta, the mind which is inactive within us. This is the drashta mind, the witnessing mind within the active, functioning, involved mind. Chitta is therefore referred to as the sakshi state, the drashta state of consciousness. It is this *sakshi,* or witnessing attitude, which stores impressions and is responsible for human evolution.

Chitta processes the impressions, the pratyayas, the memories, the archetypes, the samskaras and the karmas. As it develops understanding of the archetypes, samskaras and karmas, chitta evolves. But in the chitta which refers to awareness of vijnanamaya kosha, there is also a subtle dimension. This dimension of chitta does not interact with the senses, or with the intellect, feelings or emotions. Rather it understands various symbols, yantras, forms or patterns of consciousness. In order to activate the dormant centres of chitta, to transform the experiences in chitta, we use mantra and the symbology of yantras.

40

Mantra

Mantra and yantra are the two main practices for awakening vijnanamaya kosha. *Mantra* is a frequency, a vibration, a sound, which when repeated mentally or verbally with concentration and fixation of awareness alters the patterns of chitta. Mantra liberates mental energy from the confines of the senses; it liberates mental awareness from the experiences of material, external objects. This is one of the most commonly known and understood definitions of mantra: liberation of mind or consciousness from the bondage and influence of prakriti. With repetition of mantra we internalize our awareness, we sensitize our consciousness so as to realize the subtle transformations that happen in the deepest recesses of our personality. Mantra also acts as a tool, a medium to connect the gross mind with the subtle mind. Mantra connects the linear, logical, sequential mind with the artistic, creative potential.

Yantra

Another tool for awakening vijnanamaya kosha is yantra. *Yantra* literally means 'vehicle of consciousness'. In the unconscious, subtle dimensions of mind there are impressions that we have brought with us from our past and they determine the evolution of our consciousness. These impressions are registered in our psyche, in our DNA, in the form of figures or geometrical shapes which are unrecognized by the manifest mind but recognized, understood and realized by the subtle mind.

The manifest mind is only an agency through which to experience the world and then to transfer that experience to chitta, where it is stored. Those impressions in chitta are carried forward even after death. Therefore, in the *Bhagavad Gita* (15:7) Sri Krishna states that although the spirit is considered to be an eternal part of the immortal self, when the spirit comes in contact with prakriti, the cosmic force of creation, it brings with it the impressions of its many lives. Although the soul is immortal, imperishable and a part of the supreme consciousness, when it is attracted by the

41

gravity of prakriti it connects with nature, the dimension and realm of prakriti, and with the impressions it has stored over the period of its many existences. Prakriti gives these experiences a form, a shape, and the senses represent the ability to recognize events and situations.

Now the impressions in the unconscious which are not related to our day-to-day activities or to this present existence are recognized by chitta in the form of yantras. Yantras are defined as vehicles of consciousness because the presence of symbols and archetypes in the unconscious mind transforms the unconscious so that it becomes more refined, more sublime. It interacts with the inner world as well as the outer world, and that leads to the state of turiya.

Turiya means to be awakened internally as well as externally, to have the experience of both the inner and outer worlds. The turiya state is like a person standing in the doorway, having the ability to look both inside the confines of the room and also outside at the vastness of space. On one side you have the four walls of the room, which represents the manifest, finite world, and on the other you have the infinite experience of the cosmos, of nature, of the Self, of God, and of space. Before we merge into the state of turiya, before we become one with and identify with our universal nature, we need to release the impressions which hold and bind us to the existing plane of consciousness. Therefore, awareness of yantras plays an important role in yoga.

Awakening the chakras

In yoga awareness of yantras begins first by identifying and observing the chakras. Chakras are vortices of energy or energy fields, which have been depicted as lotuses with varying numbers of petals. What is the symbology behind the representation of an energy field in the form of a lotus? A lotus opens its petals when the sun rises and closes them again when the sun sets. The awakening of energy takes place when you become aware of the shakti inside you. When there is absence of shakti awareness the petals close again. So awareness is the sun. With the raising of awareness, or the rising of the sun, the chakras become active and the petals open up. In the absence of awareness, when the sun sets, the energy becomes dormant and the petals close.

In order to become aware of the subtle energy interaction in vijnanamaya kosha, we need to use symbols to activate the corresponding centre in consciousness. Through their investigations and research, yogis saw that certain images can activate centres in the consciousness and release certain impressions or samskaras. According to yoga, the lotus is the safest symbol, as when visualized it does not create any kind of disturbance in the personality.

When we concentrate, we focus our mind on one particular centre of the body and, because of the connection with the nadis, we are able to stimulate other centres in the brain. For example, in kundalini yoga it has been explained that if you want to activate or awaken mooladhara chakra, you need not concentrate in the mooladhara region; it is enough if you concentrate on the tip of the nose, through nasikagra drishti. Now, our rational and logical mind may ask how we can awaken mooladhara, a psychic centre, by focusing the attention at the tip of the nose. But here we are forgetting the connection with the nadis, the pranamaya kosha. When we focus our vision on this point, the sensory nerves along with the pranic nadis are being stimulated. These sensory nerves and pranic nadis are connected with centres in the brain, spine and perineum, mooladhara. Therefore, it becomes possible to awaken mooladhara. This is an example of how certain movements combined with concentration can activate the prana and the sensory nerves in order to awaken and stimulate areas in the physical body, the subtle body and the causal body.

So, when we focus on a chakra we are not only concentrating on a specific part, but eventually we also need to combine visualizations, breath awareness and mantra awareness in order to have a harmonious awakening of prana shakti, the energy aspect, and its corresponding centre in consciousness, the *chetana*. Concentration on the breath

43

combined with focusing the awareness on a chakra awakens the energy, but mantra combined with breath awareness and visualization of a yantra awakens the corresponding centre in consciousness.

Two things happen: the manifest energy is sublimated and the dormant consciousness is activated. That is the process of kundalini yoga: awakening of the chakras, then awakening prana and finally awakening kundalini, the cosmic universal shakti. As the chakras awaken, our personality undergoes a transformation and we move from the linear, sequential, logical mode of experience to the intuitive, creative and artistic mode of existence. This happens when we connect with vijnanamaya kosha.

Dharana

What is the connection of the dharana practices with vijnanamaya kosha? Let us define dharana first. *Dharana* means 'to hold' or 'to retain'. What is it that we hold? We hold our concentration, and to hold one's concentration is very difficult. We can be aware of something for a given period of time, but to be aware of something does not mean that we are focused or concentrating. Concentration is intense awareness, it is identification with awareness.

The concept of being aware and identifying with the awareness are different. I can be aware that I am my body, but when I identify with the awareness that I am my body, I become my body. I am aware that the tree is in front of me, but I am here and the tree is there. Identifying with the awareness is the process of knowing, realizing the existence of something else. When I identify with the awareness, I become the tree and the tree becomes me. We become one. Although we both have our separate body and existence, our awareness has become one. My awareness has become one with the tree's awareness and the tree's awareness has become one with mine, meaning that the two life forces have fused together, despite having different bodies, different dimensions of experience and being different forms of life. This concept of identifying with awareness is known as

44

sayujya, to become one with the object of awareness. That can only happen for a very short time, but to hold that state of identification is known as dharana.

Dharana requires a certain degree of mental discipline and training because of our active nature and the behaviour of our senses and mind. The natural state of the senses and mind is to be active. Our nature is flirtatious, dissipated and distracted. It becomes even more distracted when we are in the realm of prakriti because there are too many cravings and sources of attraction. Pratyahara is perfected to still the senses and mind, by recognizing what is happening around us. When the senses and mind have been stilled and there is no fluctuation, no distraction, no dissipation of energy and consciousness, then dharana takes place. Dharana is a state of mind, a state of consciousness which is fixed, still, one-pointed, totally identified.

There are different practices to enable us to perfect dharana. In order to train our senses to experience dharana we practise trataka – fixation of vision, fixing our gaze on an external image like a candle flame, the moon, the stars, a black point or any other form on which our vision can be fixed. That is the initial training or basic practice of dharana. After perfecting trataka, we move into the subtle mind and hold our attention there. The subtle mind has many impressions in the form of yantras and mandalas. Some of the yantras are related to our primitive experiences, the instincts. Some of the yantras and mandalas and experiences, pratyayas, are related to our intellectual concepts and knowledge. Certain forms of yantras and symbols are connected with the natural state of sattwa inherent in every being.

The natural state or quality of sattwa can be realized with the practices of a group of techniques known in yoga as hridayakasha dharana. Yantras related to knowledge, to intellectual concepts, can be realized by a series of practices dealing with chidakasha dharana. Yantras related to our instincts, the dormant energies, can be realized by a series of practices known as daharakasha dharana. So in dharana we

45

have three different groups of practices: *chidakasha dharana*, dealing with the head space; *hridayakasha dharana*, dealing with the heart space; and *daharakasha dharana*, dealing with the lower space.

Akasha

What is this concept of space, akasha, with which dharana deals? You have heard of the space of mind, *chit* plus *akasha*, chidakasha; the space of the heart, *hridaya* plus *akasha*, hridayakasha; and the lower space *dahara* and *akasha*. What is the concept of akasha, space, here? Akasha represents the vastness of consciousness without any limits, without any defined structure and area. In that vast space of consciousness are the impressions carried over from our past existence. The impressions we gather in this life do not exist in chidakasha, but what we gather in this life in the form of samskaras and karmas will become part of chidakasha in our next incarnation. Right now they are only in the form of memories, smriti. They are contained in the filing cabinet of chitta, but when we change houses we have to leave the old filing cabinet behind, and so we just take out all the files, put them in a bundle on our back and go into the next house. At that time all the classifications from one filing cabinet are put altogether, and there is no other classification. Then they become part of the akasha.

In the cosmic dimension, when we are not existing in the realm of prakriti, those memories, those pratyayas, are classified according to our evolution. People talk of the akashic records where everything that happens in this world, all that is said, experienced or known, is contained. When we change our apartment, all these files go with us and are classified according to their intensity of experience in daharakasha, hridayakasha and chidakasha. But in the next apartment we see them in cryptic forms, not in logical, linear forms. These cryptic forms or hieroglyphics are the symbols, yantras, mantras and mandalas.

You may have a certain natural inclination towards a particular image or yantra. Some people like Kali yantra, not because they have an affection for Kali, but because when they see the symbol they are automatically attracted to it. Some like Shiva yantra or Gayatri yantra. This natural attraction of consciousness towards a particular geometric figure corresponds to your state of evolution at the time. Of course, after some time you transcend that state and move on to another one. But in that state also there will be an attraction for a particular symbol or yantra. In daharakasha, yantras of instinct are dominant and active, in hridayakasha, yantras of feeling, and in chidakasha, yantras of rationality.

So in order to become established in the state of dharana, which is identifying with the awareness of the object, we again have to become aware of the subtle expressions of consciousness, to recognize these yantras and release the information stored in the yantra with the help of a mantra. In dharana, mantra becomes a tool for programming the software which allows us to retrieve the information in a particular way from the different compartments of the hard disk.

After releasing the impressions of the past, when you are absolutely free of them and not affected by the past karmas, you gain immunity from the cause and effect of the present karmas and you do not accumulate them. Your journey to self-discovery begins after cleaning out the daharakasha, hridayakasha and chidakasha impressions through the practice of dharana.

DHARANA PRACTICE

Preparation

Sit in any comfortable meditation position with the spine upright and straight, hands either on the knees in chin or jnana mudra or folded in the lap. Gently close your eyes and observe the body. Make sure that you are comfortable and at ease with yourself. There should be no tightness in the body. Make sure that you are free from physical tension. If you need to alter your position or adjust your body, do so now. Then try to become still, to minimize all physical movement as much as possible.

Observe the body, observe the posture internally. Quickly move your mind from one part of the body to another. Acknowledge the state of your body as it is right now. See each and every part of the body in one quick glance or vision, and become stable, relaxed, tranquil, still and silent.

Awareness of the breath

Now become aware of the breath. Observe the flow of breath in the nostrils. Know that you are breathing in and that you are breathing out. Not a single breath can come in or go out without your knowledge. Be conscious of breathing. Know that you are breathing. See the breath in the nostrils. As you inhale, feel the coolness of the breath in the nostrils, and as you exhale feel the warmth of the breath in the nostrils. Focus your attention totally on the breath.

Now, in order to deepen your awareness and concentration, observe your breath in the passage between the navel and the eyebrow centre. When you inhale feel the breath move up from the navel to the eyebrow centre, and when you exhale feel the breath move down again from the eyebrow centre to the navel.

Move your awareness with the breath.

In order to deepen the awareness and concentration further become aware of the movement of breath in the spinal passage.

At the time of inhalation feel the breath move up from the base of the spinal passage to the crown of the head and at the time of the exhalation watch it move down from the crown of the head to the base of the spine.

In order to deepen the concentration still further, once again watch the breath come up with inhalation from the base of the spine to the crown of the head.

And during exhalation watch it move down the front of the body, from the top of the head to the base of the spine so that there is a circular movement of breath and awareness in the body. At the time of inhalation the breath moves up through the spinal cord to the crown of the head, and during exhalation the breath moves down the front of the body to the base of the spine. Observe the circular movement of breath in the physical body.

Awareness of the chakras

Now we are going to become aware of different centres in the body, the locations of the chakras. Bring your attention to mooladhara chakra at the tip of the coccyx, near the perineum. Visualize a point of light there and focus your attention on that point of light at mooladhara. With the attention fixed on the point of light repeat the mantra Om mentally with every exhalation. When you breathe in be silent, when you breathe out mentally repeat the mantra Om and keep your attention fixed on the point of light which represents mooladhara chakra. This awareness has to be maintained at the tip of the coccyx.

Now become aware of swadhisthana chakra in the sacral region of the spine, and visualize a point of light there. With exhalation repeat the mantra mentally and focus your attention in the region of swadhisthana chakra. While repeating the mantra Om mentally, experience the vibration of Om emanating from swadhisthana chakra.

Now bring your attention to a point behind the navel and there visualize manipura chakra in the form of a point of light. Go on repeating Om mentally, and feeling the vibration of Om in the region of manipura behind the navel.

Continue repeating Om as you bring the attention near the heart, behind the depression in the chest at the centre of the sternum. There visualize a point of light at anahata chakra and experience the vibration of Om in the anahata region.

Go on repeating the mantra Om mentally and bring your attention to vishuddhi chakra. See it in the form of a point of light at the nape of the neck.

Go on repeating Om mentally and bring your awareness behind the eyebrow centre to the centre of the head. Visualize a point of light there, ajna chakra.

Now take your attention to the crown of the head, sahasrara chakra. There visualize a point of light and go on repeating Om mentally.

Hold the awareness at sahasrara, and feel the gentle warmth in the region at the crown of the head, inside the skull. Experience luminosity.

Now bring your attention back down to mooladhara. Focus yourself in the point of light at mooladhara. When you inhale feel the breath move right up from mooladhara, through the other centres up to sahasrara. When you exhale, and while you repeat the mantra Om mentally, feel the attention move from sahasrara right down to mooladhara through the frontal passage. As you move up with inhalation along the spinal passage from mooladhara to sahasrara become aware of the other chakras along with the breath, and as you move down from sahasrara to mooladhara along the frontal passage, be aware of the mantra Om which you repeat mentally while the awareness moves downwards.

Ending the practice

Now stop this practice and simply become aware of the silence and steadiness of the physical body.

Breathe normally, let go of chakra awareness, and experience inner silence, inner space and the motionlessness of the body. Take a deep breath in and chant Om three times.

Hari Om Tat Sat

Dhyana and Anandamaya Kosha

After going through the practices of pratyahara and dharana meditation, when we have been able to purify our mind, to discipline our behaviour and harmonize our emotions, the actual practice of meditation begins. This form of meditation is known as dhyana. In the state of dhyana we experience the union of individual consciousness with cosmic consciousness. Although we usually call this state the union of individuality with universal identity, we can also call it identification with our higher nature. Union is the reconnection of the individual mind with the higher cosmic mind.

Dhyana meditation is the result of inner sanyam. In the absence of sanyam, with the dissipated nature of the personality and the distracted nature of the mind, meditation is not possible. It should be clear that meditation means a pure state of mind and awareness. It is not a name given to a technique or practice. This pure state of mind is the result of sanyam.

Savishesha and nirvishesha dhyana

When we move from intuitive awareness to awareness of the existence of life at the cosmic, universal level, at that time the identification of the mind with the higher consciousness is temporary, not permanent. After the first glimpse of that higher consciousness, the mind is again brought back to the

51

world of the senses. Then again we meditate, perfecting sanyam, and again there is a connection with the cosmic consciousness. The connection lasts for some time, then again we come back. This process keeps on happening.

This process of temporary identification is known as *savishesha dhyana*, or meditation on a special attribute of our inner nature. Those attributes are bliss, or peace and harmony. We become aware of the inherent feeling of bliss, the inherent consciousness of peace, being in harmony with the environment without conflict. As that meditation progresses and we begin to identify with something manifesting within us, whether it is the sense of bliss, peace or harmony, that state of experience is further intensified by the awakening of a different kind of consciousness, which is cosmic consciousness manifesting in the body. Initially, in savishesha dhyana it is the individual consciousness which is reaching out to the cosmic consciousness. But when a connection is made, then the cosmic consciousness begins to flow into the individual consciousness. This transformation of consciousness is known in tantra as the merger of Shiva with Shakti.

Shakti is the principle which, when awakened, moves through different layers of consciousness on its way to experiencing transcendental awareness. Shakti is awakened when kundalini rises from mooladhara to sahasrara, where it merges with Shiva, consciousness. When the merging of Shakti with Shiva takes place, the two independent and defined manifestations of divinity in the form of nature and consciousness become one and fuse into one another. At that time cosmic awareness dawns in the individual mind. The transcendental consciousness manifests in the body and each and every cell of the body becomes transcendental. Transcendence is not only an experience of the mind, it is also an experience of the body. Becoming aware of transcendental reality is not only an experience of consciousness, a mental process, but also something you can experience physically in every cell of the body. Each cell of the body becomes enlightened.

In this state of enlightenment we move from savishesha dhyana to *nirvishesha dhyana*, or meditation without attributes. There the concept of duality, of the world and 'I' being two different entities, is totally lost. The raindrop merges with the ocean and becomes one with it, losing its identity and becoming universal. In this state of universal awareness, one experiences the existence or presence of God. The presence of God is not a state of mental enlightenment. It is the awakening of the total human personality, the total human nature.

Satchidananda – experience of divinity

How do we recognize the nature of God? How do we identify with it? Many people have said that God is truth, *sat*, transcendental consciousness, *chit*, and bliss, *ananda*. But my guru, Swami Satyananda, told me something different. Once I asked him, "How can God be truth, because truth is too dry. There is no beauty in truth. Truth is either an affirmation of a reality or a denial of the transitory awareness. There is no grey area in truth. How can God be recognized as truth, how can God be recognized as consciousness, and how can God be recognized as bliss?" Paramahamsaji replied, "These three words denote the three qualities that are experienced by an individual in the course of sadhana. Sat is the nature of God, but sat, the truth consciousness, is neither denial of the unreal, nor affirmation of the real. It is acknowledgement of the conditions and environment in which you live at present. Sat is an aspect of divinity."

I then asked, "If sat is neither denial nor affirmation, but rather acknowledging the continuous state of existence as we experience it, what is chit, the cosmic consciousness?" Paramahamsaji replied, "Cosmic consciousness is the auspicious quality, the uplifting, growing, evolving quality of the divine. Because we use the word 'consciousness' we immediately have an image or picture of a process of knowing, of realizing, which is very mental. We tend to identify consciousness with some inner mental process of knowing and realizing. But behind the knowing and realizing, and behind experience, there is always the aspect of auspiciousness. It is that knowledge of auspiciousness which is known as chit, and also as Shivam."

I asked, "Then what is ananda? Is it just happiness, like Archimedes sitting in his bathtub suddenly hitting upon the formula and shouting, 'Eureka, I have found it!'? Is it that kind of happiness which the mind experiences? Because, after all, in the transcendental form of being, happiness will have a form. If we use the words happiness, bliss, ananda, we are imagining a form of expression, of experience which is joyous, which is bubbling outwards."

Paramahamsaji answered, "Ananda is a state in which you appreciate the beauty that exists around you. It is not a mental expression of joy or a physical condition of happiness, rather it is an appreciation of the beauty of nature, prakriti. It is an appreciation of the interaction between nature and divinity, prakriti and purusha, which is always beautiful, *sundaram*." So, sat plus chit plus ananda equals the experience of divinity, and satyam, shivam, sundaram also equals the experience of divinity.

Self-realization and atmabhava

When one becomes established in the state of enlightenment, in yogic terminology it is known as *atmajnana*, self-realization. But this is not the end. One attains self-realization through a process of sadhana, in the form of an experience. Later, that experience has to be converted into a physical expression. It has to become part of your karma, part of your belief. It has to take hold of your senses. What is the use of an experience which does not affect and alter your senses? What is the use of having that transcendental awareness without it actually influencing the perception of mind, of manas, buddhi, chitta and ahamkara?

There comes a time in sadhana when, after going through these states of meditation, you experience nirvishesha dhyana. That higher reality then has to express itself in the world through the agency of the mind and body. The expression of cosmic consciousness in the world is known as

54

atmabhava, seeing that cosmic consciousness in everything. If you are unable to experience the existence of divinity in nature, your realization is only partial, it is selfish and again becomes confined to your individual perception. If you are going to dwell in your individuality again, you may have walked forward two steps, but you have also taken one step back. Despite your efforts, you find that you do not get very far. There is continual movement but the journey becomes very long.

As a yogi, as a sadhaka, one needs to be able to convert that transcendental realization into a physical karmic expression. That is atmabhava. Internally I may have a higher state of awareness, but until I see the same light, the same glow of divinity in others, my own realization is incomplete, because God is not invisible, God is visible.

There are many stories which give examples of this kind of realization. When a rich devotee invited Sai Baba to the celebration of a particular feast, saying, "We won't begin our festivities till you come," Sai Baba replied, "All right, I will come." At the appointed time, the man was waiting in front of the door with garlands to welcome his guru, but instead of Sai Baba he only saw a leper begging for alms. He said to the leper, "Get out of the way, my teacher is coming," and threw him out. That night, Sai Baba did not appear, so the devotee went to him and asked, "Master, what mistake did I commit that you did not come to my house despite your assurances?" Sai Baba said, "I did come but you threw me out. I came in the form of a leper." Only a person with atmabhava could have thought in this manner.

The senses and actions, the indriyas and karmas, meet to translate that higher cosmic experience into performance. It is only then that nirvishesha dhyana flows into and is experienced as samadhi. It is only then that one's personal sadhana is recognized as attainment of nirvana and moksha. It is only then that one can truly identify. It is the last temptation, the last kriya, the last action that has to be performed in the world of prakriti – conversion of cosmic consciousness and expressing it in our external life. Those

55

people who have been able to do that have become guides for humanity.

The process of yoga

This process of yoga and kundalini yoga may seem very lengthy and complicated, but remember that the journey always begins with a small step and you need to take that first step some time. If you simply make an effort to maintain the health of the body and mind and to develop the sense of well-being, that itself is one of the greatest forms of sadhana. If you become aware of your need to feel wholeness, to have physical and mental health, then you will be able to overcome much distress and conflict in relation to your nature and your aspirations. Therefore, it makes no difference whether you begin your journey with the practice of asana and pranayama, meditation and concentration, the process of relaxation, or the practices of mantra and kundalini yoga, because ultimately you will develop total health and experience completeness.

In order to understand the intricate nature of the mind and personality, you need to have willpower, conviction, faith and a vision that your life is not limited only to the expression of the senses or the mental faculties. There are possibilities of awakening your consciousness. The system is a lengthy one, but without intellectualizing too much, just begin with awareness, begin with the simple practices, and that is enough. Ultimately the whole key to individual evolution lies in awareness, in understanding and realizing where we are at present in our life.

We suffer when we are not able to fulfil our aspirations. We try to find happiness and deny suffering, but this concept has to change if we want to live the life of a true human being. In the life of a true human being there is adjustment with suffering and no expectation of happiness and joy. Happiness and joy become permanent only when you have adjusted with your suffering.

Therefore, everyone must have the basic philosophy of joyously confronting suffering, of not running away from pain, because the more you deny suffering, the more it gains in intensity. The more you try to avoid it, the stronger its grip becomes on the mind. How much are you going to struggle in search of something which can be had instantaneously if you simply adjust and learn to live with the present situation? Happiness is a temporary companion and suffering is a permanent one. If you can learn to live harmoniously with the permanent companion, suffering will not be recognized as suffering, and you will experience happiness, contentment and peace. Even this much transforms the craving, desiring, ambitious consciousness into a sattwic consciousness where you can experience luminosity. That light is the light of consciousness, the light of the Self.

People have different inclinations and tendencies, different degrees of evolution, different mentalities, samskaras and karmas. Therefore, one path cannot be suitable for everyone. The path is there, but how you walk it depends on you. We cannot follow each other's footsteps. Of course, it is said that we follow the footprints of great men who have left their imprints in the sands of time. But donkeys also leave their footprints in the sands of time. Do you have viveka, the faculty of discrimination, which enables you to decide which footprint is a saint's and which is a donkey's? It is better not to have faith in external circumstances which change continually. You need to have faith in your own inner conviction that you are going to perfect the path on which you have started walking.

Yoga says that the practices are there as guidelines, but along with the practices of meditation, observation of the senses, asana, pranayama, pratyahara, kundalini kriyas, chakra awareness and mantra, you can also develop simplicity of awareness and faith in yourself. Have faith in the direction that is given to you. That direction is always the same. The application may change from time to time depending on the changing scenario, but the guidelines have always existed. You only have to recognize and understand what they are.

It is our nature to complicate things by intellectualization and rationalization, and by becoming aware of shortcomings

57

and conflicting situations and environments in which we live. Therefore, another simple solution is just to consider that you need to learn how to focus your attention, how to experience as a drashta, a witness, the changes that happen inside your own nature, how to develop clarity of thought, faith and simplicity. If you just concentrate on these, yoga will become the blueprint of your life. It will not remain a mere concept or practice but will become your life. Living from moment to moment in a balanced way is known as yoga. Take a sankalpa, a positive resolution, to follow the path of yoga and thus experience completeness and wholeness in your own life.

DHYANA PRACTICE

Preparation

Please get ready for a short practice of savishesha dhyana.
Sit in any comfortable meditation asana with the body upright and straight, hands on the knees in chin or jnana mudra or wherever comfortable.

Become aware of the body internally and release all tensions from the physical body. Observe each and every part of the body. Become aware of any tension and tightness in any part of the body and try to release it. Be comfortable.

Now extend your awareness into the environment and become aware of the sounds around you. Become aware of all the sounds that you can hear, near and far, loud and subtle. Observe them. Become a witness to the sounds that come into the range of your mind.

Observe all sounds without thinking about them or identifying with them. Move your attention from one sound to the next and acknowledge their existence in the environment around you.

Awareness of symbol

Now focus your attention in chidakasha behind the eyebrow centre and visualize the symbol or the image of a tiny bright flame, jyoti, the symbol of consciousness.

Try to observe it, watch it. At first, seeing this symbol is a process of imagination, but as the concentration develops and intensifies you will gradually be able to see the outline and vague shape. Then, in the course of time, with the deepening of awareness and concentration you will see the symbol in its full glory and colour, vibrant and alive inside you. Right now, focus your attention and visualize the symbol of the jyoti at the eyebrow centre.

Om chanting

With the attention fixed on the symbol of the jyoti, we shall begin to chant short Oms. Breathe in deeply and while breathing out chant as many short Oms as you can do comfortably: Om . . . Om . . . Om . . . Om . . . Om

Do not strain or become breathless. You do not have to chant loudly. With each Om feel the vibration emanating from the centre of the symbol of the jyoti and vibrating throughout the entire body from inside. The visualization of the jyoti and the vibration of Om must be combined. When you feel the harmonious vibrations of Om pervading the entire inner space of the body also experience silence and luminosity within your being.

Go on with the practice at your own speed, in your own time. You do not have to wait for anyone, just do it yourself with total concentration and awareness on the symbol of the jyoti and the chanting of Om, feeling the vibrations of Om.

Experience the silence inside, experience the immobility inside. Merge your mind totally with the symbol of the flame. You are not this body, or the pain and pleasure associated with the body. You are not the mind, nor the thoughts, nor the feelings nor the experiences. Identify completely with the luminous nature of your being and experience silence and stillness inside.

Ending the practice

Now take a deep breath in and chant the mantra Om three times.

Hari Om Tat Sat

59

Pranava Meditation

Pranava dhyana, or meditation on the mantra Om, has been described widely in the yogic tradition and also in the *Mandukya Upanishad*. It is important for the perfection of dhyana and to enable the practitioner to become aware of the inner nature. When we practise yogic meditations, whether pratyahara or dharana, we tend to observe the activity of the mind or the images that come into our chidakasha. Our area of observation and psychic experience is related to the mind. That is important, of course, but human experience takes place on three levels.

The first level of experience in yoga is physical, where we are concerned with realizing and knowing the state of the physical body, experiencing comfort and discomfort, health and disease, tension and relaxation. This generates an in-depth awareness of what is happening at the physiological level, thus enabling us to eventually transcend the physiological or physical awareness and experience harmony in the body.

A similar definition is given in Patanjali's *Yoga Sutras* (2:46): *Sthira sukham asanam*. Asana does not mean a posture, rather it is a state of harmony in the body. Once you attain physical harmony, no matter how you sit or what you do, there is no pain or discomfort and you are at ease with yourself. *Sthira* means stability, *sukham* means absence of discomfort. So it is the physiological aspect that is known as asana. Here we are not referring to asana as the form of exercise we do in a yoga class, but as a state of the body. The body is one area of our identification.

The second level of experience in yoga is mental. Mental and emotional conflict, tranquillity, creativity, dormancy, pleasure, suffering, attraction and repulsion are some of the experiences of the mind with which we identify every day. Sanyam is awareness of the harmonious, balanced mind. All the practices that we do for relaxation or concentration are actually directed at providing stability, tranquillity and balance to our psychological nature. This balance and harmony is known as sanyam. In the *Yoga Sutras* it has also been written that samadhi or inner realization is the result of sanyam in pratyahara, dharana and dhyana. Mental expression in the outside world is pratyahara, mental containment in the inner world is dharana and mental realization is dhyana.

The third level of experience in yoga is awareness of spirit, which has been loosely defined by the name *atma*, soul, or *jivatma*, individuality, by different traditions. Inner experience or the experience of spirit takes place through individuality, through an expansion of consciousness where one is in tune with the universal nature. In order to train our limited personality to realize this transcendental nature, we have to dissociate ourselves temporarily from the body and mind. The two magnets of body and mind which are attracted towards each other have to be temporarily taken apart. This process is mentioned in the Upanishads.

Vibration of Om
In tantra and yoga, pranava dhyana is a practice of dissociating the mind from the body, and the spirit from the mind and body, with an eventual emphasis on focusing on the nature of the spirit. The nature of the spirit is threefold. We recognize this when we chant Om three times in class. When we say Om (Omnipotence), Om (Omnipresence) and Om (Omniscience), these are not just concepts but actual

awareness of the deeper nature. With the chanting of Om softly and slowly, the different body vibrations merge with the vibration of the mantra. The heartbeat merges with the chanting of Om. The pulse merges with the chanting of Om. All the different natural physical vibrations merge with the vibration of Om.

Speech is a distraction. When we speak we tend to ignore the other vibrations in the body. But there is a point where speech, if uttered at a certain frequency, joins with the frequency of the body. When you are frightened you are aware of your heart, but that is due to a physiological process. Increased circulation and increased adrenalin in the blood activates the nervous system and you can feel your body becoming tense and tight. There is a rush of energy through the body, haziness in front of the eyes, rapid breathing and palpitation. It is a physiological process.

In meditation, when you lower the frequencies of your speech, of your senses, that low frequency merges with the frequency of the body. It intensifies the natural frequency inside and therefore you feel the heart. Without actually experiencing anxiety, agitation or fear, you become aware of the natural throb of the heartbeat. You become aware of the natural pulsations in the body, and you can even hear the sound of the blood circulating throughout the body. Sometimes it can become very uncomfortable because we are in tune with our senses, not with the vibrations of the body, and the lowering of the mental, sensory and physical frequencies leads to *indriya nigraha* and *indriya nirodha*, blocking of the senses. There comes a time when we can just go beyond that. It is like the last barrier before you experience infinite consciousness, just for a split second. That can happen in day to day situations too.

So, in order to connect with your inner nature pranava meditation should be practised only once a month, but not every day or you will isolate yourself from active participation in life. For twenty-nine or thirty days of the month you are out in the world and for one day you are inside the body.

62

When should we practise pranava meditation and for how long?

If you do it at night, five minutes can often feel like one hour, and one hour can feel like five minutes, depending on how you are able to focus. Therefore, time is not a factor in pranava dhyana. Do it at night, you will have twelve hours in hand.

Which posture is best?

Any posture in which your spine is straight. You can even sit in a chair, but keep the spine straight because the moment you bend your spine, muscular constriction will inhibit your ability to be aware of and to experience the internal vibrations. So, try to keep the muscles in their normal position. The normal position of the muscles is straight when they are fully extended, yet relaxed.

Is lying down OK?

Preferably not, but you can recline against the wall. When you lie down you are more aware of your physical posture and often that can distract your concentration. If you sit, the pressure of the circulation is in the lower parts of the body, and there is a feeling of lightness in the upper regions, which is conducive to meditation. Therefore, we generally say that meditation should be practised sitting in a proper meditation posture such as sukhasana, siddhasana, padmasana or vajrasana. Of course, if there are physical conditions which do not allow you to sit for very long, in that case it is all right to at least concentrate while lying down. But I would recommend sitting if you can manage it.

In nadi shodhana pranayama should we start with the left or right nostril?

Start your practice with whichever nostril is open and clear. If the right is open and clear, begin with the right; if the left is open and clear, begin with the left. If both are blocked or both are open, then begin with the left. The purpose of pranayama, apart from revitalization, is also to activate the right lobe of the brain, which is the intuitive, creative side. The right nostril, which is connected with the left lobe, is the worldly side.

What is the difference between Silva mind control and yoga?

Silva mind control claims it can enhance the alpha waves of the brain within a minute. To increase the frequency of the alpha waves is actually not difficult. If you measure your brain waves, the moment you close your eyes, alpha intensifies and the moment you open your eyes, beta intensifies because the brain waves are very influenced by our sensory activities. For many people it is a major experience because they are not aware of the natural processes of the body.

However, scientifically, the moment you stop sensory interactions by closing your eyes, plugging your ears and blocking your nostrils, alpha begins immediately. Naumukhi mudra, also known as shanmukhi mudra, achieves this. Many people use this mudra as a practice to advance the pranayama techniques. You can do different things with it, like incorporating bhramari. The practice of nada yoga also uses this mudra, where you become aware of the sounds that are generated internally such as the music of the flute, bell or conch or the sound of thunder. Just the practice of shanmukhi or naumukhi mudra will enable you to pass into the alpha brain wave. Beyond alpha is theta and delta, and beyond that is *Brahmanda*, the cosmos.

The Path of Yoga

The topics for discussion are the four wheels of life, sannyasa and mansarovar. The physical Lake Mansarovar exists near Mount Kailash, but the real mansarovar exists within each one us, and the recognition and realization of this mansarovar is the aim of yoga. There have been many definitions of yoga from time immemorial. According to the time, people have propagated yoga in different ways and given it different names. Maharishi Patanjali propounded the system of raja yoga. Maharishis Swatmarama, Matsyendranath and Gorakhnath propagated the science of hatha yoga. Other sages throughout the ages have propagated jnana yoga and bhakti yoga, and avatars have propagated the science of karma yoga.

Freedom from bondage
We can see that a lot of thought has gone into the presentation of yoga. Although there are many branches and names, yoga is one and will remain one. The final aim of yoga is to discover the potential, the inherent nature, of the human mind. There is a song, "I am neither freedom nor bondage, I am Chidananda roopa, Shivoham Shivoham." This sloka conveys the entire meaning of the word 'yoga' – harmony and balance, not moksha or bondage.

You may wonder why it has been said, neither realization nor bondage, and why harmony, balance, equilibrium? This harmony and balance relates to every individual. Moksha, realization, is an outcome of the harmony that one feels within. You cannot strive for moksha, nor can you attain it. It is difficult to be liberated from the bondage of life. How do you become free? What makes you feel you are in bondage? These are not philosophical questions; they are related to our day-to-day life. We become sick because we think we are sick, we feel bondage because we believe there is bondage and we can experience freedom when we begin to feel the freedom inside.

My guru, Swami Satyananda, used to tell a story about a caravan travelling from one place to another in the desert. In the evening the camels would be tethered with a rope and everybody would rest. In the morning the camels would be untied and everybody would resume their journey. One evening there was a rope missing. So the camel driver decided to go through the ritual of tying up the camel. He pretended to tether the camel, which lay down, thinking that it was bound.

In the morning all the camels were untied as usual, but the camel that had not been bound would not get up. They started pushing and shoving the camel, trying to make it stand up, but the camel would not budge. Suddenly the driver realized that in order to free that camel he would have to go through the ritual of unbinding it. The moment he began to remove the rope from the camel's neck, the camel stood up and began to walk. So who is bound and who is free? Nobody is bound and nobody is free.

What do we experience in our life that we relate to freedom and bondage? The stuff inside the head, which is known as the mind. Many of the scriptures and thinkers have tried to define the mind. Is the mind a bundle of samskaras? Is it a bundle of thoughts? A bundle of impressions? Is it a collection of desires, ambitions and aspirations? No one has actually defined the mind. Ideas have been presented, but a proper definition has never been given to this energy, this concept, this faculty known as mind.

Yoga is equanimity

Samkhya has described four aspects of mind: manas, buddhi, chitta and ahamkara. The Samkhya system has said that these four aspects can be further classified as: *chetana*, conscious mind or *jagrit*; *avachetana*, subconscious mind or *swapna*; *achetana*, unconscious mind or *nidra*, *sushupti*; and *parachetana*, superconscious mind, *turiya*. The entire expression in life revolves around the images, impressions and memories that are gathered by these four aspects of mind. Our behaviour, actions and performance are determined by the impressions we have within us. Our beliefs, aspirations and ambitions are also guided by those impressions. But whatever we experience at present is not the real thing. Therefore, yogis have said that instead of trying to harness a transcendental experience with an untranscendental mind, the gross mind has to be recognized, accepted and made into a friend. This is the area of conflict in our life. We can't make our mind our friend, rather we want to suppress, subjugate and subdue the mental expressions and activities.

For example, when you sit down to meditate you expect your mind to become still and not to run here and there. But this is impossible. It is the nature of the mind to be active, because if the mind becomes inactive all your faculties, expressions and experiences will stop. In other words you will cease to exist. You will have your body, you will have your senses, but you will not function.

In order to harness, channel and focus the energies of the mind, different traditions prescribe different methods. Yoga says, "Meditation is the way, and through meditation we want to control the modifications of mind" – *Yogah chitta vritti nirodhah* (Patanjali 1:2). There are other ways too. You can become aware of the conscious, subconscious and unconscious impressions through observation and you can harmonize those expressions. Only when you are able to harmonize these inner expressions will wisdom dawn: *Ritambhara tatra prajna* (Patanjali 1:48). Therefore, yoga has always been a system of discovering the mansarovar within.

Just as you harvest the potential of nature, the moment you are able to harmonize the potential of the mind, you will experience tranquillity, harmony and balance, *samatvam*.

In the *Bhagavad Gita* (2:48) Lord Krishna has said, in one of the many definitions of yoga: *Samatvam yogah uchyate* – yoga is equanimity. That harmony is of the utmost importance in life, not God-realization, because self-realization is a by-product of the harmony you gain in your life. If you are not harmonious there is no realization. If you can be in harmony with yourself, your nature, your body, your mind and your spirit, and if you can live according to the principles of dharma, then you experience God within.

Four purusharthas

Do not differentiate between the concept of God and the action that you perform in the realm of prakriti. Prakriti, the manifest world, and our involvement, relationship and performance in the manifest world are not different to God experience, they are one and the same. It is for this reason that our tradition has also said that in whatever purushartha or work you perform become aware of that purushartha, that work, and be harmonious in that. Whether it is the purushartha of artha, kama, dharma or moksha, be aware of your actions and do not allow them to negate the existence of divinity in your life.

However, we allow our actions to negate the existence of divinity, and this is where all our problems arise. Once you become engrossed in action you find these actions have a beginning and an end: cause and effect. The cause can be positive or negative, sattwic or tamasic; the effect can be positive or negative, sattwic or tamasic, attractive or repulsive. We become engrossed in the play of karma in our life. How can we rise beyond the play of karma while following the path of purushartha? In everything that you do, be aware that you are doing it. If you think, be aware that you are thinking. If you walk, be aware that you are walking. If you breathe, be aware that you are breathing. If you sleep, be aware that you are sleeping. But in order to be aware, you do not have to remain focused at all times. Awareness has to be natural and spontaneous

In Hindi, awareness is known as *sajagata*, where you are aware of the awareness. An example is a mother whose children are coming home after having been absent for many months. Joyously, she cooks for them. She does not repeat their names as a mantra while she is cooking, but in the back of her mind there is continual awareness of them. In the same way, you do not have to continually think, "I am aware, I am aware", awareness should not become a mantra, but you should always know in the back of your mind that "I am aware." This awareness comes after you have acknowledged and recognized the role of purushartha in your life.

Often you are working for *artha*, money, external security, financial security. In whatever you do, the feeling of needing that security, that money, is utmost in your mind. You may be thinking of totally different things while you do your work, but you know you are working for some attainment, some result, some gain, some achievement. Even if you are sick you make an effort to go to work because there is a desire, an aspiration. Whether that aspiration is for money or some other reason is irrelevant; it is that desire which motivates you to do your work regardless of how you feel. It has been stated in the tradition, that among the purusharthas artha comes first, so that you are content, happy, satisfied, secure and there is no fear or insecurity about the future.

The second purushartha is *kama*, the fulfilment of all desires, sensorial and sensual, physical, mental and emotional. This is what we try to do all the time. We are trying to fulfil our aspirations, our desires, the needs of the senses and the sensual needs of the mind, which continually desires something exciting, new and unique. We are continually attracted towards those objects that can give us a sense of joy, contentment and happiness.

This is where the purusharthas stop. We have four wheels on the car but two are punctured – they are the tyres of dharma and moksha. What is dharma? Dharma is not religion; it is the sense of justice, the sense of righteousness that is inbuilt in you. If you can be aware of that sense of righteousness, justice and goodness that is inherent in your personality, then you are following the dharma of humanity. This is known as the manava dharma or the sanatan dharma.

If you follow this path, you can never go wrong. The moment you begin to follow this path of dharma by becoming aware of righteousness in your life, there will be the dawning of knowledge, the dawning of the wisdom that "I was never in bondage". That is moksha. Therefore, moksha is a symptom of a balanced personality. Moksha is the result of an awakened personality in which there is no difference between your thoughts, your inner belief and your performance in life, in society.

The attitude of sannyasa

In order to fully follow the path of dharma, it becomes necessary for one to become a sannyasin. Not the tradition of sannyasa that consists of wearing robes and renouncing the world, but an attitude of mental sannyasa. *Nyasa* means trust and *sam* means the sum total of yourself. When you have excess money you establish a trust and put it in the trust with the hope and belief that it will be utilized in the right way, for the purpose that you created the trust. Sannyasa is the same. You have to put in trust the gifts, the faculties, the strengths that are inherent in you. You have to recognize the qualities with which you were endowed when you took birth. How are you using these qualities? How aware are you of your personality, actions, beliefs and thoughts in your life, in your family, in society, in the country, in the world? What is your contribution? That sense of contributing to the growth of humanity is awake in the life of a sannyasin.

Sannyasa is an attitude and sannyasa is also a tradition. We are talking here, not of the tradition, but of the attitude of sannyasa. You can adopt this at any time, because the main components of sannyasa are *viveka*, the faculty of

70

discrimination, and *vairagya*, non-attachment. You have everything, but you are not attached, not possessive, not greedy about your possessions. They are there to assist you to free yourself, to make your life simple, easy and smooth, so you don't have to worry about shelter, or food, or money. You should not deny the pleasures of life, but enjoy them along with viveka and vairagya. If you can do that, then that is sannyasa.

The attitude of sannyasa also has to bring about a definite qualitative change in one's life, otherwise we have wasted our time, we have not made enough effort to realize sannyasa. If we want to be successful materially or spiritually, we must have the attitude of a sannyasin, not as a renunciate, but as one who is aware of himself, who is using the faculties of viveka and vairagya to expand the horizons of the mind. In this context sannyasa is definitely relevant to everyone.

This is exactly what the tradition has said. There are different *ashramas,* or stages of life. First is *brahmacharya ashrama,* where you learn skills to help you find security, happiness and contentment in life through education. The second stage of life is *grihastha ashrama,* in which you can attain all that you desire: prosperity, a happy family, fulfilment of all your urges, ambitions and aspirations. You remove the samskaras of sensuality and satisfaction from your personality and mind so that you can move naturally into the next stage of life, which is *vanaprastha ashrama.* There you can follow and pursue the path of dharma, righteousness. After vanaprastha comes the stage of *sannyasa ashrama* where you can experience absolute balance and harmony, samatvam, which eventually gives the awareness of "I am what I am". This is the process of yoga.

You have to understand the relationship of yoga to your nature, mind and beliefs. Yoga is not a set of practices you perform to gain health and to experience mental peace. Yoga is a state of living. It is a condition in which you learn to live properly, doing the things that you need to do yet maintaining clarity, harmony and balance.

Bhakti yoga

Apart from formal yoga teaching we have also started thinking along the lines of bhakti yoga, because ultimately the faculty of bhakti can purify a person. Through asana you can purify your body. The practice of shatkarmas such as shankhaprakshalana removes the toxins from the digestive system and the body becomes like new, there is a purity of body. Similarly, through bhakti one attains purity of consciousness, and consciousness in totality is the sum and substance of our existence as *jivas*, individual beings.

The teaching of yoga is given in Munger, and the teaching of bhakti is given in Rikhia. Hatha yoga is to purify and harmonize the body, and bhakti is to purify and harmonize the activities of consciousness. Bhakti is not something you learn, it is something you have to imbibe, it is something you have to discover. Bhakti is not worship, it is not adoration. Bhakti is not belief in a form, it is not belief in God. Bhakti is neither *karmakanda*, ritual, nor *upasana*, personal worship. Bhakti is discovering your relationship with your higher nature. That is all. It is jnana, knowing, it is realizing what your relationship as an individual being is with God.

When you realize your relationship with the higher nature, you can claim to be a bhakta. That relationship can take any form. For Jesus, the relationship was of father and son. For Mirabai, the relationship was of husband and wife. For Uddhava, the relationship was of a friend, a companion. Bhaktas have realized their relationship with God. That is the only reason they have been recognized as bhaktas, otherwise they are ordinary people. Bhakti is realization of that relationship. Just as externally we have relationships with other people: my brother, my sister, my father, my husband, my wife, my child, my friend, my enemy, in the same way bhakti is *bhava*, an awareness, an attitude which defines your relationship. It can happen at any time spontaneously, provided you are willing to empty yourself of preconceived ideas and notions about God. God is not Rama, God is not Krishna, God is not Devi, God is not Durga. These are symbols, manifestations, images, visions

72

of certain experiences that somebody had. You can have a vision, you can have a symbol too, but you will need to think about it.

Bhakti is fulfilled when you have *atmabhava,* the feeling of oneness. That feeling of oneness is spontaneous, not imposed; it is a feeling that everyone is mine, everything is mine and I belong to everyone. Another journey begins after samadhi, because in samadhi you have realized your nature, and now that nature has to manifest externally. Samadhi is not the end, it is a medium, a means by which you can express and realize outside what you have felt inside.

Bhakti and yoga are not two different things. If you call samadhi a PhD in yoga, then bhakti is a DLitt, it comes after the PhD. If you speak of yoga as being from body to spirit, from health to samadhi, there is a complete cycle up to the PhD in samadhi. It is an extension of that education which gives you the degree of DLitt. Therefore, bhakti is another step beyond yoga. We should make an attempt first to realize yoga and then to realize bhakti.

It is not a difficult path; we can do it. We are imbued with the faculties and energy, the mind, consciousness, emotion and rationality which can take us through this journey. We just have to make proper use of the faculties we have, and this is the training we require from yoga. If you attain good health in this training, well and good. If you attain mental peace, well and good. But the journey does not stop when you attain peace, it begins. Until you attain peace you are just preparing yourself.

From chaos to peace

There is always chaos in the world, and to attain peace from that chaos is the first trial. When you achieve peace, the unending journey of life begins where all your brilliance, capacity and energy culminate in one direction and you come to realize yourself, to know yourself and to understand yourself in the form of light. Then you understand that dream of India when it was said, *Atmadeepo bhavah* – you yourself become light.

In this journey of life, it is up to you how far you go. The process is within you: pratyahara, dharana and dhyana. In pratyahara you start to become aware of the sensorial and mental experiences one by one. After you have identified each one independently, combine them and have the complete picture. Once you see the complete picture and focus on it, that is dharana. To establish oneself in the state of concentration, contemplation, without any distraction or deviation of thought or mind is dhyana.

The senses can distract you, the thoughts can distract you, the samskaras and karmas can distract you. Even tapasvis like Vishwamitra were distracted by the senses. The senses are nothing but an interplay of maya in your life. In the desert you see a mirage of water. There is no water but you continue to see it. Why? This is projection of the mind combined with natural phenomena. Prakriti in itself is as powerful as purusha; maya is as powerful as Brahman. Therefore, when you have the initial picture of the totality, that is known as dharana. When you identify with the totality and not with the fraction that is dominant at present, everything is in prakriti, and it is through prakriti that you realize purusha, Brahman.

In spiritual life there is no end to distraction, but the basic principle remains the same. Do not allow yourself to be distracted; remain focused, remain firm. If siddhis come, do not use them, disregard them. There are temptations. Buddha had to face temptations. Christ had to face temptations. We all have to face temptations in our lives, and they capture us. But if we can say no to them and be happy about it, without feeling their absence, then that is the state of dhyana, constant, permanent, established dhyana.

One Family

If one child in a family of four children is handicapped, which child will the parents care for the most? You may say that the healthy ones will receive the most care, but this is not so. The parents will provide the healthy children with all the facilities they need to complete their education and stand on their own two feet, but the handicapped child will receive the most care. In exactly the same way, some people in the family of God are handicapped because they are not able to enjoy the same facilities as healthy children.

A healthy child receives an education, and after completing his studies in India he may be sent abroad so that he becomes well trained and able to earn name and fame in the world, and is thus able to stand on his own two feet. In this way, the healthy child receives facilities automatically and later contributes to the growth and upliftment of the nation. The handicapped child, who is dependent on his parents at home, cannot be educated to the extent where he can be called an intellectual, or be given facilities through which he can become wealthy. But the spark of God is also burning in the handicapped child and that child also wins God's affection.

Widening the vision
If we adopt this viewpoint, then definitely the misconception in our mind today regarding our own status in society will

become clear. Feelings such as, "I am high, he is low", "I am big, he is small", "I am rich, he is poor" are inherent in the Indian way of thinking. In the very beginning we understood that the whole world was one family, that the whole earth, even the whole of creation, was our family. But today our actual family is limited to mother, father and children, and this way of thinking is becoming narrower. Once the family planning slogan was: "A small family, a happy family". Then it changed to: "Two of us, two of ours". Later it changed again to: "The first one not now, the second one never". In the future it may possibly become: "I am not yours, you are not mine".

There is no certainty in the human mind. It is a characterless mind without ideals, because we have come to believe that character and mind are imbibed from outside. We have forgotten that feeling comes from within. This state has become the cause of man's downfall. The disputes and disturbances that exist in society and the world today stem from this belief. People have limited their feelings, and are concerned only with self-fulfilment. Even if the other person starves to death they do not care, as they want to become wealthy at any cost. This is selfishness. When a person's thinking is negative, he definitely has to face negative circumstances.

The same attitude is reflected in society today. People have become negative and the environment has also become negative and destructive. If we want to safeguard our future, we will have to take the necessary action. Firstly, we should discipline ourselves so that we experience the thoughts and ideals that we consider spiritual and wish to achieve from external sources and efforts. They should flow out of our inner self spontaneously. So, experience of the self and internal discipline are needed.

Secondly, our actions should not be for our own selves. The actions we perform should be done with the feeling of service. These actions should also extend to others. Our guru, Swami Satyananda, calls this process of thinking 'atmabhava'. He says that you definitely care for your own

76

self and for those whom you believe to be your family. When a near relative falls sick, has an accident or dies you express sorrow. You keep in touch with incidents happening to distant relatives, but you do not pay any attention to the person who is not your relative, who is not connected with you in any way. You just say that they are suffering due to their karmas, that they are experiencing poverty or wealth due to their vices and virtues. This thinking is not based on right knowledge, nor does it show the proper connection you should have in relation to mankind. It is associated with your narrow vision. But, sooner or later, in the life of every human being who wants pleasure, satisfaction and spiritual upliftment, a time should come when the emotions encompass those to whom you are not related. This is called atmabhava.

Spiritual education
When our actions and conduct include thinking and worrying about others, they are helpful in the upliftment of mankind. Swami Satyananda has said that there would be no poverty in India if people thought of their family not just as 'two of us, two of ours' but as 'two of us, three of ours'. Add one more to the number. If there are four in the family, then make it five. If there are five, then make it six. Provide one extra person with the same sort of facilities that you provide for yourselves. If you buy two pairs of shoes for your two children, buy one extra pair also for a deserving child. If you buy two pairs of trousers for your two children, then buy a third pair also and give it to whoever deserves it. India's wealthy citizens have the capacity to help those less fortunate in this way.

The meaning of the word wealthy is not owning Tata. After all, we are also wealthy; there is no poverty or neediness in our lives. We definitely think about how to increase our prosperity, how to invest our money, but we are not dying of hunger. So, if we, the wealthy citizens of India who lack nothing, were to provide patronage to a needy person, then rather than waiting for a generation, in only one year the

77

signs of poverty would vanish from the face of India. Such programs are being undertaken by those who are aware and who understand. It has also been added to our institutional programs, because we do not just teach yoga. We also go to the backward regions of India and try to perform some service according to our capabilities. This is spiritual education.

Service is not charity. Service is not done for name and fame. Donations are not given for name and fame. Today people run after name and fame. If they build someone a small mud hut with a roof made of husks, they stick a big marble stone on the front with their name as donor written on it. Even though the hut may be washed away in one rainy season, their name must not be rubbed off the marble stone. Such is the mentality, and if this mentality continues, then even God cannot come and stop humanity's downfall. God is also becoming disappointed.

If your child goes on the wrong path and you try to correct him, but he does not understand and keeps on committing the same mistakes, then won't you also become disappointed? When your child lies, cheats, steals and speaks ill of others, then you get hurt too. You undergo a nervous breakdown. The same lies, cheating and theft have a wide effect, even causing heart failure. Do you think that God is immune to those feelings? No, God is not immune.

If we have come here in His form, then the emotions within us, the samskaras within us, the thoughts within us, are in God too. Your child is not born with feelings different to yours. The emotion is the same. The emotion in the child, the father and the mother is the same although the behaviour may be different. Just as a parent desires the happiness of his child, God also desires the happiness and upliftment of humanity. Just as a parent feels pain and disappointment seeing his child going on the wrong path, in the same way, God is also filled with sorrow and disappointment to see humanity going on the wrong path.

In the same way that a parent abandons his child after suffering from his misdeeds, God also abandons man when

78

He feels distressed by his misdeeds. If you maintain the belief that the Lord is an ocean of love and compassion and that even if you keep on committing mistakes He will keep forgiving you, then you have forcibly applied this thought in your life to escape from your guilt. That thought is false. You believe God to be an ocean of compassion, but how long can He be compassionate? Man takes birth and dies. In his whole life compassion is never seen. Humans take birth many times. In *Bhajo Govindam*, Adi Shankaracharya says,

> *Punarapu jananam, punarapi maranam,*
> *punarapi janani jathare shayanam*

Birth unceasing! Death unceasing!
Ever to pass through a mother's womb.

However, although we take birth and die so many times, we never realize God, we realize only sorrow, pain and grief. No matter how many times a man or woman takes birth, the experience is just suffering, grief, distress and affliction. Humanity never experiences God in each and every moment, action and thought. Only a few unique people understand this fact, ones to whom the Lord gives His darshan, and says, "O child, you are my beloved! All are beloved but I love you most," because they have given meaning to their life and their emotions. They have made their lives successful by their deeds, attitudes, thoughts and behaviour.

How do the concepts of yoga relate to the concepts of heaven and hell?

Human beings should adopt two things in life. One is an attitude by which they achieve self-discipline, and the medium for this is yoga. Yoga has been given importance in Samkhya philosophy. Maharishi Patanjali was a Samkhya yogi and in the *Yoga Sutras* he has said in the first sutra, *Atha yoga anushasanam* – "Now you know that yoga is a discipline". Why did he use the word *atha*, now? When we use the word 'now', it is understood that we are continuing on from something else, that the situation has been explained to

79

some extent by a previous interaction or thinking. For example, now we are talking about how people should behave, what type of care should be taken and which process or solution has to be followed. Tomorrow, we may say, "Remember that you can make your life better through this process." In the same manner, by using the word 'atha' the sages refer us to a process through which we can expand our knowledge and make our attitude and behaviour pure. This method is yoga.

They have not described yoga just as a curiosity. If there is curiosity to know God, if one is a *Brahman jignasu*, then discipline is needed to purify that curiosity, *atha yoga anushasanam*. So, this fact of disciplining oneself has been separated from our life and accepted as being part of the process of sadhana. But this is not the final solution. This is just a stage in which our thoughts and intellect are balanced, in which we see, understand and associate our behaviour and actions with the well-being, not only of ourselves but of the world.

We have often said that yoga is the means and not the goal. Yoga is considered to be the goal when it becomes an inseparable, intimate part of our life. Until then, it is only a means, a path of endeavour. We should try to become harmonized internally and act in such a way that the whole word is benefited and uplifted. This is the first point.

Secondly, we must endeavour to transform our selfish attitudes and awaken a feeling for humanity. We should try to associate ourselves with everyone. If another's happiness can be our happiness, then another's sorrow should be ours also. In the same way that we try to get rid of our own sorrow, we should try to relieve other people's sorrow. This is called service. If we believe yoga to be self-analysis, the study of our own life, and transform our actions into service, then we can even achieve the stage of surrender through this self-analysis and service. And in that surrender we can also achieve God-realization.

Most of you know the story of Saint Ekanath, who went to Gangotri to offer water to Rameshwaram. In those days

80

the journey was very difficult and took many months. At the entrance to Rameshwaram, he saw a donkey dying of thirst. Other people were offering their water at Gangotri, but Saint Ekanath fell into a dilemma. He had brought water to offer to the Lord, but he did not know whether to offer it to God or to one of his creatures who was dying of thirst. Finally, his inner self told him, "Give the water to that thirsty donkey, it is an immortal fragment of God." Ekanath left the temple and gave the water to the donkey.

What would you have done in his place? Search your heart and say what you would have done in such a situation. How many people would have given water to the donkey with an open heart? This world is called paradise and it is also called hell. Paradise is not different from this world and hell is not different either. If there is a heaven, it is in your own life, and if there is a hell, it is also in your life.

People don't focus on heaven at all because if they did they would be caught up in unnecessary problems, worried that the day their bank balance ran out their stay in heaven would be over and they would be thrown out. If seen clearly, heaven is just a hotel where there is good food, dancing and pop music playing. Everyone comes in their Sunday best, sprayed with sweet perfume, clean-shaven, well groomed and well dressed. They sit there with honour, smoke, dance and listen to music. Famous people like Michael Jackson perform so you feel pleasure. But the day your pocket is empty, they take you by the scruff of the neck and throw you out. When the good karmas are exhausted, then you are thrown out of heaven. So never desire heaven in life. If God says, "I will take you to heaven," then say, "No, take me anywhere else but not to heaven." Never say that any place looks like heaven. Rather than accepting the concept of heaven, accept the concept of hell because hell is real. The imagination of heaven is not real. Hell is where man, somehow or other, tries to become good so that he will be free from sorrow.

There is both heaven and hell in this life itself, but if anything is to be desired at all, we should desire to live happily in hell. Why live sadly in heaven, always in fear and doubt that at any time you may be thrown out when your credit is up? That is fear. Never desire to live with that fear and doubt. In our philosophy it is also said that the best place is the mortal world, earth, where you achieve whatever you wish for by your endeavour. The happiness that you can gain in the mortal world through your own efforts and sadhana cannot be gained even in heaven. The happiness you can get on earth, you will not get anywhere else. There is no such place as heaven and hell in the physical form, they are just forms of our own thoughts, behaviour and attitudes. If you can give a good form to your thinking, behaviour and attitudes, you can achieve closeness and union with God.

There is a short story about a devoted saint who used to meet with God every day. Once he asked the Lord to come for a walk along the seashore, and the Lord agreed. The devotee asked for a boon: "If I happen to stumble, please hold me." "I won't let you fall," the Lord replied.

Both walked together in silence because the means of conversation was not verbal. The way to talk to God is not through words but the language of silence. Suddenly the devotee turned around and on the sand behind him he saw the footprints of two people in some places and the footprints of only one person in other places. The devotee felt very hurt, thinking that maybe God had disappeared when he was looking ahead. "Does He have another friend?" So he said to the Lord, "You said that you would go with me, but in some places there is only one set of footprints." The Lord replied, "Son, when the journey became difficult, then I carried you. The footprints you can see are mine, not yours."

Faith, trust and belief

When man achieves happiness and pleasure as a result of his own endeavours, then he achieves closeness, union, with the Lord. So do not feel frightened, suspicious or hopeless. All these are different states which relate to prakriti. They are produced naturally within us, they relate to maya and

82

are a natural part of our lives. But if our attention becomes diverted to God, then the voice of the Lord becomes true. In the *Ramacharitamanas*, it is said, "When the jiva turns towards me, then I put an end to all his karmas in a fraction of a second." The same thing is said in the *Bhagavad Gita*: "When the jiva becomes united with me, then I break all his bonds." In the verses of Kabir Das it is said, "If you search for me, you will find me. O disciple, where do you seek me? I am right beside you."

It is essential to have faith and belief in God. The *Ramayana* also begins with these words. Faith in God is necessary and trust in oneself is essential. These are two small resolutions that we should introduce into our lives. Keep this faith and trust that you are never alone: "There is a blessing hand above me and I have faith in myself, in my behaviour and in my efforts. I am not weak." If this feeling grows in your life, then your way will be clear. So, at every step keep reminding yourself that you have faith, trust and belief.

If at some time you feel the need to intensify this faith, if you think you need more sadhana as a process to intensify your faith, then there are also ways. One way is mantra. In reality there are two forms of mantra. One form is faith. If we have faith in the mantra, we will have realization of the name of God. If our mantra is 'Om Namo Bhagavate Vasudevaya' or 'Om Namah Shivaya', our faith will take us to realization of the name and attribute associated with the mantra, whether it is manifest or unmanifest. From the mantra 'Om' also we get an indication of something, even though it is a formless form. This is the relationship between faith and mantra.

The vibration of mantra
The second relationship is between the mantra and our inner personality. It deals with our internal expressions which remain unmanifest, formless. There is no name, no form and no attribute for the internal expressions. Name, form and qualities are the attributes of something which has been identified by the human mind. This identification is

intellectual, it is based on a concept, a belief, an idea. It is an intellectual analysis of appreciation and acceptance of something which we have imbibed, either through direct sense cognition, or through belief in our tradition, culture and religion, or because someone whom we respect has told us to believe it. Thus it is still related with our mental process. But when we go deep inside the name, form and idea, we experience one that does not exist.

For example, if you reach inside the molecules and atoms of your body, in the middle of the atom you will feel the vibration of a force. The feeling of that vibration is very subtle and it can be experienced only after reaching its subtleness. In the centre of all the atoms in your body there is a basic vibration. The gross perception does not hear the sound or vibration of the force in the body, but at the atomic level, of neutrons, electrons and protons, you feel only vibrations. You do not feel solidity or stability. In that form you do not feel the body. In the same way, the experience of the body is also not only of the physical form. There is a stage in which vibration becomes everything.

When the force of mantra becomes associated with our inner nature, then the gross form does not remain, neither does name, form or quality. What form is there? With the help of the vibrating force of the mantra we are awakening the vibration within us. In western countries, when we give a mantra to someone, whether it is Rama, Krishna or Shiva, we do not explain that this is the mantra of Shiva who lives in Kailash, who has a snake round his neck, wears ash, drinks poison and has the moon and the Ganga flowing from his hair, etc. We just give the mantra. They have no mental image of Shiva. There is a lack of attributed qualities, but there is no lack of faith, and they perfect and awaken the mantra, experiencing peace within the self only because of faith.

Mantra japa is also a sadhana and one can achieve perfection in mantra by many methods. Sometimes the guru forcibly takes hold of a person and whispers the mantra in their ear, because he sees that the person needs that mantra, but is being drawn away by materialistic attitudes. Many people receive a mantra of their own free will. If a person wants to take a mantra of his or her own free will, then there will be a resolution and the possibility of the mantra being perfected.

There is also another way. According to how you feel, you can select an image of the Lord in which you have faith. You may choose the mantra of that form yourself. If your faith in that particular form is very intense, the guru is not necessary at that time. However, this is only in the context of mantra, not in any other context. Whatever form you have trust in, whatever form captures your feelings, you must choose its mantra and perform japa. But there is some danger in that. We think that the more powerful the mantra is, the quicker our development will be. We forget that our capacity is very limited.

Keeping the mind under control

If you light a small cracker in your room, it will make the sound 'pat' and there will be no chance of breaking the windows. But if you set off a big bomb inside your room, what will happen? The small cracker gives enjoyment whereas the bigger bomb blasts the eardrums. You can get hurt; if it is a big blast you can die. Similarly, if you choose a mantra yourself, it should be small, beautiful and charming. Do things in a natural way. Do not desire a lot of power. Go for a little power which you can keep under your control. Can you control your mental balance? No! If you become unbalanced, then you approach your guru and say, "My mind has gone wrong." What will the poor guru do? You did not ask him whether or not you should repeat the mantra.

Do you know the story of the monkey with a sword in its hand? A king had tamed a monkey and the monkey was very clever, always caring for the king's security. One day the king was doing yoga nidra after lunch; he was a yogi king. While he was doing yoga nidra, a fly buzzed by and sat on his head. The monkey was sitting there making sure that the king was doing yoga nidra, when he saw the fly. He thought his master was being disturbed, so he shooed it away. The fly flew around and then sat on the king's nose. The monkey again waved the fly away.

The monkey had good intentions and was trying to ensure that his master's sadhana was not disturbed, so that better and better concentration would be achieved and the yoga nidra would be successful. He spent a lot of effort on driving the fly away. Sometimes the fly sat on the king's nose, sometimes on his eyelids, sometimes on his ears, sometimes on his neck and sometimes on his head. The monkey got irritated and thought, "Why not do something? I will kill the fly." He saw the king's sword nearby, picked it up and waited. The fly sat on the king's throat and the monkey killed it with the sword. But the fly did not die – the result was that the king went from yoga nidra to maha yoga nidra!

So, do not let your naughty monkey have any weapon which can take you from this world to the next. This is the secret of mantra. If you are given a good mantra, then sadhana, faith and trust can definitely be awakened. After that awakening, your effort takes the form of service. After that achievement, life becomes disciplined, and only then will your life be successful.

A Gathering for Friends of Yoga

European Yoga Fellowship,
Aix-Les-Bains, France, 24–27 April 1997

The Beginning of a Dream

This gathering for friends of yoga is the beginning of a dream to see different people from different traditions and walks of life coming together under the umbrella of yoga. The European Yoga Fellowship was formed with this intention. The first event of the European Yoga Fellowship is definitely the beginning of a dream that we will all cherish with happy memories and with the inspiration to incorporate the science and subject of yoga in our lives.

We need to understand yoga and how to apply it. A long time ago, when humankind was still in its primitive stages, someone discovered how to make fire, wrote a book on the subject and printed three copies. Then he started to tour the world. He visited three different tribes and gave the book to each one with these instructions: "In this book I have written down the process of creating fire. Fire is definitely beneficial for providing warmth, for cooking food, for protecting oneself from predators and for providing light." After describing the various benefits of fire, he continued on his journey.

The first tribe said, "Wonderful! This book contains the answers. Let us keep it and worship it." They never learned how to make fire. Although the knowledge was there and they worshipped and adored the book, they remained totally ignorant.

The second tribe said, "Fire is something that does not exist and we have no knowledge, understanding or inclination to discover what fire is. So let us throw the book in the river."

The third tribe looked at the book and read it. They learned how to create fire by rubbing sticks together. They learned how to use fire to cook their meals and to provide security and light.

Many years later, when that inventor of fire again visited these three tribes, he discovered that the first tribe, even with all the knowledge contained in the book, had never understood or learnt the use of fire. The second tribe had thrown the book away, believing that fire was impossible to achieve and attain. But the third tribe had actually studied and used the potential of fire to enrich their own lives, community and tribe.

Similar things have happened with yoga too. It has been around for a long time and people have used it in different ways. Some thought yoga was a process of enlightenment and looked at it from a mystical, spiritual viewpoint. Some said, "It is not our cup of tea," and ignored it. Others said, "Let us try to discover what this is all about and reap the benefits."

We belong to the third category. At least the speakers, guests, delegates and friends who have come here in the spirit of yoga, with the aim of understanding and incorporating the principles and practices of yoga in their lives, belong to the third category. Our combined efforts to discover our nature and potential in order to enrich our lives will make us see a better dawn for the whole of humanity. That is why this is the beginning of a dream, and with your help one day it will become a reality.

The Vision of Yoga

Yoga has always meant connection. Yoga believes that there is an intimate and subtle connection between the individual, the world and the cosmos. Once we become aware of this connection, which is individual, global and cosmic, our creativity becomes alive and we become fulfilled in all spheres of life. Connecting with nature, whether personal or cosmic, has been the aim of yoga.

Nature is multidimensional. Externally, in the physical sense, we connect with each other through the breath. We are breathing in and breathing out, but it is not only you or me, as individuals, who are breathing in and out. The entire world and all of nature is breathing in and breathing out. Plants breathe in and out, animals breathe in and out and human beings breathe in and out. Through the breath we are connected with our environment, with our fellow human beings and with all sentient beings. Just as we are connected with each other physically through the breath, another connection also exists. That connection is consciousness. In German the word 'atmen' means to breathe, and in Sanskrit the word 'atman' means 'spirit'. The breath is the connection in the external dimension, and the atman, the spirit or consciousness, is the connection in the internal dimension. When we breathe in or out, there is a process of expansion and release – liberation, freedom. Even the statement, "Give me air," indicates the desire to expand and experience freedom.

This expansion and freedom is also internal. In tantra this concept has been defined in very beautiful terms as Shiva and Shakti. Shakti is the force, the energy. In the physical dimension, this energy is the breath. The subtle aspect of Shakti is energy – vitality, dynamism, movement. The other aspect is Shiva – consciousness. It is the awakening or the expansion of consciousness and the experience of freedom, liberation of energy, which come together. The practices to give you this experience are the systems of yoga.

There is another symbology. You may have heard about the dance of Shiva and seen the Indian icon of Shiva dancing. Many people may think that Shiva is a religious figure, but he is not. The word *shiva* means the auspicious nature or the auspicious consciousness, consciousness which is conducive to positive, harmonious, and balanced growth. Therefore, this symbology and the icon of Shiva dancing represent a process of connection between the individual and the cosmos.

Multidimensional experiences

Just as nature is multidimensional, so yoga sees a human being as having different dimensions of experience. The first dimension of experience is the physical body. We identify very deeply with the body or the physical structure because it is visible, we know that it exists. How do we know? Because of our thoughts, our rationality, our contemplation, the beliefs and ideas that we try to implement in our life. This subtle activity makes us aware that there is something known as the mind. In the same way, another area of human experience is energy, the dynamic force known as prana. At the physical level this prana is experienced as warmth in the body, as motion and as energy and vitality. At the subtle dimension, it is experienced as the life force, the breath, in the absence of which we would not exist.

There is a relationship between the breath and the spirit. When we stop breathing, when the breath finally leaves the body, we die. Is it only the breath leaving the body and the

92

body not breathing any more that makes us dead? Or is it the exit of the spirit from the body? Initially I used the German word atmen and the Sanskrit word atman to show that there is a link between the breath and the spirit. Not the physical breath and not the internal, subtle spirit, rather as a process of expansion and liberation, freedom, growth, and overcoming of human limitations.

The aim of yoga has been to experience this growth and freedom. Various methods have been adopted. Yogis have believed that in order to experience the different dimensions of the body and the different levels of experience in life, one needs to develop awareness of the nature that governs our existence. They give the example of milk which is one substance but from which butter, yoghurt, cheese and many other things can be made. In its original form, cheese is not seen in milk, nor is yoghurt or butter. In order to extract yoghurt, butter, cheese or any other form of milk product, you need to churn the milk. Through a process of churning these different items are separated.

The four outcomes of practising yoga

In the same manner, although the body is perceived as one thing, there are four different outcomes and results from having a harmonious and balanced body. The first outcome is physical health. Nowadays many people have researched the benefits of yoga in the management of various physical disorders. Researchers have shown that psychosomatic illnesses such as asthma, diabetes, hypertension and other physical problems and ailments can be helped by the practices of yoga. Although yoga provides us with a sense of well-being and physical health, it is not a form of therapy. Please remember this. Yoga is not a therapy, rather it is a system by which you are able to harmonize and remove the imbalances from the body. The moment you are able to remove the imbalances and harmonize your body, your body experiences total health.

The second result of yoga is in the mental dimension – relaxation, rejuvenation and revitalization of the mind. Why do we sleep? We sleep to revitalize and rejuvenate our mental structure as well as our physical structure. The moment a state of relaxation is experienced in the body, tiredness, fatigue, and tension leave. The mind feels quiet, tranquil, and balanced, and we experience focus and concentration of the mental faculties.

Normally, in our day-to-day involvement and participation in the world of the senses and sensuality, our mind is continually moving from one object of pleasure to another. Whether this movement is conscious, subconscious or unconscious makes no difference; the mind is looking for pleasure, contentment and satisfaction. In this quest it looks for different experiences which can give us that feeling of pleasure, contentment, satisfaction and happiness. But then we look for new, better mental stimulation. This is a natural human process, but at the same time diversion of the mind creates deep internal, unconscious stress which does not allow the mental faculties to become charged with the energy, vibration and harmony of the individual and the universe.

So, relaxation and concentration is the second outcome of the yogic practices. Many people attempt meditation to find relaxation and concentration. But the object of meditation is not to provide one with relaxation and concentration, rather it is to expand the mind which is manifesting at present. With the expansion of the mind, the creative faculties become predominant and one becomes creative. That is the purpose of meditation: expansion of mind and awakening of creativity.

The third result of yoga is seen at the level of prana, energy. You connect with the source of energy and you do not permit your physical and mental energies to be depleted. So there is constant alertness and a sense of well-being, dynamism and vitality. This is attained through the practices of pranayama or breathing techniques. The purpose is not to teach you how to breathe, but how to awaken the energy, the power, the prana inside.

The fourth outcome of yoga is connecting with the subtle nature, the intuitive nature beyond the intellect or

94

rationality. Intellect and rationality are functions of the manifest mind. Nature is visible and manifest and also invisible and unmanifest. Initially, when we work with the mind, we are dealing with the manifest and the visible nature – intellect, emotions, feelings, rationality, thoughts, interactions, ideas, concepts, beliefs, etc. But when we move into the subtle dimension of our consciousness, there we transcend the intellect or rationality and connect with the cosmic consciousness. That cosmic consciousness manifests in our lives in the form of intuition.

In time that intuition is transformed into wisdom, where there is no difference between our belief and our lifestyle. At present there is a split between our personal philosophy and our actions. Because of the split, we undergo a lot of psychological, mental and emotional stress. Often we cannot come to terms with our lifestyle, or what we do, or how we behave or interact with our environment, with people or with society. We have knowledge but we do not have wisdom. Wisdom is applied knowledge. Regular knowledge is intellectual knowledge. So the fourth outcome of yoga is connecting with wisdom and applying the knowledge in our lives in order to become better and to become responsible for positive growth. This happens when we transcend the mind, when we connect with the intuitive nature, and when we convert our intellectual knowledge into wisdom.

Experiencing perfection
As a result of these four attainments in body, mind, energy and psychic consciousness, the final outcome is one of bliss, contentment, happiness and fulfilment. That is the culmination of the human effort and journey. This has been the vision of yoga. No matter how we begin to incorporate yoga in our lives, whether we do it with the practice of physical postures, or with the application of meditative techniques, or with other different systems, the final outcome is to experience perfection in life. In the course of this gathering there needs to be an effort to understand the

95

whole spectrum of yoga, not only the part with which we are associated.

A long time ago people believed in truth. Truth was like a long piece of cloth. Everyone wanted to have the truth in their possession, so they tore up that long piece of cloth into many millions of pieces. Each one held on to a piece, and said, "This is the truth! I have the truth!" But each fragment of fabric was not the complete truth. Even today we hold on to our piece of fabric and say, "For me this is the truth." But yoga says, "No, what you have in your hands is only a fragment of the fabric known as the truth. If you put all the pieces together, then you will have the complete picture." Therefore, right at the outset I would like to say, "Give yoga a chance in your life."

Human Health
and Applied Yoga

To understand how yoga is applied to gain health, it is necessary first to understand the yogic concept of human health. If we look at the idea of health from a very basic viewpoint, we see that as individuals we go through different levels of stress and tension in the course of our interactions with life. This stress and tension determines our health and our creativity.

Stress is a very common word nowadays. It is a necessary ingredient in everyone's life, enabling one to function optimally and to interact creatively. When the stress is unmanageable, it is known as distress. When the stress is euphoric, light, it is known as eustress. These are the three levels of stress in our lives: balanced, positive stress or eustress, and negative stress or distress, and we move from one level to another in the course of our daily activities. This stress determines the health of the body, mind and emotions. Even the word 'disease' represents an unbalanced state of personality. The word 'ease' means comfort, and when the state of comfort, harmony and balance is somehow disturbed, due to our interactions with the environment and with other people, then the disturbed ease is known as 'dis-ease'.

We fluctuate constantly from one level of stress to another – physically, mentally, emotionally, morally and also spiritually. Our life is like the continuous swing of a pendulum. Sometimes we are on the right side, sometimes on the left side. Through this movement we are trying to find a balance. Yoga is a method of finding the right balance.

Yoga is a method of utilizing stress to enhance and develop human potential, and in order to develop this potential, it is important that we accept ourselves as we are. It is a human tendency to put on different kinds of masks in different situations at different times. Whenever we put on a mask, we see ourselves in that image. In order to experience spontaneity and to become natural, we have to remove these masks. The process of yoga is one of removing these masks and seeing ourselves as we are. This idea has been conveyed in the traditional yoga of the sage Patanjali, who first described yoga in the *Yoga Sutras*. He said that the purpose of yoga is to realize one's true nature and to become established in one's true nature. In order to do that, we have to learn to manage the situations and conditions that arise in our bodies, our minds, our emotions and in the dimension of our spiritual experiences.

Three stages of stress

There is a story about an early eighteenth century Sufi saint. During a walk with his disciples, he came across a fair where there were many different kinds of contests. One was an archery contest. Many of the disciples asked their master to participate in the contest and he agreed. Each contestant was given three arrows and had to try to hit the bull's eye, which was placed about fifty metres away. When the renowned Sufi master appeared in the arena, the crowd gathered to see how he would fare in this contest.

The Sufi master adjusted his body posture, lifted the bow, fitted an arrow, adjusted his cap and with an air of pride and confidence released the arrow. Unfortunately the arrow went very wide of its mark and the crowd started to giggle and laugh. However, one of the disciples thought to himself, "There must be a purpose behind his missing the mark." He said to the Sufi master, "You advocate concentration, merger and union, and yet you are unable to hit the bull's eye. Why?" The master replied, "I missed the target because I was behaving like an overconfident person. An overconfident person doesn't have the necessary faculties and control, so it is quite possible for that person to miss the target."

He picked up another arrow, but this time more carefully and gently. He took aim and shot the arrow, but unfortunately it flew half the way and then fell down. Again there was laughter from the crowd, and again the disciple came to his master's rescue by asking the same question: "Please tell me which one of your personalities shot that arrow?" The master replied, "The underconfident one who is never sure and who always falls back. That person will never hit the target."

Then he picked up a third arrow. He looked neither to left or right, nor did he bother about the wind velocity, he simply let the arrow fly. This arrow went straight to the centre of the bull's eye. There was great applause, the master collected his prize, which was a basket of fifty different varieties of French cheese, and started to walk away. His disciple said, "Master, please tell me who shot the third arrow?" The master looked at him and said, "That was me."

This story describes the three stages of stress: the overconfident person represents eustress or positive stress; the underconfident person represents distress or negative stress; and the third person, the natural person, represents the balanced state of stress. There is this swing of the pendulum, this swing of life from positive to negative and from negative to positive. We know that negative is bad, but we should also know that positive is equally as bad. Positive simply represents plus, while negative simply represents minus. If the minus can be bad, then the corresponding part – the plus – is also bad. What do we need to attain in life? The centre, and it is this centre which represents total health.

Finding a balance
The World Health Organization has defined human health as being physical, mental, emotional and spiritual. If there is

balance in the physical, mental, emotional, moral and spiritual dimensions, then a person enjoys total health. Previously the concept of health was simply confined to the body, to the management of disorders and the removal of defects and imbalances from the body. When this concept of health was defined by the World Health Organization, many people started to think, "What is human life? What is the body, what is the mind and what is the spirit?" Yoga said the same thing many thousands of years ago. This concept of yoga is evident in the raja yoga of Patanjali. In the *Yoga Sutras*, Patanjali, one of the ancient propagators of yoga, defined eight different stages of yoga in the form of yama, niyama, asana, pranayama, pratyahara, dharana, dhyana and samadhi.

Yama and niyama, the moral disciplines, relate to our moral health so that our attitudes, behaviour and interactions are harmonious and balanced. Asana and pranayama relate to our physical health so that with the proper performance of postures and breathing techniques, we are able to remove the blockages and imbalances from the body and the brain. Pratyahara and dharana, the aspects of concentration and relaxation, give us mental and emotional health. Dhyana or meditation, along with samadhi, the advanced state of meditation, provide us with spiritual health or spiritual well-being. This is the yogic idea of health.

Other experiences included in yoga are the states of stability and comfort. In the *Yoga Sutras* stability and comfort are associated with the performance of postures, but they represent two different areas of influence that a posture has on the human personality: physical stability and mental ease. Physical stability and mental ease are byproducts of performing a posture or asana. However, if we take this concept beyond the practice of asana, we will discover that the imbalances and tensions in the body do not allow the ease of the body to emerge. It is the same with the mind. The mind is in a state of continuous tension, dissipation and distraction. For the mind to become active, dynamic and creative, it is necessary for it to experience tranquillity,

100

ease and comfort. So, physical stability and mental ease or comfort are the two areas of experience that we try to attain through the practices of yoga.

Yoga is a process of finding a balance; it is not therapy. But because the body plays a dominant role in our life, the practices of yoga begin with the body. When we are unable to manage distress in the body, that imbalance manifests and is experienced as a disease. When we are unable to manage our stress, we have hypertension, we cannot sleep, we become nervous, our digestive function becomes sluggish, our circulatory function becomes slow and our respiratory system takes a different form. Slowly, slowly, this imbalance begins to affect the weakest organ of the body, and it becomes diseased.

In the *Iliad*, we hear of Achilles' heel, which was the weakest point in this warrior's body. Similarly, each one of us has a weak organ. In some people the weak organ is the digestive system, in others it is the immune system and in some it is genetic. This weak organ is usually affected when we undergo a lot of distress. Initially, the disease begins to manifest through that weak organ.

If twenty of us are put in similar situations with similar levels of stress and tension, that stress and tension will manifest differently in those twenty different bodies. Some people will find that their digestion plays up; some will find that their blood pressure goes up; others will find that their breathing is affected and they will become hyperactive and unable to maintain their balance. Some will find that they cannot go to sleep and others will find that they become nervous. Although the stressful condition is the same for each participant, the actual manifestation of stress in the body will be different in each person. This shows that we all have a weak area in our personality which needs to be balanced and harmonized.

Applied yoga
When we look at the yogic principles, we find that with the simple practices of postures, relaxation techniques and

concentration we are able to realign the body, mind, emotions, behaviour patterns and attitudes, and the outcome or by-product of this alignment is maintained. Many scientists and doctors throughout the world have conducted research to evaluate the benefits of yogic practices in the management of various disorders. We will look at this research briefly, beginning with India. First let me make it clear that just because yoga comes from India does not mean that Indians are more prone to accept yoga. Indians may have an understanding of yogic principles, but their misconceptions about yoga are universal. It is difficult for them to accept yoga as a science of life. Therefore, when research work was done in India, it was with a lot of scepticism that they found there was a scientific basis to the yogic practices and principles.

The research started in the late 1960s when some medical doctors began using yoga techniques to assess their benefits in the management of cardiac problems and heart disease. They found that yoga was very successful in rejuvenating and strengthening a weak heart, and that hypertension could be managed through relaxation practices and breathing techniques.

In the 1970s, research into the management of psychosomatic disorders was carried out. With non-insulin dependent diabetes, medical professionals found that within forty days of yoga practice it was possible to regain health and overcome the condition. With bronchial asthma, it was found that with regular practice of postures, it was possible to overcome the condition and to develop immunity to various allergies. In this way an interest developed in India in the management of health problems through yoga.

Since 1994 we have been teaching the principles of yoga therapy in the medical colleges of Bihar state, India. The government of Bihar has identified thirty-six psychosomatic diseases which will be treated with the practices of yoga only. It may be because there is a lack of medical facilities, but nevertheless it is a big step to accept yoga as a

102

therapy, so much so that the Indian Medical Council has also received a recommendation to include yoga as a subject in the medical syllabus. We are confident that, in the course of time, yoga will emerge as frontline therapy, not as an alternative therapy.

While this was happening in India, doctors in Australia also investigated the role that yoga can play in the management of cancer. Dr Ainsley Meares, from the Australian Cancer Research Foundation, experimented using relaxation techniques, breathing techniques and mantra to overcome cases of cancer. This is a very positive development, because it gives a different insight into the human body and human nature. In England, yoga is being tested and tried in the management of HIV/AIDS. These are some examples of the physical research into yoga being conducted by professionals, not by yoga teachers.

Similarly, for the management of mental disorders, psychologists, psychiatrists, and psychoanalysts have incorporated yoga techniques into their practice to improve mental attitudes, to harmonize and balance behaviour, to remove aggression, anxiety and fear from the mind, and to remove various blocks which act as inhibitions and complexes.

Simple yoga techniques have also been tried with prisoners, who are highly volatile, aggressive and have a lot of suppressed anger and frustration. Since 1995, we have been teaching yoga in prisons in Bihar, India. From a psychological analysis of the data collected, we have found that there is a marked improvement in the personality, behaviour and attitude of the prisoners after learning yoga. After seeing these results, the Bihar government gave us the opportunity to train lifers as yoga teachers. They are now going to different prisons as yoga teachers, having overcome their aggression, guilt and suppression, and are on the way to becoming responsible members of society. This is a brief summary of how yoga is being applied in the management of physiological and psychological disorders.

Health management

Yoga recognizes that health is not the absence of disease but the proper management of diseased conditions. It would be impossible for us to envision a person who is totally free from every kind of illness. We have a body, and the body is influenced by climate, environment and diet. The body is influenced by so many different factors, including genetic conditions, that it is impossible to say that one can be totally and absolutely free from disease. Yoga says that in the process of life, between birth and death, there are two conditions we cannot avoid: old age and disease. We have taken birth and we will suffer from disease. We will also become old and the body will become more susceptible and prone to influences which will alter its natural state of ease and comfort, and the body will suffer.

So, yoga does not say that we will never suffer from any kind of disease. Yoga says we will suffer because that is the natural law, but if we can manage the disease, then that management is health. Therefore, according to yogic principles, health is based on common sense. Health is based on how efficiently and effectively we utilize our body to perform its various functions, without sliding into levels of disease or imbalance which are the cause of illness. Therefore, health is not the absence of disease but the proper management of disease. That is the theory of yoga.

This theory is being experimented with by professionals all over the world and also by many people who suffer from chronic illness. There is a large range of yoga practices which give us the ability to function optimally in life. Hatha yoga, the most commonly known form of yoga in the West, is a system by which we detoxify the system and organs of the body, and with the elimination of toxins, the physical body experiences health. Raja yoga, another common yoga, helps to bring about flexibility in the physical body as well as balance in the movement and flow of the vital forces in the body. It also helps to bring about balance and harmony in the mental dimension, giving one the ability to cope with stress. So remember that yoga is not a method or a technique that allows us to escape from the responsibilities of life. Rather, it is a process which makes us face life with optimism and clarity of mind. If you are able to understand this, then the concept of yoga therapy will become clear.

Anxiety management

There are many new ailments and diseases that we encounter every day, but there is one form of disease for which there is no solution: DIFS or Disease Induced Fear Syndrome. Cancer, HIV/AIDS, hypertension, arthritis, digestive problems, diabetes and respiratory problems can be managed very easily provided we can treat DIFS, the fear syndrome. It is the fear that feeds the illness, and it is the fear that makes us diseased. In yoga, through the process of relaxation, through the process of creating and circulating the life forces in the body, then through the process of managing the mental states of anxiety and stress, we are able to overcome fear. Once the fear is overcome, disease has no place in life. This is the concept of human health and yoga, applied yoga and yoga therapy. Let us hope that you are inspired to face the conditions of your life with a positive frame of mind, thus experiencing optimum health at all levels of your personality.

Yoga and Total Health

Illness is the outcome of unresolved problems. When we are unable to resolve the problems we face, whether environmental, social, personal or family, the effect of those unresolved problems manifests in the form of an illness. We can also say that the patient is not the victim of a work of nature, an unhealthy lifestyle or of pollution, but is suffering because of unresolved problems.

We have to learn how to cope and deal with these problems at various levels of our personality. It is not enough to say, "Okay, I am suffering from ill health, I am suffering from disease and I have to treat it physically or psychologically." Human beings are all subject to the influence of circumstances, events and the environment and, therefore, we also need to develop an awareness of how we interact with and react to such situations.

Each one of us, all the time, is continually reacting; there is never a proper, spontaneous or reasonable action. We react to people, we react to what they say, we react to our pleasure and to our pain and suffering. Our entire life goes from one stage to another through a process of reaction; there are no original or spontaneous actions. These events and conditions have to be interpreted in order to understand their meaning. Only when we are able to interpret a situation properly will it become meaningful. This is an important

106

point to remember, because it is from this point that we begin the process of realigning our body with our nature, our mind and our consciousness. This is the beginning of the first step towards the attainment of total health.

Yoga says that there is form and content in life. To give an example: the body is a form but inside the form there are many different contents: emotions, rationality, logic, thoughts, ambitions, desires, feelings. These are the contents which we experience in the form of the body, but we see them as experiences, as conditions, as events which continually change and alter our perceptions and attitudes. Remember that the content of the physical form has to be harmonized to experience health, happiness, fulfilment and satisfaction. A painter is a good example. A painter uses the canvas on which to create an image or picture. The picture is the final outcome of the concept or image inherent in the painter's mind. The canvas and the paints are only the mediums through which an expression is given to the image already existing in the painter's mind.

Body, mind and consciousness
In the same way, there is a link between the body, meaning the human personality manifesting at present in our life, and consciousness, which is invisible, unmanifest and subtle. Consciousness is manifesting throughout the body. We can imagine consciousness in the form of radio waves and the body in the form of the radio. When the body is in tune with the consciousness, the projections of consciousness into the body will be harmonious. When the body is not tuned to the consciousness, the receptive signals will never be heard or seen. There has to be a tuning between the body or the personality which is manifesting, and the consciousness, which is unmanifest.

For example, we have different channels on a television set. If we want to see one channel, we have to change to that channel; if we want to see another channel, we have to change again. Imagine, for a moment, what would happen if all the channels were seen together on one channel. It

107

would be very difficult to decipher what was being seen on the screen. There would be no tuning and all the images and frequencies would be coming through on one channel. There would be no clarity. There would be a mixture of images with no meaning, a mixture of sounds with no meaning and a mixture of impressions with no meaning. This is similar to what happens when our consciousness interacts with the body in a very disturbed, distracted and dissipated way.

We have to make an effort to tune each frequency properly to a different channel. Once different frequencies are tuned to different channels, the images and sounds will be perfectly clear and sharp, and we can look at, understand and give a meaning to them. So, when consciousness is manifesting in our body and it is not tuned in properly, the body is going to react. This is the beginning of an illness. Illness is not a physical condition, rather it is a state of disharmony between our subtle nature and our gross nature; it is a state of imbalance between the consciousness and the body. Therefore, yoga says that if you wish to experience health or well-being, you have to approach your nature from different angles. We work with our body, but at the same time we have to work with our mind as well as with the expressions of consciousness which are filtering down into the mind and the body.

Intellect, emotions and instinct

Consciousness has three major areas of expression: intellectual, emotional, and instinctive. The first expression is intellectual, representing the head: understanding, rationality, analysis of a situation, a condition or an event, and living harmoniously with the intellectual aspect of consciousness. The second expression is emotional: the heart, feelings and sensitivity. When our heart is in disharmony, there will be suppression of emotions and feelings. This suppression is unnatural to the normal state of the body and mind, and when suppression happens we will suffer. So the release of blockages from the heart centre

108

leads to health. The third expression is instinctive; we react instinctively to many situations in life.

To understand how yoga views these three different expressions of consciousness in our life and body, we need to look at the concept of chakras in kundalini yoga. Chakras are centres in the body where consciousness manifests in a particular form and where energy manifests in a particular form. Those who have studied yoga will know that there are seven psychic centres or chakras in our body. The first chakra is mooladhara, at the base of the spinal cord, in the coccygeal centre; the second is swadhisthana, which is known as the sacral centre; and the third is manipura, behind the navel in the spinal cord, which is known as the solar plexus. These first three chakras or centres represent the instinctive dimension of our personality: fear, insecurity, sexuality, vitality, motivation and power. The fourth chakra, anahata, which is known as the heart centre, and the fifth chakra, vishuddhi, which is known as the throat centre, represent feeling, the emotional aspect of human nature. The sixth chakra, ajna, the eyebrow centre, represents the higher mind.

If you look at this description of the six chakras, you will see a very interesting pattern emerging. The first three centres deal with instinct, the two middle ones deal with the emotions and the upper one deals with the higher mind. The highest centre, sahasrara, on the crown of the head is the command centre for all these different centres of consciousness and energy.

The heaviest concentration of consciousness changing, directing, guiding and affecting our physical nature is at the lower level where the first three centres are active. In the middle area, where consciousness interacts in the realm of emotions and feelings, we have two centres, and the intensity of consciousness interacting at this level is less. At the higher level we only have one centre and the intensity of consciousness interacting with the higher mind is very little.

Now, this goes slightly against the normal belief that we are intellectuals. We are intellectuals, no doubt. We have developed our sciences and our beliefs to a great extent, but even that development of knowledge in society and in the world is not the final indication of knowledge which filters down from the consciousness into our life. Many people say that today we work with our head. We think we have access to information and to many different things through which we can improve our life. But all the knowledge and understanding we have, although it may be logical, precise and clear, is connected and linked with the three first psychic centres, which are instinctive. All our achievements have been in search of fulfilment, satisfaction and pleasure. Science has manipulated nature to make our lives more comfortable and pleasant, and to give us a sense of satisfaction, joy and happiness. The search for satisfaction, joy, happiness, pleasure and security are the expressions of consciousness at the lower centres.

We have ignored the middle aspect of feeling and emotions, thinking that rationality is above feeling and emotions. In early times, thinkers said that every expression in life came from the head, meaning the higher centre. Later, thinkers said that every expression in life came from the heart centre; that what we feel and what we believe in determines how we act and live. More recently, when psychotherapy was being developed, Freud and other eminent psychoanalysts said that everything that happens to us comes from the lower centres. When Einstein entered the picture, he said that everything is relative! The point to consider here is that we need to find a balance between our instinctive nature, our emotional nature and our intellectual nature. Once a balance is found between these three different natures, then transmissions from the consciousness into the body will be more harmonious, balanced and integrated.

The body is part of the consciousness manifesting externally. It is a unit of the cosmic, universal, all-pervading consciousness. The body does not contain consciousness, rather consciousness expresses itself through the body at these different levels. Therefore, we can say that the body is never ill and never healthy. The body is simply

110

responding to what is filtering down from this higher level, to what is coming down from the consciousness. If something coming down into the head centre is distorted, we go through head trips and have headaches; if what is coming down into the middle centres is distorted, we go through heartaches; and, if what is coming down from the higher to the lower centres is distorted, we go through a lot of frustration, aggression, suppression, anxiety, fear and insecurity. It is these mental states which later alter and influence the performances of the body and manifest in the form of illness and disease.

Pratyahara – consciousness therapy

How does yoga attempt to clear the transmission passage, the transmitters of consciousness into the body? Asanas, pranayama and the relaxation techniques can be used to induce different states of flexibility, comfort and ease into the physical, muscular, endocrinal and respiratory systems. But therapy does not stop there; therapy also has to continue at the subtle level.

The best form of therapy is consciousness therapy which clears the channels through which consciousness transmits into the physical dimension. An indication of consciousness therapy is seen in the practices of pratyahara. Pratyahara is the fifth stage of raja yoga, and the beginning of introspection, of reflection, of experiencing silence, of going within and finding stability, and of finding the focus. Pratyahara is also divided into many different segments and groups.

How do we become aware of something subtle, something that is happening internally at a subtle dimension at the level of consciousness? If the fruit is on the highest branch of the tree, you have to start climbing from the lowest level in order to reach it. This climb from the lowest to the highest level begins with awareness of the senses. There is an extension of awareness into the sensory perceptions to know how they are affecting and altering the mind and the consciousness. So, first, there is an extension of consciousness into the senses, and then, after we know exactly what is

111

transpiring at the level of the senses, there is a focusing of the consciousness.

The second stage of pratyahara is an extension of awareness into the mind, to know how our mind is interacting with situations, conditions and events which influence our life, and then there is a focusing of this awareness. The third stage of pratyahara is the extension of awareness into the emotional dimension, to realize and understand the nature of our emotions, feelings and sensitivity, and then focusing of this awareness. The fourth stage of pratyahara is the extension of awareness into the instinctive dimension and then, again, focusing of this awareness. This is how we gradually train ourselves to observe and analyze how we are responding and reacting to different situations that create an imbalance in our personality.

After we have observed the interplay and interaction of our consciousness with the senses, with the intellectual aspect, with the emotional aspect and with the instinctive aspect, we move on to the next stage of introspection which is known as dharana. Dharana is holding the consciousness stable and identifying with the tranquil consciousness. When we are able to identify with the tranquil consciousness, then meditation, dhyana, begins.

This process of self-observation or self-understanding leads to the experience of optimum health and well-being. Yoga therapy does not aim for removal of the symptoms of which we have become aware; yoga therapy is not a method of treating an illness or a disease. Rather it is a method of treating the person who is suffering from a condition by making him or her aware of their personality, and how the personality is interacting in the world at the external level and with the consciousness at the subtle level.

When we are able to do this, we find that our habits change and our lifestyle changes. We also find that our attitudes, perspectives and vision change, and there is a feeling of completeness and wholeness. With this sense of wholeness, the journey into yoga begins. We move forward to experience our life unfolding, growing and evolving.

Improving the quality of mind

Here is an example of how habits change. Once I had the opportunity of going to the source of the river Ganges in the Himalayas. Along the way there are little hamlets where people can rest and prepare for the next journey. One evening, when I was at one of the hamlets, it had snowed quite heavily and in the evening I went for a walk. There was also an invalid with a wooden leg who could not walk properly. He was hopping and trying to keep his balance on the snow and ice. I was behind him.

At first I did not pay him much attention. However, there came a point when I felt that he wanted to cross the street, but was afraid because he felt that he would slip on the ice. So I decided to help him out and said, "Can I help you cross the street?" He looked at me and replied, "I am frightened that I will slip on the ice and fall and hurt myself." I said, "Do you want a permanent solution to your fear, or do you want me to help you across the road?" "Both," he replied. "Please help me across the road and, if possible, give me a permanent solution to overcome my fear." I said, "Well, if you want both, then you have to follow my instructions." "How?" he asked. "First let me blindfold you," I replied. I took my dhoti and tied it around his eyes so he was totally blindfolded. Then I said, "Turn around five or six times so that you lose your sense of direction completely."

He turned around five or six times and then I guided him to dry, clear ground, held his hand and said, "Don't worry. You are walking on snow and ice, but I am holding you. Just keep on walking." That was not true, but well worth it. I made him walk both a short distance and a long distance on ground which was totally free of ice and snow, without telling him that he was walking on dry ground. When I found that he was walking upright with confidence and not faltering, then I simply took him across the road and removed his blindfold. Then I told him, "Look, for the first twenty minutes I made you walk on clear ground and when you felt able to walk without fear, then I simply took you across the ice on the road and you did not slip. Overcome your fear, develop self-confidence and an awareness of what is happening to you. With awareness, self-confidence and by overcoming fear, you will be able to go anywhere, even climb mountains, without worrying about slipping and falling."

This was not a good deed. I simply applied a yogic principle. If I had said to him, "Look, I can guide you to the other side," he would have been very hesitant and constantly watching where he was putting his feet. But by blindfolding him so that he lost his sense of direction, he was able to walk on dry, clear ground and develop his confidence and, in the same way, he walked across the ice.

This was a yogic principle applied to help an individual overcome his fears, to develop his self-confidence and to help him get in touch with his nature, which was not fearful and lacking in confidence. Once he got in touch with his nature, he was able to overcome his difficulties easily and happily.

Yoga gives many hints and ideas on how we can manage our life. It is up to us to apply these ideas and to become aware of those hints in order to improve the quality of our bodies, minds and interactions. Once we can improve the quality of the body and the mind, that is total health.

Mind Management

Management of the mind is a subject that has to be analyzed in relation to one's day-to-day activities, otherwise whatever is said is simply theory. Yoga has certain ideas and thoughts as to how the mind functions. It has defined mind as *manas*, the process of reflection, *buddhi*, the process of intellect, *chitta*, memory, and *ahamkara*, the ego principle. Many books have been written on these four subjects, but no one is quite clear about how the mind interacts in life and we only have our personal experiences to go by.

We can observe the various aspects of the mind and how they manifest, without trying to define the mind. In our lives there is a very beautiful process in which something subtle in the form of an idea, a desire or a thought manifests and implements itself at the gross level. There is an intimate link between our subtle nature (the mind), the nature which is more subtle than the mind (consciousness) and our life (the visible world of objects and senses). There is a flow of information which comes from the consciousness to the mind and into the body; the body is simply a medium through which the mind expresses itself.

From unmanifest to manifest
Therefore, it is important not to differentiate between the thinking nature and the acting instrument, which is the

115

body. We have to see it as the flow of one stream of an idea, coming from the subtle, the invisible to the manifest, the visible. In this context, look at this example: an idea evolves at the deepest levels of our nature; the idea becomes a desire; the desire then creates a plan of action, and that plan of action is later implemented by the senses, the body.

So we have a concept, which is related to the ahamkara aspect, the ego principle or the 'I' identity. All concepts in life generate from this dimension of the 'I' identity, the nature of individuality. Later, this concept filters down to the lower levels of the mind – the intellect, the memory and the reflective processes – and is identified as a desire or a need. This desire or need is then linked with our aspirations, our strengths and our weaknesses. It takes a definite form to fulfil a vacuum that we feel when we engage in self-reflection.

What is a desire? Desire simply means a wish to attain something that we find lacking at present in our life. How do we identify what is lacking? An intricate process of analysis happens at the unconscious level where the subtle mind – the ego principle – observes and analyzes the needs which we then try to fulfil in the course of our lives. The concept is converted into desire, desire is converted into a need, the need is converted into an action and the action is converted into a result. In this process, the consciousness, mind, senses and body work as one integrated unit. At present there is no direction to this flow of mental energy and no control over the channelling of the mental forces that manifest in the body. There is internal confusion, psychological confusion, unconscious confusion, but we are not aware of this internal confusion until it comes to the forefront of our manifest conscious mind.

Modern psychology says there is the conscious mind, the subconscious mind and the unconscious mind. Yoga says there is the active mind, the passive mind and the dormant mind. The active mind is linked with the conscious mind, the passive mind is linked with the subconscious mind and the dormant mind is linked with the unconscious mind. However, beyond this there is another state of supermind, or awakened mind, where there is no differentiation or distinction between the different aspects of the mind such as manas, buddhi, chitta and ahamkara. Whatever state of mind we talk about, we have to know whether it is the unconscious state, the subconscious state or the conscious state.

The SWAN principle

There are certain principles that guide the desires, aspirations and motivations. In yoga these principles are known as the SWAN principle. SWAN is an acronym: S stands for strengths, W stands for weaknesses, A stands for ambitions and N stands for needs. These are the four principles that make up our personality. In some people, inner strength, mental strength, strength of will or the strength of the self is predominant. In some people, weaknesses which can be lack of willpower or mental clarity are predominant. Some people identify more deeply with their ambitions and aspirations and try to fulfil and attain them. Some people identify more deeply with their needs, which are physical or social, in relation to their family, work performance and society.

It is the expression of either strengths, weaknesses, ambitions or needs that defines our personality and makes us what we are today. When we are able to project the strength of the self, a particular nature is defined in an individual. This does not mean the higher Self, but the self which is contained in this personality, combining our knowledge, our mind, our senses and our ability to become part of the whole picture. When the self is manifesting at the level of strength, we say that person is very creative, dynamic, outgoing and compassionate, has a clear mind, is helpful and a guide to many people, who derive inspiration when they come in contact with such a personality.

When the self expresses itself through the areas of weakness, we identify that person as unclear or weak, without force, energy, strength or dynamism, as uncertain and unsure. When the self is manifesting at the level of ambitions and aspirations, we identify that person as being ruthless and arrogant, as trying to get his or her way at the expense of others, and as uncaring. When the self is manifesting in the dimension of need, then we identify that person as being self-centred, as only making an effort to look after his or her self, and as uncaring.

This is how we recognize and define a personality from the yogic perspective. If we analyze the psychological perspective, we find that there are many similarities between the modern concept of psychology and the yogic concept of psychology, but we are using the yogic model because you are already aware of the existing psychological models. The yogic model says that there are two dimensions of self: one which is manifesting as the SWAN principle and another which is unmanifest, dormant and subtle.

Developing inner awareness

All the efforts that we make to somehow manage our internal and psychological imbalances are in the manifest area. We try to improve our behaviour by enforcing an idea or a concept. It has been said that when we try to live or bring a concept into our lives, it becomes a philosophy or an idea with which we identify. But when the concept becomes a philosophy, it is not translated into action. There is a split between our personal philosophy and our actions in the outer world due to lack of discipline, lack of awareness. Yoga has been very clear in saying that the beginning of yoga is through a discipline which is not enforced, but which is the outcome of the awareness spanning all the different dimensions of the human personality.

In the *Yoga Sutras* Patanjali uses the Sanskrit word *anushasanam* in the first statement. Yoga is anushasanam. This word has been translated in English as 'discipline', but it is not discipline. It means awareness of the inner personality which is manifesting in the outer world. *Anu* means subtle, *shasanam* means to rule, to govern, to be in control of. Therefore, according to Patanjali, yoga is a form or method of governing and directing the inner nature harmoniously

118

so that it can manifest externally. This is the beginning of yoga.

In this process how do we become aware of our inner nature? Not by enforcing certain concepts and ideas upon ourselves, because, if we try to enforce anything on our mind or nature, there is going to be a reaction. We will reject it because it is coming from outside, not naturally and spontaneously from inside. Despite this awareness and understanding, many yoga practitioners make the mistake of enforcing certain ideas and disciplines in their lives in order to change – and they have failed. One has to begin gradually. Here are two examples.

When I first joined the ashram I was the type of person who identified with sleep. People could pick me up and take me from Munger to Timbuktu without my waking up. They could turn me upside down and I would stay fast asleep. They could put a bomb under my bed and I would not wake up. I would set the alarm clock for four or five o'clock in the morning but still remain fast asleep. It was definitely a big problem and I wanted to find a solution.

I spoke to my guru, Swami Satyananda, who said, "Wake up at a time which is natural for you. Don't try to change it. Always make sure that you are up at that time, even if it is seven, eight, nine or ten o'clock, and maintain the same time every day. Try to understand the natural rhythm of your body." I tried it and in five or six years I was able to overcome my sleeping pattern.

When we enforce a routine or discipline, we try to do too many things with it. People often come to me and say, "I wish to wake up early." I reply, "All right, set the alarm for five o'clock." After one week they tell me, "After waking up at five o'clock I go into the bathroom, have my shower, do my daily ablutions, do my asanas, pranayama and meditation, have my breakfast and then I feel tired." I reply, "Yes, you will feel tired because it is not in your nature to wake up at five o'clock and go through your yoga routine. You have to adapt gradually. Wake up at five o'clock, don't get out of bed, turn off the alarm and go back to sleep. You wanted to wake up early. You woke up at five o'clock when the alarm went off. Be happy that you are up at five and go back to sleep at five minutes past five. Gradually adapt yourself to waking up at one time, gradually increase the duration of your waking state. For a week, open your eyes, look around the room, turn off the alarm and go back to sleep. In the second week, when the alarm goes off, wake up, go for a walk around the room, get back into bed and sleep. In the third week, when the alarm goes off, get up, walk around the room, go to the bathroom, get back into bed, sleep and so on. This is how to train yourself."

Befriending the mind

Swami Satyananda used to tell the following story. Once upon a time there lived a king who had four beautiful but absolutely wild horses. All the trainers in the world had failed to train and tame those horses. But the king was very fond of them, so he issued a proclamation throughout the kingdom that anybody who could tame those horses would receive the hand of the princess and half the kingdom. Many people came to try their luck. Who wouldn't want to marry a princess and have half the kingdom? But the horses would not allow anybody to ride them. Those who tried to saddle them, to put on a bridle, to ride them, to rub their necks, all failed.

The king gave up hope. Finally, my grandfather went to the king and said, "I will attempt to tame the horses." The king said, "Are you sure?" My grandfather replied, "Yes, I don't want to marry the princess or have half the kingdom. I want to tame the horses. But I have a condition. Give me the horses for one year and I will return them to you properly trained." The king agreed, and my grandfather took the horses away.

One year later, when the king had given up hope, he saw my grandfather coming down the pathway, riding a very beautiful horse with three other horses following behind. "How did you do it?" the king asked my grandfather. "Simple," he replied. "From the very first day I never tried to put on a

120

saddle or bridle, rather I let the horses be free. When they ran in the fields, I would run with them. When they stopped to drink water, I would make my coffee and drink it. When they ate grass, I would also cook my rice and vegetables and eat it. By developing closeness to them the horses recognized that I was one of them. Slowly I became their friend.

"One day I placed my hand on the back of one of the horses. That horse did not like my touch. He jumped and gave me a big kick, but in the course of time he accepted my caress and my touch. I did the same with the other horses until they accepted my presence and my touch. Then I put a blanket on them. They did not like the blanket, but eventually they got used to it. Then one day I put on a bridle. They did not like it, but they got used to it because they saw me as a friend. I developed that friendship and as a result today I am able to ride on them."

Reflecting on one's SWAN

Swami Sivananda said, "If you want to direct your mind, become a friend of your mind. Don't try to become the ruler of your mind." You have to make yourself acceptable to your mind. This is the concept of discipline. Discipline is not something you enforce in yourself, rather it is a spontaneous outcome of your proximity and friendship to your nature. When we talk of the mind, when we talk of changing our views and attitudes, when we talk of changing our nature, we make the mistake of enforcing a system, a rule, a law, which is unnatural to our nature. Then in the course of time there is a rebellion.

If we try to make an immediate change in the structure of our mind, it is not going to work. A dog's tail will always be crooked. If you want to straighten the tail, you can put it in a pipe, but the tail will only be straight for as long as it is in the pipe. The pipe represents rigid discipline. When you remove the pipe, the tail will again curve. Another method of keeping the tail straight is cutting it off so you can't see the curve and only a stump remains. That stump will always be straight. Now, don't think that this cutting off is an

121

impossible or difficult process. It is simple. Cutting off simply means altering or changing a pattern which is at present predominant and manifesting in the nature.

If you suffer from any kind of mental problem, the first requirement is meditation, reflection. That is the first thing you need to do because when you identify a problem you are simply seeing the symptom that is manifesting on the outside. You are not aware of the cause of the problem, whether it is sleeplessness, loss of memory, a psychological, emotional or moral problem. You see its manifestation on the outer dimension, which is identified as a problem, but you do not see the cause that is creating that problem.

For that reason, meditation is the first requirement in order to know the cause of that mental or emotional imbalance. How can you manage and improve your nature, personality, attitude, behaviour, thinking process, inter-actions or motivation? Through the process of meditation in which you analyse the areas of your strengths, weaknesses, ambitions and needs. Make a list of the things you consider to be your strengths, weaknesses, ambitions and needs. Be objective. Don't confuse ambitions with needs or needs with ambitions. Don't confuse strengths with weaknesses or weaknesses with strengths. Reflect, think about them, and make the list. Don't show it to anybody; it is your personal list. Look at it every day and add or remove something from the list. In three or four months time, you will have a big list or a small list as your understanding and awareness develop. As the ability to cope with different mental states develops, you will realize that management of the mind is a very simple process. You don't need a psychoanalyst or a psychotherapist for it and it is a great thing for your personal satisfaction and attainment. So, meditation is the first step in order to identify your strengths, weaknesses, ambitions and needs, and the second step is to list them.

Mantra and inner harmony
The use of mantra is the third tool to go deeper and to harmonize your inner nature. Mantras are collections of

sound vibrations. We know that every kind of sound evokes a particular psychological response. Every sentence evokes a response. The sentence, "You are wonderful" will evoke an emotional response, a feeling, a sensation, and you will feel bright, happy and free. The sentence, "You are hopeless" will evoke another form of response. It will make you feel restricted, inhibited, closed, unsure and uncertain of yourself. "You are wonderful" or "You are hopeless" are sentences which you understand intellectually, but the responses they evoke are not intellectual responses, they are feelings. You cannot identify or analyze feelings instantaneously.

Similarly, mantras are combinations of different sounds or syllables which evoke an unconscious response. That unconscious response, which is non-intellectual, stimulates the psychic personality or the psychic centres, and you feel more tranquil, balanced and harmonious internally. Mantras are used to harmonize the inner distractions and dissipations. Mantras are used to freeze the frame of mental images.

When you travel in a train and look out the window, you see the scenery moving by. While watching the scenery, can you freeze one image in your mind? Nowadays there are television sets in which you can see different channels in square boxes simultaneously in the bottom right or left hand corner of the screen. You can freeze one picture while watching another one. Can you do the same with your mind while you are in a moving train and observing the scenery? Can you just go click and freeze an image, let the scenery flow by but maintain the image in your mind? It is very difficult. But that is exactly the training or effect of the mantra: stillness of the unconscious and subconscious agitation, and identification with the state of silence and stillness which is your own internal harmony. In the state of internal harmony, there is strength.

When a light is focused to a point it becomes a laser beam. When the same light is dissipated it provides illumination, but it does not have the power to burn through steel, or to do very precise eye operations. It is all a play of focusing the light, concentrating the light to a point. The mantra applies the same principle with the human mind. The word 'mantra' also means freeing the mind from its external distractions and focusing and centring it inside. When you centre the mind inside, in the state of stillness and silence, and when you are able to freeze the image or picture, then you have the source of your inner strength.

Changing the perspective

Meditation, identification of the SWAN principle and the use of mantra become very powerful yogic psychotherapeutic tools to overcome personality, mental and emotional imbalances. When you are able to combine meditation with a change in your daily routine and when you are able to combine meditation with awareness, then you begin to live life in a joyous way. We cannot change circumstances and situations, but we can change our perceptions.

A person once came to me and said, "Swamiji, I am suffering from hypertension." I asked him what he was doing for it and he replied, "Well, I am taking the normal medications, but I am going through a lot of mental turmoil and agitation." When I asked him why he said, "Somebody in my family, in a fit of anger, told me that I was a dog (in India there are many street dogs and they are thin, with protruding bones, fleas and sores on their bodies) and I imagined myself to be a street dog and I can't get that image or idea out of my mind. The thought comes to me again and again. Why did the person call me a dog? Why did the person identify me with a dog? I can't sleep. It has become a big problem and I am sure my hypertension is due to this state."

I gave him this solution: "Instead of thinking that you are a street dog, why don't you think that you are Fifi, the dog of a multimillionaire who travels in absolute luxury, in an air-conditioned coach, sleeps on a beautiful feathered bed and is groomed every day."

The man said, "Swamiji, I came to you looking for a solution and you have simply made me a multimillionaire's dog rather than a street dog." "Yes," I replied, "because when you become the dog of a multimillionaire, you will have your solution."

When I saw that man one month later, he said, "I am not taking any more medication. My hypertension has gone. I am absolutely fine." I asked him why and he replied, "Initially, I used to identify with the suffering and pain of the street dog, but now I identify with the pleasure of a dog who lives in luxury, and I don't have any mental problems."

The situation did not change; his perspective changed. I did not say, "No, no, no, you are not a dog." I suggested, "Yes, you are a dog, but you think you are a happy dog." Of course, it is idiotic to believe that if somebody tells me I am a dog or a donkey that I will become a dog or a donkey. If I begin to feel that I am a dog or a donkey, it means I am prone to other people's suggestions and do not have a will of my own. I have such a weak nature and mind that I cannot be myself. Of course, I can be myself. You can call me a dog or a donkey a hundred times over, but it won't make any difference to me because I know what I am.

Manifesting harmony

People have to be happy knowing who they are. We are very weak. We become very influenced by the negativity and the positivity we encounter in life, and our responses are guided by those negative or positive inputs. Where is our natural being? We are not aware of what we are. We become what other people project onto us, and that is where meditation comes in handy. It allows one to realize the individual or personal nature, identify with that nature, overcome the quirks of the nature and personality, and thus experience inner growth.

There is no point talking about how the mind, the ego or the intellect works. They work, that is enough. We must know how we can handle the situations and conditions which alter our self-perspective. For this there are three processes: (i) meditation as the means of reflecting and discovering our strengths, weaknesses, ambitions and needs; (ii) identifying these four areas, known as the SWAN

125

principle; and (iii) harmonizing the inner being through the use of mantra. These are the tools that will lead to enhanced awareness and harmonious participation in life. You will then be known as a balanced person. If somebody tells you that they find a balance in you, that is the biggest attribute you can have, because that harmony and balance is manifesting in your life. That is all that we need in order to make our lives and the world beautiful.

Practice, Philosophy and Lifestyle

If we are committed to the principles and vision of yoga, we should also be aware that there are three areas involved: yogic science, yogic philosophy and yogic lifestyle. These three combined make up the structure of yoga. Yogic practice alone is incomplete if it is not understood as a system of thought. Yogic philosophy is incomplete if it is not understood as lifestyle. We have to look at yoga from these three different perspectives and try to apply the concepts, techniques and principles in our lives. It is not important to know many things if we are unable to implement them properly. It is better to know a little and implement that properly in our lives.

Yoga practices for busy people

For people who are involved in the world and who have obligations and responsibilities to the family and society, yoga practice should be limited to techniques which can be performed and practised in the shortest time possible, postures to free the body of tightness and tension and to move the energy in the body.

The first posture suggested is *tadasana*, the palm tree pose, which involves contraction of the different joints and extension and expansion of the muscles. It is a very good practice to do in the morning because it helps to free the joints of the accumulated blockages and tensions which give a feeling of stiffness and tightness. The second practice is *tiryaka tadasana*, the swaying palm tree pose, in which there is extension and contraction of each side of the body. This helps to improve the movement and circulation on the lateral side of the body. It also helps to use the little used muscles of the sides of the body.

The third practice is *kati chakrasana*, the waist rotating pose. It is like squeezing out a wet cloth. Imagine your body is like a sponge and you have a lot of fluid to squeeze out. In this posture you have to make sure that the spine is rotated properly. It frees up the blocks and mobilizes the body. The fourth practice is *surya namaskara*, salute to the sun, twelve postures in which the body mainly bends forward and backward. These are the two major movements in this practice. The final practice is *sirshasana*, the headstand pose.

These five postures are the ideal ones for a healthy being. They can be performed every morning to free the blockages, to release the tensions and stiffness, and to improve the flow of energy. It should not take long – five or ten minutes. After that, two pranayama or breathing practices can be practised.

Pranayama

Remember that this program is for those people who are rushing from job to house, and don't have time to wind down, rest and relax. This does not mean that winding down is not necessary – it is very necessary. One has to learn how to sit back and observe, to sit in silence. What is silence for you? Your head still ticks away, your thoughts still go on; you are not silent. The clock inside the head still ticks and you lack the ability to be quiet. Learning to be silent or quiet comes through training in yoga.

When you are in a rush, there are certain simple breathing practices that can be performed. One is known as *bhramari pranayama* or humming bee breathing. First you have to plug the ears with the index fingers so that the external noise does not come in. A word of warning: if you have long

128

fingernails, don't put them inside the ears; rather, block the ears by closing the flaps with the fingers. Then take a deep breath in and make a sound like the last part of the mantra Om – m-m-m-m, in one gear only. Don't change gears while you are practising; don't go up and down. Move the sound in one gear only. While you are practising this pranayama with the eyes closed, focus your attention in the centre of the head by drawing an imaginary line across the centre of the head, or by thinking of the centre as the place where the two fingers would normally meet if your head was hollow. Just find the source, the centre. After you have exhaled completely while humming, again take a slow, deep and gentle breath, not a forced breath, and again exhale while humming. Practise five rounds.

Bhramari pranayama has a very soothing effect on the nerves, especially for those people who are physically and mentally in a rush. We have found that this practice stimulates the alpha brain waves. You will feel this even more intensely when you come home from work. After three or four rounds of bhramari you will feel a state of deep relaxation, awareness and alertness, because the sound vibrations you emit in this practice, and your concentration in the centre of the head where the sound is being felt, help to tranquilize and relax the agitated state of the brain by inducing alpha brain waves and by relaxing the nervous agitation. We have also found that bhramari is a very effective technique to lower hypertension.

Bhramari, combined with psychic alternate nostril breathing, or *nadi shodhana*, completes the practice of pranayama. Just sit quietly and close the eyes. Imagine you are breathing in through one nostril and breathing out through the other nostril. Imagine that you are breathing in through the left nostril, breathing out through the right nostril, breathing back in through the right nostril and out through the left nostril. Again, at the time of breathing in the breath flows in through the left and out through the right, in through the right and out through the left. Become aware also of the temperature of the air as it passes through the nostrils. At the time of inhalation there is a cool sensation inside the nostrils and at the time of exhalation there is a warm sensation. Become aware of the changes in temperature at the time of breathing in and breathing out. Continue imagining the flow of the breath in through one nostril and out through the other. This is known as psychic alternate nostril breathing.

You can practise this for two, three, four, five or ten minutes, whatever time is comfortable and convenient for you. You will find that it also induces a state of deep physiological and psychological relaxation. If you can do these five postures and two breathing techniques in the morning on waking up, you will have plenty of energy, vitality and dynamism throughout the day.

Yoga nidra and antar mouna

In the evening when you come home, instead of immediately going to the bar or fridge, taking out a glass and pouring yourself some fermented grape juice, just practise a short *yoga nidra*, yogic relaxation or psychic sleep, for ten or fifteen minutes, or half an hour, whatever time you can devote to it.

Combine the practice of yoga nidra with *antar mouna*, inner silence, by observing the flow of thoughts that come naturally into the mind. Don't identify with the thoughts, don't try to think or bring in thoughts; simply become aware of what is coming naturally without any effort. The thoughts may be related to your job, your family or to a party which you have to go to in the evening, or they may be related to certain problems or difficulties you have encountered. Observe them and finish. This is how to incorporate asanas, pranayama and pratyahara into the daily routine.

Karma yoga in daily life

The concept of karma yoga can also be incorporated in the day-to-day, moment-to-moment activities. Whatever you do, do it with awareness. Whatever work you are involved in,

130

don't let it be an unconscious activity, rather make it into a conscious activity. If you are writing, be aware of the process of writing, the handwriting, what is being written. If you are driving, extend your attention and awareness into the driving. Become the car, become the road, become the traffic light and become you, the body. Don't allow things to happen mechanically, but bring the concept of awareness into every activity. This is the first step of karma yoga, extending the awareness into every activity you are involved in. This is the simplest form of karma yoga.

In the course of time, as you progress in your yogic practices, you can incorporate many other techniques. You can have a separate time for kundalini yoga and a separate time for meditation. You can join different seminars and courses and learn about these techniques in depth. That is your choice. In this way, gradually incorporate one practice at a time into your daily routine. You will find that yoga becomes an effortless process as it becomes part of your routine. It is not necessary to go to a seminar to awaken your kundalini, your chakras or your pranas, because you will be able to do that only while you are there. Once you return home, you fall back into the same old patterns. So it is necessary to incorporate some element of yoga and awareness into the normal patterns of our lives, in our homes and in society. This is how we have to understand the concept of yoga practice.

The beginning of yogic philosophy

The next aspect is yoga philosophy. What is yoga philosophy? The word 'philosophy' means 'love of knowledge', but in Sanskrit it means 'darshan'. *Darshan* means 'to realize, to see'. In English we use the words 'yoga philosophy' and in Sanskrit we use the words *yoga darshan*, meaning 'to realize yoga'. How do we realize yoga? Paramahamsaji once said that a human being is a composition of the qualities of head, heart and hands – intellect, emotions and actions. These three qualities are important. If you remove feeling, your life has no meaning; and if you remove intelligence or intellect, your life has no meaning. So, if an individual is a composition of the qualities of head, heart and hands, these three need to be balanced and harmonized. This is the beginning of yoga philosophy.

Yoga philosophy does not begin with high-flying ideas of divine consciousness manifesting in the human body. Yoga philosophy begins with recognition of the qualities that are inherent in our lives, that can be unified and harmonized: the qualities of head, heart and hands. The moment we are able, through observation, to know the qualities of the mind, the reactions, actions and expressions of the mind – the mental nature; when we are able to know, through observation, the expressions of the emotional nature and how we interact with other people and with our environment, and we are able to bring these three different areas together, then yoga philosophy is being lived.

The first stage of meditation – pratyahara

Observation of the mind happens through meditation. Meditation is experiencing three different forms. In the first stage of meditation, which is the beginning of pratyahara, we have to become aware of three things. When you were asked to close your eyes and meditate, what did you focus on? You were focusing on the impression or the image that you were told to observe. This needs to be defined in detail because it is important. Meditation reflects different states of mind. In the state of pratyahara, the fifth stage of raja yoga, three things are involved in the process of meditation: the seer, which is me; the object of seeing, the object of meditation; and the process of meditation. I am sitting down; I am focusing on my symbol; I am directing my attention to remain firm and stable on the symbol. So there is myself as the body, the flow of consciousness towards the object or symbol, and the symbol. These are the three things: the observer, the process of observation, and what is observed. This is how meditation has to begin.

132

If meditation is not like this, there is a danger of falling into slumber. Slumber is not sleep, slumber is loss of direction, clarity, awareness and concentration, like a person who walks like a zombie and doesn't know what is happening or where he or she is. In pranayama it is taught, first of all, that you must become aware of the body, the posture and how you are sitting. You must become aware of the stresses and tensions. You must also analyze and observe if there is any tightness in the body, then release that tightness and be totally comfortable. Become aware of the body from the top of the head to the tip of the toes. Try to have a vision of the whole body in one glimpse, in one thought.

After this stage, the practice is taken further. After becoming aware of the observer, the meditator, there is an awareness of the process of meditation. We begin to observe the movement of the breath, the spontaneous activities that go on in the body, which become the tool, the medium, through which we reach the point of concentration. Then the object of meditation is added, which can be a symbol, a mantra, an image or an idea, and one has to try to identify with that image, idea or symbol.

Dharana

Following the stage of pratyahara, the form of meditation changes. In dharana, which is the next stage of meditation, we move into consciousness of the object of meditation and the process of meditation, and the meditator dissolves. It can be explained in the following way. You have a target and a gun or bow and arrow in your hand. You line up and take aim. The target is the object which you have to attain. Your body is the meditator, which is observing the object. But in order to attain the object, to hit the bull's eye, you have to pull the trigger, to let the arrow or bullet fly. Then it is the arrow or bullet which has to find its mark, not you. You become redundant after shooting; the important thing is the arrow or bullet and the target. After shooting, you may even want to look the other way and not bother watching the target. It is the arrow or bullet you have guided which has to find the mark.

So, the process of meditation and the object of meditation become important in the state of dharana or deep concentration. When this deep concentration converts into meditation, it means the arrow or bullet has hit the bull's eye, and the process has become one with the object of meditation. So, there is you, the arrow or bullet, and the target. This is the first step. In this first step, you have to align yourself with the target; you have to be aware, alert and shoot. After you have let the arrow or bullet fly, the next step is dharana. You can go for a walk and allow the arrow or bullet to find the target. Once the arrow or bullet has hit the target, that is dhyana or the attainment of the object of meditation.

Integrating head, heart and hands

Meditation allows the practitioner to realize the faculties of the head, the intellect. So meditation is the process through which we become aware of the head aspect. The qualities of the heart are awakened by combining the attainments of the meditative process with karma yoga. What you experience here, you express out there. What you experience inside, you express outside. The feelings associated with that expression have to be unconditioned feelings, not for any personal, selfish reason or gain, but as part of your giving help and support to people around you. Sentiments and emotions will flow, oneness will be experienced, the qualities of the heart will awaken, and this will eventually become an action of which you are an integrated part.

Union between the faculties of head, heart and hands is the purpose of yoga philosophy rather than God-realization or realization of the divine nature. The expression of divinity is in life. It is the coolness of the air, the warmth of the sun, the fragrance of a flower, the taste of water, which is contentment, unity, perfection, the manifestation of the supreme consciousness or the higher consciousness in life. This is what yoga calls the higher Self. We have to understand yogic philosophy from this practical perspective, not as a mystical subject.

134

Yogic lifestyle

The third aspect is yogic lifestyle. Yogic lifestyle is based on the foundations of awareness. What do you do when you get up in the morning? Turn on the news, read newspapers and immediately begin to participate actively in whatever is happening around you. Imagine that while you sleep at night, your mind becomes tranquil and passive, like a still lake where there is no agitation or movement on the surface of the water. As soon as you wake up in the morning, what kind of impressions are you giving to that still nature of yours? Impressions which you read or see or hear about. These create a distorted picture and image of reality in your mind. Therefore, as a part of yogic lifestyle, yoga says give yourself and your mind time to become fully alert and aware and move gently from the state of sleep to the state of wakefulness. It takes about two hours.

Don't listen to the news or read the newspapers for at least two hours. Don't think about any scandals, problems or difficulties because it is those impressions which are creating images or imprints on the still mind, and for the rest of the day your mind is disturbed and agitated. Yogis have said that in the morning one should spend at least two hours practising something useful, which allows you to grow and to find your balance. Either you practise yoga, or you simply sit near the window and observe nature and the scenery. Become one with the scenery, go for a walk, don't talk to anybody, be silent and talk only when necessary. Gradually your mind begins to adapt itself to what is happening outside and then you have a greater participation with the world.

At night, when you go to bed, see the events of the day like a movie showing how you interacted, what your response was, what you said and what you did. Become aware of every moment that passed from the time you woke up till the time you went to bed. See the entire day in the form of pictures, like a film or movie, and try to discover where you failed and how you can improve your communication, interaction and dealings with people. See if you reacted in any way and if

135

that action was justified? If you have been in a similar situation before, how did you respond? This is how you start living a yogic lifestyle. Therefore, the foundations of a yogic lifestyle are based on awareness.

Yogic philosophy, yogic lifestyle and yogic practice have to be combined if you wish to see a new you emerge from the ashes of the old one. If you combine these three, then without practising kundalini yoga, your kundalini will awaken. Without practising kriya yoga, your chakras will awaken. It is the concept of mind over matter and the concept of energy over mind and matter. If you are able to manage the energies which manifest naturally and spontaneously, that harmony will alter the mind and body. One learns to live in simplicity and openness. These are the two legs of yoga. In your own process you need to incorporate these principles and obtain the maximum benefits.

Satsang 1

What does perfection mean?

Perfection cannot be defined, and if you do define perfection, it is not perfection any more. According to yoga, perfection is an ongoing process of becoming better and if you can become better every moment of every day, you are on your path. Therefore, don't attempt to define perfection because it is an evolutionary process. Make an effort to improve yourself, your performance, your life and your attitude every moment of every day, by living in the present. One can become perfect, if there is a concept of perfection, by living in the present. Generally, people live in memories of the past, are fearful and apprehensive of the future and ignore their present state. When you are attached to past experiences and apprehensive or fearful about your future, then you tend to miss many things in the present which can be improved and changed. Therefore, the yogic theory is to live in the present in order to experience the process of ongoing perfection in life.

Why is it almost impossible to guide the kundalini up to its final destination without the help of a guru, even if a very good purification of the chakras and the nadis has been done previously?

The awakening of kundalini is preceded by two other awakenings. The first is the awakening of the prana shakti,

137

the vital life force. If you study kundalini yoga, you will know that in our body the life force or prana manifests in five different forms, and each form has a specific function and job to perform. Each form of prana controls a particular activity of the physiological system and also a particular centre in the brain and its corresponding aspect in consciousness. So the pranas have to be awakened, balanced and harmonized. This is the first step.

The second step is the awakening or opening of the chakras, the removal of blocks from the different psychic centres. Here we have to work with each chakra individually and independently through the yogic processes known as chakra shuddhi and tattwa shuddhi. After that, we move into the area of kundalini.

The awakening of kundalini takes place when the pranas are activated and when the chakras are opened. If you go through a systematic process, then kundalini is not dangerous at all. But still one needs to be guided because there are so many different experiences, unconscious and subconscious in nature, which manifest at the time of kundalini awakening. If you are not able to handle these psychic and unconscious experiences, then you pass through what is known as kundalini crisis. This is where the assistance of a guru is required to guide and help one to overcome and understand these experiences. Therefore, it has always been advised that you learn, practise and perfect kundalini yoga under the guidance of a competent teacher. You have to realize that you do not know what kind of experiences are going to manifest eventually from the depths of your personality. The path is uncharted and only a person who has gone through that experience can guide you through the process.

How does yoga view sexual rapport? Can it help us on the spiritual path?
The concept of the sexual act in tantra and yoga is that it has three purposes: pleasure, progeny or sublimation. The pleasure aspect is dominant in society today, the progeny

aspect is important in society today and the sublimation aspect is generally not subscribed to by people today. This is where the problem arises. Yoga and tantra say that sex is not a sin. Definitely not. When two people come together with an immense feeling of affection, love and unity, then that feeling is always a very positive and transforming experience in human consciousness. If you can become aware of that underlying feeling of unity and deeply embedded love and identify with that, then the normal sexual act takes on a spiritual meaning. It links you with your inner spirit and your inner nature. If you combine meditation with that, then it elevates the consciousness from the gross dimension to the transcendental dimension, which is known as sublimation.

Therefore, yoga and tantra do not deny sexual activity or say that it is bad. They accept it because they see a different reason and purpose behind the act. But in order to understand this process you have to search yourself and your thoughts and make the effort to realize the transcendental aspect of the sexual act, beyond pleasure and progeny. There is a training and a discipline that have to be understood before you jump into the waters, thinking, "Oh well, tantra and yoga accept it, so let me try to transcend myself."

Being economical with your sexual life is also a very important aspect, because you can of course exhaust your energy. The energy which is released in the sexual act is known as virya and ojas in yogic terminology. **Virya** is the material substance while **ojas** is the energy substance.

In India, and amongst all yoga practitioners, the word 'guru' is a most respected term. However, today the word 'guru' is used by journalists and the media in a way that contradicts its original meaning. They use this word to mean a conman or a crook or even worse. This creates major confusion in people's minds and brings prejudice to yoga and the true spiritual masters. People have mixed yoga up with sects, fanaticism, exploitation, etc. Lies and misinformation create a lot of damage. Could you shed

some light on the concept of guru and on the true role of the guru?

The word *guru* means 'dispeller of darkness'. It is a word which has come down to us from ancient times when all science and philosophy was being propagated by certain thinkers and masters who were known as the gurus. In fact, we can say that originally the word guru meant a person who had completed a doctorate in spiritual philosophy or in spiritual practice and who was teaching or propagating his or her discoveries for life improvement and for getting in touch with the higher nature. Therefore, the word guru means dispeller of darkness.

In today's society the word guru means many things, not only in the West but in the East and also in India. A thief can be a guru, a robber can be a guru, a conman can be a guru, but not in the original sense of the word. It is very difficult to even think about defining and clarifying the meaning of the word guru. If those people who understand the concept are clear in their heads and hearts, they will be able to help others clear their own misconceptions and ideas. So, rather than trying to change the image in the media, on TV and in the newspapers, I would suggest you develop a clear picture within yourself first. Know what it means. Identify with the word guru. Develop a relationship with the concept of the word guru and only then will you be able to present this term and concept with clarity to others.

What is tantric philosophy?

Yoga and tantra are father and son, or mother and son, or father and daughter, or mother and daughter. Yoga is an offshoot of tantra. Rather than having a specific philosophy, tantra and yoga deal with the discovery of human nature, the awakening of consciousness and the liberation of the energy that is inherent in every being. Kriya yoga and kundalini yoga are part of tantra and the entire yogic thought pattern is tantric. So when we use the word 'tantra', we are using it in its broad sense referring to meditations, attitudes, practices and disciplines which are physical, social, moral and personal, and referring also to the ability to accept life.

Tantra is not a mystical subject, science or philosophy. There is no mysticism in tantra although many authors have made the subject mystical. Mysticism simply refers to an unknown process in which experiences manifest that are not common. If you see light in meditation, you would call that a mystical experience. If you see an image, a figure of God or the Goddess or a saint in meditation, you would call that a mystical experience. If you see a demon or a devil in meditation, you would not call that a mystical experience. You would call it a horrible experience because of a belief that something mystical is always related to a transcendental and divine experience and that anything which is not transcendental or divine is not mystical. Tantra does not say that. Tantra says that in life you have all kinds of experiences, which are gross, subtle, transcendental, instinctive, animal-like, human-like and divine in nature, and they all form part of your personality.

It is the realization and understanding of this wide range of human experiences which is the aim of tantra. Yoga is a method by which you can train yourself physically, mentally and emotionally to understand the meaning behind these experiences inherent within us. So yoga and tantra are one and the same. Yoga is the practical side of tantra and it leads you to the realization of the transcendental nature.

How does vibration work on human consciousness?

The questioner is referring to vibrations as emanations from an individual, reflecting a particular mood. We are continually, consciously or unconsciously, emitting and projecting our innermost thoughts and moods. When those thoughts and moods reach a critical stage, either on the negative side or on the positive side, they are recognized and given a name. You project a mood at the time of depression, you project a mood at the time of anxiety, you project a mood at the time of frustration and anger, you project a mood when

141

you are at peace and relaxed. These projections are recognized by other people either as a mood, as a vibration, as a good feeling or as something which you experience without knowing what it is. Therefore, if we have to consider the effect of vibration on consciousness, we should say that it is the projection of consciousness.

You can definitely guide and channel that projection and make it more harmonious and balanced through meditation. In meditation, as you alter your inner perception and inner mood, your projection will undergo a change which you and other people will recognize as balance, tranquillity and harmony.

How can we progress with our spiritual development if we are married and have a child?

You can definitely lead a yogic lifestyle, practise yoga and have a yogic mind in the family, whether or not your husband or wife supports you or whether or not your children or other family members support you, provided you are able to practise karma yoga.

'Karma' means action, participation. We are continually, every day and at every moment, participating in activity. Whether that activity is confined to the family, to a job or to a person, we are continually interacting and performing action. Yogis have added the word 'yoga' to 'karma' with a specific purpose: balance in action and awareness in your participation. Balance in action and awareness in participation is karma yoga. So when a child screams at you or when you are running behind schedule and are rushed, allow one part of yourself to observe yourself and see what is happening to you. How are you rushing? How are you interacting? What is your mental state? How is the adrenalin flowing? Are you agitated? Just that much will make a big difference to your involvement and participation in work, activity and action. This is known as karma yoga.

You don't need to practise yoga as a discipline if you don't have the time. You don't need to practise yogic postures or meditations for an hour every day, morning or evening, if you don't have the time. You can practise karma yoga any moment, anywhere and that in itself will lead you to the experience of the yogic lifestyle and yogic mentality. So begin with karma yoga and later, when you have the time, practise hatha yoga, raja yoga and other forms of yoga.

Satsang 2

Does a yogi live in his or her world or in the world?

Yogis do not live in a world of their own, they live in this world. But there is a difference. An example is the lotus flower which grows in the mud. The flower comes up, grows through the water and then rises above the water. One of the beauties of the lotus flower is that the petals are totally unaffected by the mud and water, by their immediate surroundings. You can pour buckets of water on the petals and they will never become wet. That is the example which the tradition gives us on how yogis have to live.

You have to understand that yogis are people who practise yoga, and you also have to understand that they are the offspring of people who live in society. Yogis do not drop from heaven into the world. They are children of parents who live in society, in a cultural and social environment, and who have their own natures to overcome. A person who becomes aware of the need to improve, who adopts certain disciplines to experience inner unity and who, in the course of time, expresses that inner unity in the outer world is known as a yogi. The roots of a yogi are in the world and the consciousness of a yogi is beyond the world. That is the traditional concept.

Often yogis are portrayed as people who like to do the headstand. If you see a picture or a comic strip, you will

144

often find an icon of a yogi with a beard and long hair standing on his head. Now, of course, in the West the headstand is a posture which represents the complexity of yoga, but in the East it symbolizes something else. Normally, our feet are on the ground and our head is up in the clouds. But, as a yogi, you have to earth your head and walk in the higher dimensions. So yogis have an opposite polarity to most people, which represents their personal discipline and understanding.

You will not find a yogi who is born perfect. Practitioners of yoga have to work with their mind and with their nature and become better. That is the ideal of a yogi according to yoga. Yogis live in the world, yet are unaffected and not attached to the pleasures of the world. This would be the most common characteristic of a yogi.

Somebody once asked our guru, Swami Satyananda, how to know if one is evolving spiritually. He simply gave a short answer, saying, "As you evolve spiritually, you will find your desires becoming less and less." In material life, we are in a state of technological and material hypnosis and in this state we increase our desires instead of reducing them. As the desires increase more and more, our consciousness becomes more gross and material and craves pleasure. Here the rat race begins.

When you begin to practise yoga, when you begin to analyze your personality, when you begin to overcome the conditionings that are detrimental to the growth and unfoldment of human nature, and when you overcome the conditionings which limit the inherent creativity and expression of wisdom, then many unnecessary desires and attachments are simply left behind. This is the concept of renunciation.

Generally, people think that renunciation means leaving behind many things that are dear to them. In fact, renunciation is not something that you leave behind, but something which you attain. If you have to come up on to the stage, you place your foot on the first rung of the ladder, and only when the foot is firmly placed on the step will the

145

other foot leave the ground and go to the next step. When the other foot is firmly placed, then this first one will leave that step and reach up to the next step. So attainment always comes before renouncing.

Similarly, if, as a yoga practitioner, you start worrying and going through different head trips about the futility of the world, the environment and the ills of society, that simply represents the state of your own confused mind. But, if you can remain true to your commitment, your inspiration and yourself, then there will be no head trips or anxiety, and you will be able to flow from one stage of life into the other without any pain or suffering. That is true spirituality. That is the life that yogis try to lead, a life based on the principles of simplicity and inner innocence, not on intellectual complexity, a life based on the foundations of awareness. So, we can come to the conclusion that yogis live in this world with a different attitude and perspective on the world.

With the increasing development of scientific research into aspects of yoga, ranging from research into practices for health, to research into practices of faith, devotion and bhakti, is there any possible danger presented by all the scientific inquiry to the more direct spiritual approach of higher experience? For example, if an experience is dissected, measured etc., then isn't something lost?

Scientific discoveries don't demean or belittle human experience. You have to remember that science is still in its infancy. Science can only observe and monitor the physical parameters that can be measured with the help of an instrument and with what is physical in nature. But a human being is not only a physical being.

In previous talks we have referred to the different dimensions of human experience, in which the body is one dimension, the mind is another, energy is another, consciousness is another and the experience of inner unity or perfection is another dimension. When we talk about measuring something scientifically, we only measure what is

146

happening at the physical dimension. Up to a point we can measure what is happening in the energy dimension, because the energy is manifesting physically. It is absurd to believe that everything that is invisible and subtle can be measured by a physical process. So I don't have that fear or thought that if science monitors the attainment of a human being, it will belittle or negate the entire range of human experience, perception, attainment and realization.

We have heard during this gathering a lot relating to yoga and the mind. Could you comment a little about yoga and the heart? Swami Vivekananda once said, at the beginning of the century, that in the battle between the head and the heart, one should follow the heart. Could you comment?

It is a very true statement. Consciousness manifests at three different levels: the instinctive level, the heart level and the mental level. Somehow we are caught at the mental level and even when we have an experience of the heart level, we try to understand it at the level of the mind. We are unable to do that properly and we miss the point. It has become a human tendency to believe that we hold the answer to every problem in the head, which may possibly be a shortcoming of human nature.

If we use the yogic model, we will understand that the intellect is only one area of consciousness that allows us to understand the process of the senses in the world of objects. The intellect allows us to understand the interaction of the body and the personality in the world of name, form and idea, nothing more than that. It has been the belief of every enlightened being, not only Swami Vivekananda, that the heart is the subtle force. The heart contains the subtle energy where the human qualities are given the opportunity to flower. These qualities are unconditioned, expansive human nature.

What is love? Does love generate from the heart or from the head? Think about it for a minute. If you love somebody, can you define what you love about that person? Person X loves person Y. What is there to love? You love somebody and somebody loves you. What do you love? Do you love the body? Do you love the nature? Do you love the expression of that person? What is it that you love in another person? You can't convert that experience of love into intellectual analysis, but you tend to do that and, therefore, when your love from the heart moves to the head, it gives you headaches, it becomes conditioned, it becomes associated with expectations, with the desire for fulfilment, of wanting to own or possess another. Love becomes attachment, possession; love becomes the fulfilment of personal expectations; love becomes sensory and sensual fulfilment. Is this the definition of love? No. This is an example of how the heart feelings are totally changed and altered by the head.

This is an area where a lot of discoveries are going to be made in the next millennium. Swami Satyananda has said that the coming millennium will be the millennium of bhakti. This millennium was the millennium of buddhi or intellect. In the twentieth century we have tried to categorize and analyze events, situations, experiences and attainments through a rational process. We have reached a block and we feel this block or conditioning in our lives.

Bhakti is generally thought of as devotion, but it is not devotion. Bhakti is an emotion. When an emotion is directed towards children, it takes the form of affection. When an emotion is directed towards somebody you love, it takes the form of love. When that emotion is directed towards some material object that you want to possess, it takes the form of greed. When that emotion is directed towards a person whom you consider to be your friend, that emotion is recognized as friendship. When your emotion is directed towards somebody you feel is threatening you, it is recognized as enmity. When the emotion is directed towards somebody whom you see as your competitor, it is recognized as jealousy. When the same emotion is directed towards the experience of inner unity, it is known as bhakti.

Therefore, Swami Satyananda has said that the coming millennium will be the catalyst to discover one's own bhakti, or the emotion that gives one the experience of personal and cosmic unity, and this will represent the culmination of human attainment. So, the heart experience – what is known as feeling or emotion or sentiment – in its true form, without any conditioning or alteration by the intellect, leads one to the opening of the inner spirit.

It will be a good step if we can gradually make the effort to shift our awareness down from the head into the heart. Yoga aims at that. Of course, initially yoga emphasizes awareness of the mind because at present the mind is active within all of us, and we have got into the habit of analyzing and rationalizing everything intellectually. For this reason, yoga emphasizes observation of the mind. Let us see how it functions and, after we have observed and know the functioning of the mind, when we have realized the conditioned nature of the mind, then we can learn how to break the conditionings of the mind. Of course, it is not necessary to break the conditionings of the mind until and unless they are recognized as limiting, suppressive, detrimental and negative to your free, creative, harmonious expression. If you live with that form of conditioning which is already free, creative and harmonious, then you do not have to change it. So you have to recognize the state of the mind before attempting to understand the experiences of the heart.

In the *Yoga Sutras* this has been clearly stated. You have heard about controlling the patterns of the mind, the vrittis, through yoga. Vrittis are the intellectual, rational and analytical impressions. After we are able to harmonize them, what happens? We become one with our true nature. Try to understand that in a practical way, not in a philosophical or theoretical way. Further on in the *Yoga Sutras*, it has been stated that one who has attained understanding of their nature lives and expresses the qualities of their life in a determined way. One who has attained unity within expresses friendship, compassion and happiness with all beings who live in their vicinity or environment. It is an internal process which, after realization, becomes external; it is a personal process which, after attainment, becomes universal. So yoga is a process of moving from the personal to the universal. If you can understand this, then you will know that eventually, in the end, it is the opening up of the heart that is the most important thing in life.

How do you see the role of women in the coming millennium and what qualities should a woman of the coming age develop?

Women have always had a very vital role to play in the forming of the individual personality, and they have to become more dynamic in playing this role more efficiently and effectively. In India we have a saying that the body is provided by the father and the nature is provided by the mother. The union of parents is physical and, at the same time, it is subtle. In the physical process, the formation of the physical body happens because of the father, but the mind, the nature, samskaras and impressions are given by the mother. So, women have the greatest responsibility in shaping the life of an individual, the life of society and also the life of civilization. They are the shakti, the force. They are not for the pleasure of others; they are not there to be exploited. This has been the Indian belief, the tantric belief and the yogic belief.

When a child is born, the mother is the first person the child sees. It is the mother who has to identify the father for the child. The mother does not have to identify herself, because there is a very intimate connection existing between the child and the mother, which does not exist between the father and the child. What does this indicate? That at a deeper subtle level there is a connection existing between the mother's consciousness and the child's consciousness.

It is only recently that doctors and scientists have begun recommending that pregnant women should lead a very balanced lifestyle. In America and Australia doctors recommend that during pregnancy mothers should avoid smoking and drinking, that they should avoid the stress and tension of their job and family, and that they should listen to gentle, soothing music. Many such ideas are now being promoted by professionals in the field, because they say the mental and nervous conditioning of the mother influences the foetus. In India, we have many stories of people who are born with wisdom because, while they were in the womb, their mothers led a very balanced lifestyle. Personally, I am thankful to my father because he gave me my body, but I am thankful and grateful to my mother who made me what I am today through hard inspiration and hard input.

This has to be the role of women in the future. They have to actively participate in the making of human society and in the making of an individual. If they are aware of yogic principles and practise yogic disciplines, if they are able to harmonize their mental and emotional processes, develop a balanced attitude and vision of life, the credit will go to them for bringing enlightened people into the world who will then guide the destiny of humankind.

What sort of attitude should one have to partake of life joyously and happily? You mentioned that the highest quality of an individual is to have understanding. Perhaps this attitude and your concept of understanding are linked. Could you comment on this?

There is a prayer that is the appropriate answer to this question: "God grant me the serenity to accept the things I cannot change, courage to change the things I can and the wisdom to know the difference." This prayer tells what kind of attitude we need to develop in order to flow more smoothly. "The wisdom to know the difference" is the important point. That can become the sadhana, practice, effort and sankalpa or resolution of everyone. The wisdom to know is understanding.

Love is an expression of understanding and compassion is an expression of understanding. If there is no under-standing, including modesty, then how is love going to flow? What form will it take? How is compassion going to flow? What form will compassion have? Understanding is the wisdom to know that one can change positively, constructively and creatively. Let this be our sankalpa and resolution.

Festival of Yogic Life

Satyanandashram, Aube, France,
30 April–3 May 1997

Spiritual Lifestyle

We are meeting here to experience a festival of the yogic way of life. In the yogic and spiritual traditions, the word 'festival' means an event full of joy, happiness and opening up. So the aim of this meeting is to experience joy and happiness together and an opening up of the heart and the head together. The two words linked with festival are 'yogic' and 'life'. However, before talking about yogic life we will look at the different traditions that have existed in the world since antiquity. These traditions have made an effort to understand the nature of an individual and how we, as individuals, can experience unity deep down within.

There is a difference between spiritual life and religious life. Sometimes we tend to confuse spirituality with religion, but they are poles apart. Spiritual life means a process by which we can understand the harmony that exists in different areas of our personality and by which we can realize the oneness of human nature, because in essence we are all one and the same. In order to experience this oneness that underlies every aspect of creation and existence, different ways of thinking and living have been devised. Externally they may seem different, but they all aim at the experience of unity between individual consciousness and higher consciousness. In fact, according to many traditions that is the purpose of life, and it is a natural process of evolution as well.

We are continually evolving. Our evolution goes from a finite, limited understanding and appreciation of what we are, to a broad, unlimited and infinite realization of what we truly are. In the process of moving from a limited under-standing to a broader perspective, we utilize the different qualities and faculties that are inherent in us. These qualities and faculties are the head and the heart. In yogic terminology, they are known as *buddhi,* representing the head, the intellect, and *bhavana,* representing spontaneity, the heart.

Limitations of intellect

In this modern age, we have reached a point of deep identification with intellectual experience. We have also come to believe that the intellect or head provides us with solutions to all the different problems and processes that we undergo in our lives. However, there is a problem which the intellect has been unable to answer. How do we experience, understand and realize something which is beyond the intellect? The intellect has a strange habit of rejecting things that it cannot comprehend.

It is like the story of the ocean frog and the well frog. One day the ocean frog decided to go on a world tour. He left his ocean and started hopping around the world. In the course of his hopping, he fell into a well where he found another similar looking animal, which was a well frog. The well frog asked the ocean frog where it came from and the ocean frog replied, "From the ocean." The well frog asked, "What is the ocean?" The ocean frog replied, "An immense body of water."

The well frog was curious. "How big?" he asked. "You can't imagine how big it is," the ocean frog replied. "You can't see the other shore. If you look to your right, all you see is a vast expanse of water. If you look to your left, you can only see water. If you look ahead, there is nothing but water. No matter how hard you try, you cannot reach the other shore."

The well frog was now very curious about the size of the ocean. He took a mighty leap inside the well and asked, "Is the ocean as big as my leap?" The ocean frog replied, "No, it is much bigger." The well frog then called up all his reserve forces and took another mighty leap in which he cleared his previous record by a few feet. He again asked, "Is the ocean this big?" "No, it is much bigger," replied the ocean frog. The well frog then said, "I don't believe that anything else could be bigger than my well."

This is the conditioning of the human intellect. The human intellect is trained to find solutions to its problems by using the inherent intellectual faculties which are conditioned by the culture, society, education, personal limitations and also by personal beliefs or religious concepts. This conditioning causes us to analyze and convert any kind of understanding to an intellectual, sequential process. But there is a problem. We are simply jumping inside the well of our own creation, the well of our own life.

There have been some wise frogs in the world who have come from another body of water, maybe a bigger well, a lake, a river or an ocean. They have told us, "There is something bigger out there, outside your perceptions and limitations, but to know what exists outside you have to come out of your well." It is this process of coming out of our individual wells that has been the aim of the different traditions which have existed in the past and which exist today.

In antiquity, only one tradition existed. It emphasized discovery of the inner nature and harmony with the outer nature. In this process, people from different parts of the world learned how to go within, and devised practices of meditation, contemplation and introspection. At the same time, they tried to harmonize with and understand the outer nature, and to build a bridge between the inner nature and the outer nature. Their form of understanding the outer nature was through a process of worship, going back to nature, appreciating the environment, worshipping the cosmic forces. They realized that the cosmic forces are represented inside and the internal forces are represented in the cosmos. It was a very natural and spontaneous way of life.

Overcoming suffering

Something happened along the way and the spontaneity of life was overshadowed by another kind of search. That search was to find happiness and to overcome the suffering and pain that we encounter in our day to day lives. The spiritual traditions have said that there are three kinds of suffering. One form of suffering is personal, which is generated within our minds in the form of anxiety, fear and unhappiness. It is related to the body, mind, emotions and society.

Another form of suffering is fear in the form of a threat coming from other people or other beings. Imagine what would happen if a tiger suddenly appeared here. You would all run into your homes and be afraid to come out until you were sure that the threat no longer existed. The third form of suffering is cosmic, over which there is no human control.

The Samkhya tradition has spoken of these three kinds of suffering as adhidaivic, adhibhautic and adhyatmic. *Adhidaivic* suffering is cosmic, beyond the control of a human being. *Adhibhautic* is the suffering inherent in existence. *Adhyatmic* means suffering that comes from within: insecurity, fear, anxiety, unhappiness. Overcoming this suffering became the focal point of many of the ancient traditions. For example, Buddha spoke about overcoming human suffering. He spoke about knowing the cause of suffering, knowing what suffering is and overcoming it. He said that when we are able to overcome all suffering, that is the state of *nirvana*, freedom from pain and suffering.

In this way, many other masters, thinkers and philosophers have said that evolution in life depends on how we are able to overcome and manage personal, social and cosmic suffering. Each belief and tradition evolved a philosophy and a set of practices with which they felt it was possible to find harmony in life. Buddhism, Samkhya, Vedanta, Tantra and Yoga all came into existence as a result of this search. Each philosophy took the idea of overcoming suffering one step further.

Buddhism said: Overcome the suffering which affects your personality, mind and nature through a process of

158

meditation. Tantra said: Overcome the limitations and suffering by observing life, by expanding your consciousness so that it will not be confined to your personal experience, but will be able to encompass a broader range of experience. Overcome the limitations and suffering in life by awakening and harmonizing both the personal and cosmic forces.

Vedanta said: Overcome the limitations of life by realizing the true nature of the self. The true nature of the self is unlimited, whereas all the events and experiences of the world are limited. The vedantic concept said that truth is real and the world of name, form and idea is false. This world does not represent reality, but is only a reflection of the cosmic reality. Vedanta described this by saying that the reflection we see of ourselves in a mirror is not the real self. In the same way, the self sees its reflection in the world and identifies with the world. The self identifies with the body, the mind, with events and conditions, but it is only a reflection; it is not the real identity.

Similarly, yoga also said that it is possible to realize and know the inner self. You have to find a balance between the outer and inner life, which is your true nature. These ideas show that the different traditions and beliefs have only one aim: to improve the quality of life and to overcome the conditions of the mind and personality which inhibit the growth of human nature.

Search for harmony
Apart from these practices, thinkers also believed that a way of life is important to hasten the process of finding tranquillity. In the beginning, there was one human civilization. When we first appeared on the planet, we all had similar minds, natures and aspirations, but the local environment of the place where we lived guided us to excel in only one aspect of life.

In the course of time two different mentalities evolved in human civilization. One mentality tried to modify and alter the forces of nature to suit itself, while the other mentality learned to live according to the laws of nature. The result of these different mentalities can be seen today. The occidental culture tried to manipulate nature, to make it more amenable to its own mentality, and the oriental culture tried to understand nature and to live according to the laws of nature. One exploited nature, the other lived in harmony with nature. This is also evident in the ancient civilizations which existed in China, Japan, India and other parts of Asia.

Most of the thoughts and beliefs that have guided or are guiding human beings in their quest for harmony have come from the East, including the most recent traditions of Christianity and Islam. This does not mean that there is a vacuum or absence of ideas in the occidental culture, simply that the direction of thinking was different in both cultures.

Now a time has come when we are all trying to integrate the positive aspects of both cultures in order to find our source of harmony and balance. That is why we are meeting here today, that is why we have come together in the past and that is why we will come together again in the future, with a belief and a conviction that we can bring together the positive and beautiful aspects of the two cultures. We are meeting to learn how we can live the human way of life, transcending all the different cultural, social and dogmatic limitations.

Development of a spiritual lifestyle

While a search was going on into how to live harmoniously together by devising certain practices and techniques which would enable people to balance their internal and external lives, some people also pointed out that practice alone is not enough. Thinking about a utopian concept alone is not enough. Rather, there has to be an understanding of our routine, of our day-to-day activities, no matter where we are. Somehow we have to manage our day-to-day routine with a greater perception of how we act, interact, think and live. So the concept of lifestyle came about.

Before then the spiritual lifestyle had been limited to only a few, who were known as recluses, renunciates or

160

tyagis, people who had left one set concept of living and adopted another form of living. In the course of time, people found that the practices of the different traditions worked with the human mind and changed the perceptions. It was not only the perception or attitude or thought that changed, but the practices also became a catalyst to alter our social behaviour and way of thinking.

Initially, this change was too hard. The transition from one way of life to another, from active social participation to passive withdrawal, created more problems than solutions for human beings. The thinkers said no. We have found a method by which we can make people look within and understand their personality and nature. However, when people can feel and identify with their inner nature and personality, they find it difficult to again be part of the social life and social mentality; they become somewhat like outcasts in society. So there has to be another method which will allow people who want to experience, or who have experienced, inner harmony to live in the world with a different kind of attitude and awareness.

Four principles of spiritual life

Adaptation of a spiritual practice within a social lifestyle became known as the spiritual lifestyle. The spiritual lifestyle was founded upon the precepts of practice, awareness, attitude and action. Practice involved techniques of introspection which allowed one to find out the source of disturbance, anxiety or ill-feeling, and to harmonize it. Awareness involved an understanding of the environment, conditions, situations and events that influence us. Attitude involved a knowledge and understanding of how we, as individuals, can have a positive and creative outlook on life. Action involved an understanding of how we act, think and interact in the world, alone and with others. These four concepts became the foundation stones of the spiritual lifestyle. Why do we call it a spiritual lifestyle? Why are we unable to call it a more humanistic way of living? Spiritual lifestyle simply means a form of living in which one is aware of the spirit.

161

What is spirit? It is the root of existence. In the *Bhagavad Gita* there is a very beautiful concept. Krishna states that all creation and existence is like an upside-down tree, which has its roots high up in the heavens, the trunk coming down from the heavens to the earth, with the branches, leaves, flowers and fruits growing in the earthly dimension. We are all caught up in the branches, we all look to the beauty of the flowers, which are earthly, and we all want to eat the fruits of the tree, which are earthly. However, there are ways by which we can get out of this intricate web of branches, twigs, leaves, flowers and fruits and climb the trunk until we reach the roots, which are in heaven, centred in divinity.

The leaves represent knowledge and wisdom. There are many leaves on a tree, endless forms of knowing, thousands of ways of understanding. The leaves are the knowledge, the flowers are the flowering of knowledge, the fruits are the results of an individual's participation and action in the world. The straight trunk is the path. When Christ said, "I am the way", when Krishna said, "I am it", they were both referring to the process of climbing the trunk from materialism to spiritual experience, to spiritual realization.

Detachment and discrimination
However, while we are lost in the complexities of the trunk, leaves, flowers and fruits, we become engrossed in the experiences that are there. That engrossed nature is known as attachment. How can the attachments be overcome? When we are at the level of the fruits, flowers and leaves, we want to possess the beautiful, uplifting things that satisfy our nature. So another theory emerged. Do not be so caught up with and attached to sensorial and sensual experiences that you are unable to withdraw from their attraction and their grip. It is human nature to try to possess everything that is beautiful and good. However, at the same time, one can also make an effort to 'unpossess' what is already possessed. These kinds of ideas took root in different spiritual traditions and also became part of the spiritual process.

162

These concepts are known as *viveka*, which is the faculty of discrimination, of knowing just from unjust, right from wrong, broad from limited; and *vairagya*, which is detachment from the experiences of the sensory and sensual perceptions. The thinkers further explained that viveka and vairagya are like the two wings of a bird, enabling it to fly up in the sky. If you only have viveka, one wing, or vairagya, one wing, it is difficult to fly. In order to fly you always need two wings. So a combination of viveka and vairagya, along with the four principles of lifestyle: action, attitude, awareness and practice, became the foundations of spiritual life.

Think about these six things: practice, attitude, awareness, action, detachment and discrimination. Try to understand how you may apply them in your lives. Analyze it objectively, look at your lifestyle, know where you live, what you do, where you work. Know how you interact with your family and with other people in society, and how you respond to them and how you become a part of that environment. Know if you are able to maintain your sense of detachment and discrimination while you are part of it. Know if you are able to maintain an awareness and attitude which allows you to be harmonious and balanced while in that social environment. Know if you are able to guide your actions and whether or not you are able to practise what you feel like in your life.

Evolution and Spiritual Life

Swami Satyananda has always spoken about the need to harmonize the activities of the head and the heart. There has to be a balance in the functions of the head and the heart. The head, or intellect, with its faculty of analysis, rationality and understanding, leads to a limited perception of the reality around us. The head can only see what is understood and experienced by the senses of the body and the senses of the mind. These instruments or organs feed our intellect. Just as our body has arms and legs and other parts that are used to give us a complete picture of our interactions during the day, in the same way intellect uses the faculties of the senses and mind in order to reach a conclusion, to know and understand something.

However, there is another area which is invisible. The Samkhya tradition has described this by saying that the realm of *prakriti*, the realm of nature, is composed of experiences in two dimensions, the visible and the invisible. In the realm of nature, the visible dimension is what we interact with, and the invisible dimension is what we experience in states of subconscious and unconscious awareness. The words 'subconscious and unconscious awareness' mean a part of awareness that is active even when the awakened or dynamic faculties of the mind have become passive. When the awakened, outgoing faculties of the senses

164

and mind become passive, one enters the dimension of images, symbols, vibrations, energy and a different quality of awareness which cannot be either explained or understood with the intellectual mind.

Paramahamsaji has stated that realization is a transcendental experience which cannot be understood or experienced by an untranscendental mind. At present, our lives, minds, natures, attitudes and perceptions are not transcendental. So, with an untranscendental mind how can we understand something which is transcendental? We have been conditioned to live in a particular way. How can we experience what lies beyond that conditioning?

In the same way, awareness and experience are twofold, the manifest and the unmanifest. The intellect sees the manifest, whereas the emotions, feelings or sentiments have the ability to feel the unmanifest. It is the quality of the heart that has to be awakened in order to establish oneself in spiritual life.

Spirit – the roots of life

Why do we use the word 'spirituality' and not the word 'humanity'? Why do we say this is a spiritual tradition, a spiritual subject, a spiritual thought? Why don't we say it is a humanistic subject, a humanistic tradition, a humanistic thought? To answer this question there is the example of the inverted tree, the tree of existence, as defined by Krishna in the *Bhagavad Gita*. Another example is that spirituality is realization of the whole picture, whereas humanitarianism is the spontaneous and natural expression that comes after seeing the whole picture. Spirituality is the foundation on which a humanistic culture is built.

You may have heard or read about the story explaining that the most important part of a tree is not the trunk or the branches but the roots. If we are unable to take care of the roots, then the tree will be infirm and weak; it will fall down whenever there is a storm, and the flowers and fruits will be of an inferior quality. In order to make the tree strong, it is not necessary to provide it with different kinds

165

of props and support. In order to make the fruit sweet, it is not necessary to inject it with sugar. In order to make the flowers more fragrant, it is not necessary to spray them with Chanel No.5. If we can simply take good care of the roots, provide them with water, compost, energy, light and air, that is enough. The tree will become firm, strong and sturdy.

The roots are underground and cannot be seen. What is seen externally is the trunk and the canopy of branches and leaves. Similarly, in our lives too we have roots that are underground, and they are known as the spirit, the *atma*, the soul. The trunk is the physical body, the *annamaya kosha*, the body of matter. The mind is the canopy over the trunk, the little branches and twigs that are covered with leaves, flowers and fruit. The canopy is the mind, the *manomaya kosha*, the mental body. Our method of taking care of these two bodies is to provide them with health.

Our concept of health has been a state of harmony in order to experience pleasure and contentment. If there is a physical hurt, the pain is definitely not pleasure, it is displeasure. If there is mental anxiety or emotional imbalance, that is definitely not pleasure, it is displeasure. We are feeding our body and our mind with ideas and items of pleasure. If we cannot get the kind of food that nourishes and sustains the body and mind, we move into a state of depression, isolation, anxiety and frustration.

So the human effort has been to nurture annamaya kosha and manomaya kosha, the physical and the mental bodies. In broad terms, there is the visible or sensorial and the invisible or feeling, but yoga and the different traditions say that there is another aspect, which is the atmic or spiritual. The atmic aspect is our roots which have to be nurtured. If we are not able to nurture our roots, life will be full of pain and suffering. How to realize the atmic level? How to get to the source of our tree of existence? The process and the methods have been described in different traditions as spiritual practices.

The process of evolution

One point to consider is the concept of evolution. What is evolution? What is the evolution of a seed? Think about it for a moment. In its final form a seed does not become a tree, a seed evolves into a seed. That is the final evolution of the seed. When you plant the seed in the ground, over the years it becomes a tree. If the seed simply remained a tree, it would have no purpose; it would be finished. From a tree, the seed that was planted becomes a seed contained in a fruit. The covering of the seed is known as the fruit. A funny thing happens here. You cannot plant the fruit in the ground. First you have to eat the fruit, then take out the seed and plant it. This is the concept of life and karma. The seed of life is planted in the ground and the same seed of life is contained in the fruit of karma. In order to bring out the seed of life, you have to eat the fruit of the karma.

So evolution goes full circle; evolution is from seed to seed, not from seed to tree. In this context, our existence as human beings is only half of the circle. We are in full use of our sensorial, intellectual and emotional faculties. We think that by expanding these faculties even more, we will become enlightened. We think that by opening up our head or intellect and by opening up our heart, we will become enlightened, realized. But we won't! The opening of the head and the heart is only a process that allows us to exhaust the karmas and samskaras.

Take meditation as an example. Why do we meditate? We meditate to exhaust and realize our karmas and samskaras. Only when the karmas and samskaras are exhausted does the seed containing new life begin to sprout. So, spirituality is knowledge of this entire process of evolution which goes full circle, from seed to seed, from life to life, from pure consciousness to externalized consciousness, back to pure consciousness.

Developing spiritual awareness

The process that we go through in this circle is the sadhana, the effort. Sadhana means the effort which one makes to go around the circle. This concept has been clearly defined in the symbology of the wheel of karma, or the wheel of life, which is the bindu according to the tantric tradition. *Bindu* is the source from which everything comes out and the source where everything eventually dissolves or merges.

Opening of the intellect through the process of jnana yoga, experiential knowledge, and opening of the heart, conversion of conditioned emotions and sentiments to unconditional feelings, are only processes used to overcome samskaras and karmas. With the exhaustion of samskaras and karmas, the realization of the inner spirit dawns and one begins to live in that spirit.

First of all, we have to become aware of our personal need and aspiration to evolve. Whether we do it consciously or allow nature to take its course, it is the same thing. If we allow nature to take its course, then we have to wait, and the path is very bumpy. Sometimes the virtuous, positive nature of an individual becomes predominant, sometimes the negative nature, the vices, become predominant and the journey can be very bumpy. However, if we make the effort, then it is the force of will, awareness and conviction that clears many things for us. It clears the path so that the ride is smoother. Of course, we have to go through and experience the ups and downs, but our goal remains in focus.

It is like saying that we are walking through a very dark forest at night and the light in the distance is the only thing making us aware of the direction in which we have to go. We can see this light in the distance and we know we have to walk towards it. We go uphill and downhill, knowing that the light is in front of us, and we are constantly looking at it. Even when we are going downhill and the light is hidden behind the trees and hills, we know that we are going in the right direction because we can see that tiny glimmer of light in the distance whenever we go uphill again. That is the force of will, that is awareness, that is conviction.

The different traditions have tried to emphasize the point that one can eventually reach the end of the journey through will, awareness, discrimination, detachment, attitude and action. While we are going through this process, heart and head have to merge to give a different kind of experience, which is combining the intellectual with the sentimental. Therefore, in different kinds of meditation practices it is also said to move down into the heart space and to feel rather than think. There are different meditation techniques which emphasize feeling and not thinking.

Expressing human qualities

The outcome of this spiritual awareness is expression of human qualities, which are compassion, affection, joy, contentment and knowing the truth. When these qualities are expressed through our actions and behaviour, we become human. Right now we are not human, we only have the label human. We do not have human qualities. In many ways we are worse off than animals. Animals do not exploit fellow animals – we do. Animals do not exploit nature and the natural resources – we do. Animals do not destroy their habitat - we do. We are labelled as human beings, but we do not have human qualities. Spiritual realization aims at the expression of human qualities in life. Those people who have expressed such human qualities have been recognized as enlightened beings.

When you are sick and go to the hospital as a patient, you stay there until you are well enough to walk out, not necessarily totally cured, but well enough. The doctors will not allow you to leave if you are not well enough to walk out. Similarly, this planet is a hospital and we have come here as inpatients, but somehow, somewhere, we have confused 'in' with 'im'. Instead of remaining inpatients we have become impatient! This is where the problem lies.

We are patients in the realm of prakriti and we will not get out of this hospital until we are well enough in the head, the heart and the hands. Only then will we move out of this hospital into the other world, the other realm of existence. Swami Sivananda used to sing a song:

> *Nature throws a man into the crucible of pain*
> *In order to turn him into a sublime superman.*

169

Nature is the doctor, nature is the hospital and nature is the treatment, the medicine.

Changing the perspective

The purpose of spiritual life is to discover your nature and also to harmonize the faculties of the head and the heart. No matter what happens in between, who you fight with and how, what kind of head trips you go through, do not worry about it. When you are at ground level, the trees look big, the path looks winding and bumpy, but if you go up in a helicopter or a rocket, the view changes the higher you go.

If you are caught up in your swadhisthana with your fear, if you are caught up in your manipura with your aggression, that is what you are going to see all around you. If somebody smiles at you, you will feel he has an ulterior motive. If somebody frowns at you, you will feel he is frowning for some other reason. Eventually you will see everybody through your eyes. Your eyes, your vision, your perspective is what you are at different levels. If you think about your problems for twenty-three hours and fifty minutes a day, try not to think about them for at least the remaining ten minutes. If you can do that much, I can guarantee that your perspective and perception will change.

There is a very good practice to see how you are coping, which we recommend to everyone. You have heard this suggestion before but have never followed it. Listen to it once again and try to follow it. Then you will have no more head trips or difficulties.

When you go to bed at night, don't just go to sleep, but try to recapture and relive the hours when you were active, from the time you woke up to the time you went to bed. See what you did, what time you woke up, what you had for breakfast and so on. Live your day again, visualize your day, moment to moment, what happened, what clothes you wore, how you wore them, what you ate, with whom you ate, what you said, why you spoke, what situations you confronted, how you coped with those situations, whom you liked, whom you disliked, whom you laughed with, whom you fought with and so on. Live every moment and then make a positive resolution, a positive sankalpa, to have a better, happier way of life the next day. Then go to sleep. Do this again the next day and continue the practice for three months. Then write and let me know how you feel.

Yogic Discipline

Spiritual lifestyle is based on the principles of awareness, attitude, practice, action, discrimination and non-attachment. Human qualities manifest naturally and spontaneously when we are able to live these principles to whatever degree possible in our lives. These qualities are not based on the conditioning of the mind or the expectations of society, rather they are creative expressions. Lifestyle is definitely linked with how we live socially, how we perceive our mind and what our spiritual aspirations are for the future.

Social education

The social environment is geared to provide us with a sense of fulfilment, security and status in life. The social environment is also guided by how we have been educated. From childhood, we are put in schools to be educated. The education which we imbibe in the course of our studies is known as skill-oriented or job-oriented education, where we are given a vision of what we can be if we undergo the whole process. We can become a successful doctor or business person or engineer, we can become a carpenter or a computer electronic expert, a successful historian, biologist or chemist, so on and so forth. These become our goals in education.

Whatever the form of education, it simply directs us to excel in one aspect of life. From a more human point of

172

view, one of the shortcomings in this type of education is that it does not give us a sense of inner discipline and inner stability. It does not give us a sense of personal, mental awareness. This type of education, which is material and physical, conditions our life and makes us what we are today. However, there has to be another form of education which can bring us into contact with our inner personality. There also has to be an integration of our social responsibilities and skills with our mental stability and happiness. This is where a concept of spirituality in life becomes important, to discover the inner source.

Yogic education

In the *Yoga Sutras*, Patanjali has defined the word 'yoga' in the first sutra as *Atha yoga anushasanam*, which means 'yoga is a form of discipline'. In this sentence Patanjali has described the aim of yoga. But what kind of discipline? The word in Sanskrit is *anushasan*, *anu* meaning 'the subtle aspects of human personality', *shasan* meaning 'to rule over' or 'to govern'. So the concept of yogic discipline is knowledge of the subtle dimensions and aspects of human personality, and directing or governing the subtle nature. This discipline becomes the foundation stone of yoga, without which yoga can never be perfected. In the absence of that discipline, there is always going to be a search to find happiness and harmony, there is always going to be a sense of emptiness inside, of not being fulfilled or deriving the best from life.

This concept of inner discipline is taken further by Sage Patanjali when he is asked, "What is the result of yogic discipline?" The outcome of yogic discipline is being able to control the *chitta vrittis*, or modifications of the mind, the different states or experiences within the mental dimension – *Yogah chitta vritti nirodhah* (1:2). Again Patanjali is asked, "What are the benefits of controlling the mental modifications?" He replies, *Tada drastuh swaroope 'vasthanam* (1:3) – After you have controlled the mental modifications, the chitta vrittis, you become in tune with your inner nature, established in your inner nature.

In these three statements, Patanjali has given the complete yogic picture, which shows how one can excel in life, both socially and spiritually, by applying these principles and experiencing wholeness, completeness and fulfilment. This concept of discipline has also been the foundation of yogic or spiritual education. There is no harm in going through the normal education. One needs and one has to go through it because that is a social standard, but just as we have created a social standard, we also need to create a personal standard. This personal standard of education should be based upon the principles and concept of inner discipline or self-discipline. Only when we have this strong inner discipline will we find that we are able to manage with greater ease most of the problems that we face in life.

Yoga in prisons

In Bihar, we have taught yoga in twenty-four state prisons. The story of prisons is the same all over the world. They are overcrowded and the infrastructure is never sufficient to cope with and to manage the number of internees. We taught very basic yogic principles, such as asana and pranayama, the practices of yoga nidra, antar mouna or inner silence, and ajapa japa or mantra combined with the breath. While we were teaching yoga, a change happened in the attitude and behaviour of the prisoners. Observation of this change prompted the state government to carry out a psychological profile of prisoners undergoing the training. The results were very interesting. We had chosen prisoners who were in jail for life and who had committed the most atrocious of crimes. They were very violent and aggressive, very disturbed mentally and emotionally unbalanced in their behaviour.

A psychological profile was taken every month for a period of eight months, with the same group of prisoners. They expressed that they were feeling less guilty and less aggressive. They were feeling happier, they were able to accept their environment and the fighting had reduced. This was further validated by the profiles. Even medical expenses were reduced. In one prison, for example, monthly

174

medical expenses of about eighty thousand rupees decreased to a thousand rupees in six months. This is recorded evidence. Previously, the prisoners would not do any kind of work, but they started to grow their own vegetables. The cost of food from the market was about two hundred thousand rupees per month and it decreased to twenty thousand rupees per month. So you can just imagine what kind of motivation, inspiration and energy the prisoners gained. We can definitely attribute this to the yogic practices and principles to which they were being exposed.

There is another aspect which cannot be overlooked: the sense of fulfilment and achievement, which is definitely a subjective matter and can't be quantified. This sense of fulfilment and happiness, the sense of finding a source of inner tranquillity, balance and greater inner discipline became the cause of radical changes in their lifestyle within the reformatory.

Identifying with the inner nature

We also recommended that the state government change the numbers of the different prison wards, and give them more human names based on the names of saints, like 'Ramakrishna building' instead of building 'Number 10', 'Vivekananda building', 'Ramana Maharishi building', 'Sivananda building', 'Satyananda building'. This happened in three prisons. Just identifying with the name of the building also helped to change the prisoners' attitude and behaviour, because they were no longer just numbers.

We are moving towards a form of society where soon we will become numbers. In the past our name meant something but now we have forgotten the meaning. Once the name given during baptism, or during initiation, represented a quality, a nature with which one could identify, with which one could become one. Unfortunately, that tradition has been lost today and the real meaning of the name has been forgotten.

When I was a small child, I read a story in which the star was a magician who lived in a world where people's true names were hidden. Everyone was given a false name, because there was a fear that if people knew their true names, they would become the source of power and wisdom. Only the magicians would study the true names and they would call out the names of the birds in the air, the true names of the fishes in the water, the true names of the animals that walked on the earth, and they would also know the true names of people. The most intimate form of relationship was sharing their true name with each other.

We have forgotten the true meaning of our names and the name has simply become a label. If we can know the real meaning of our names and identify with the principle, the quality, the nature, the idea that our name conveys, we will come in touch with our inner nature. At present we are moving further and further away from our nature and our source. Why is this happening? Because we have moved into the outer world, away from the source of humanism.

Integrating inner discipline into life

The topic of yogic education is relevant because it is education which creates and becomes our samskara and also our lifestyle. If we are educated as doctors, being a doctor becomes our lifestyle. If we are trained as carpenters, carpentry becomes our lifestyle. If we are trained as engineers, engineering becomes our lifestyle. All our efforts revolve around that form of education. So we somehow need to complement our external living with inner discipline. Only when we are able to integrate these two aspects, do we find a beautiful change happening in our lives. We become human.

This is one area we will need to think about: how, in the present environment, personal at first and then social, we can bring about a change in the form of education. If it is not possible in schools, then we can definitely do it within the home environment. When children are sleeping at night, play them a yoga nidra cassette. Let them imbibe the information unconsciously. It works! When I first came to the ashram in Munger, I was a very difficult child. Paramahamsaji tried to teach me by making me sit in front

176

of him, but the moment he looked the other way I would be miles away. That education did not work and so he tried yoga nidra. When I was asleep, he would play cassettes and give me instructions. Today I realize that the information I received while asleep has guided me and formed my personality. It has given me insight into many things about myself which otherwise I would not have had.

It is not necessary to think about how we can change something that is already established in the social context, because that would be like hitting one's head against a brick wall. However, within the family environment, we can definitely create a system where children are motivated to express the positive, creative aspect of their personality. It is important to have an environment of discipline within the home. This doesn't mean enforced discipline. Discipline is a method and process by which we can come to terms with and realize our inner personality.

In the course of time, you will see a change, a flowering of the children in your homes, and that becomes the first step. When they are grown up, when they are mature and able to understand their role within the family and the social context, when they are able to understand the responsibilities of a human being, then they have to go to the next step, observation of the chitta vrittis, the mental modifications.

Observing the mental patterns

The mental aspect of yoga applies to each and everyone, because it is our mind which is our enemy. But it's a very friendly enemy! There is a hairline difference between friendship and animosity. Friendship is not affection and love, animosity is not fighting, hatred and aggression. The concepts of friendship and animosity are very close together, only a hair's breadth separates them. Friendship means to nurture the positive and the creative aspect of every individual. Animosity inhibits and restricts the nurturing of the positive and the creative and throws us into another pattern of mind, where we feel constricted, restricted and unable to express ourselves. This inability then evolves into aggression, competitiveness, jealousy and hatred. It snow-balls, and the snowball becomes bigger and bigger.

The concepts we have in our lives, whatever they may be, are simply guided by certain ideas of positivity, creativity and openness. Something is good when it can assist us in becoming more positive, more creative and more open. Something is bad when it inhibits us from becoming more positive, creative and open. When different mental traits come up through the inhibited nature, they are identified as negative qualities. When different traits come up through the open nature, they are identified as positive qualities.

Every individual has the ability, the strength and the will to become free. Because of the conditionings and lack of inner discipline in life, we are afraid of becoming free. We are attached to ideas and objects with which we identify, and when we identify with something it becomes difficult to isolate ourselves from that identification. When possessive-ness is strong, it is difficult to let go of that possessive nature. However, if we look deep down inside, as human beings we are concerned with only a few things: positivity, creativity, openness.

Meditation and the chitta vrittis

The spiritual disciplines and the yogic discipline aim at making us aware of the distractions, dissipations and diversions of the mind, which are explained in the form of chitta vrittis. We can overcome those distractions, dissipations and disturbances through the process of self-observation, which is *dhyana*, meditation. One of the benefits of meditation is that subjectively and personally, we feel at peace with ourselves. In the course of time, we feel a sense of joy within. We feel a sense of harmony existing between ourselves and other people, between ourselves and nature, between ourselves and the universe. All this happens in the course of time.

First is the sense of peace. Why do we have that sense of peace in meditation? Why do we identify with the state of silence, with the sense of quietness, in meditation? We identify

178

with it because that is the deep-rooted desire. In fact, we can even say it is contained in our mental DNA. Just as the body has physical DNA, the mind has its own DNA and the spirit has its own DNA. The theory is to manage the mental modifications and to experience peace, to live peace. Here we find another problem. When we are together, we can talk about many things, shake our heads and say, "Yes, it is true." But we can't hold on to that idea for long. After one hour, or maybe after a day, a week or a month or maybe after a year, we fall back into the same old pattern, and we say, "Oh! I find it difficult, I know it is good but I find it difficult to implement."

It becomes easier when we are controlling the chitta vrittis through a meditative process initially by looking inside, realizing the nature, realizing the personality, then by quietening the distractions of mind. For this reason, many people use the meditative process for therapy as well, as psychotherapy to overcome the distractions, dissipations and disturbances of the chitta vrittis. So, meditation is working with the mind and altering its functions.

Yamas and niyamas – expressions of a balanced mind

When we are able to quieten down our chitta vrittis, attitudes, views and ideas change. These attitudes, views and ideas have been explained as yamas and niyamas. Although the word 'yama' is translated literally as moral discipline, that is not what it means. *Yama* means a state of mind which is attained through meditation. Yama means expansion. The word 'pranayama' does not mean breathing technique. One meaning of pranayama is to expand the dimensions of the pranic force, from *prana*, meaning energy and vitality, and *ayama*, meaning expansion. Another meaning is to hold the vital energy in balance and not to allow it to be dissipated, from *yam*, meaning to sustain, to hold. These are the two meanings of the word *pranayama*: expanding the dimension of energy and then holding the energy to prevent it from being dissipated. In the same way, *yama* means to hold the mind in balance. What happens when you hold the mind in balance? The mind stops identifying itself with the sense objects, and the moment it does so it becomes free.

Once an Italian swami and an Australian swami were walking alongside the Ganges river in Munger. The Italian swami was a very free person. The Australian swami was new to the ashram and he felt the best way to become a sannyasin was to have a very pious and virtuous attitude, control of the mind, so he was behaving like a saint.

While they were walking beside the river, they saw a young lady, wearing a long white flowing dress like a priestess. She was standing beside a small stream, wondering how to get across. You can imagine what happened! The Italian swami picked her up, carried her across, put her down and then continued walking. The Australian swami, his head going out of gear, began to ask, "How can a sannyasin touch this woman?"

When he arrived back at the ashram, there was Paramahamsaji sitting in the garden. The swami said, "Swamiji, I am very disturbed." Paramahamsaji asked, "What happened?" The swami replied, "Well, we are taught about piety, about control of the mind and the senses, and this Italian fellow breaks all the rules and has no control over his senses." After Paramahamsaji had heard the full story, he said, "So what was wrong with that? He left her on the other side and you are still carrying her in your mind!"

When we identify with something, it becomes very difficult to sit back and observe. We get caught up in the complexity of the thoughts related to the world of objects. We think, "What is my role?" "Where do I belong?" "Do I belong or not belong?"

A person once asked Buddha, "How I can attain peace?" Buddha replied, "You have to stay with us for some time and learn the process." The man said, "No, I want you to tell me now. If peace is my birthright, then I want to know how to attain peace."

"Is that what you really want?" Buddha asked. "Is that what everybody really wans?" "Yes," the man replied, "you are not a man of the world, you are a recluse, a renunciate. I am telling you that everybody in the world wants peace."

Buddha said, "All right, go around the village and ask everybody what they really want in their lives. Write it down and bring the list to me. If there are two people who want peace, I will change my philosophy."

The man took out his paper and pen and walked around the village. When he returned in the evening, he had a long list. One person wanted prosperity, another wanted children, someone else wanted recognition, status and fame, another wanted a good marriage and a good education for their children. Everybody wanted something different but nobody wanted peace.

The man said, "I have realized that there are certain things in life which we desire, which are deeply embedded, but we can't attain those things because we can't dissociate the mind from the world of objects and pleasures." Buddha replied, "Yes, and the moment you can dissociate your mind from pleasures and objects, accept them when you have them and don't bother about them when you don't, then you will know peace."

The lesson in this story is dissociation, not by cutting off the connection, but by accepting situations as they appear in our lives at any given time, so that there is no struggle, no conflict. We have to train ourselves to get to this point, to the yamas and niyamas, the ability to hold the mind still without allowing it to dissipate. It has to be done through awareness, knowing when to sit back and observe and when to be a dynamic participant in the events of life. The yamas and niyamas are the natural outcome.

The Yamas and Niyamas

The yoga of the future is not going to be hatha yoga or raja yoga. The yoga of the future is going to be discovery of the human mind and management of the different personality traits in order to become one with the underlying harmony. Human qualities manifest only when we are at peace and in harmony with ourselves. This harmony is then projected outside. It is a personal experience which is later converted into a social experience, a social environment. In this way it becomes possible to bring about a qualitative change in the individual as well as in society. This has always been the aim of yoga.

Changing the vision through re-education

Yoga has never been a system to replace other beliefs, cultures or mentalities. In fact, Paramahamsaji calls yoga the emergency medicine. When you are having a heart attack you go to an intensive care unit until you are well enough to move on to another form of treatment. Similarly, when there is degeneration of the mind, when the faculties are suppressed, when you are not able to cope with life's situations, yoga comes in as an emergency medicine. This emergency medicine allows you to cope with the present circumstances until you are able to develop a different, higher vision and perspective of yourself. Then you can go out and lead a normal life, with control, discipline and awareness.

When people find their balance, yoga will again recede into the background. In the state of balance, other qualities will be expressed which may not necessarily be yogic but which will be relevant in this club of prakriti of which we are all life members. We move with that level of awareness for some time, situations change, conditions change, the environment changes. When we again feel we are being inhibited and unable to express our nature and personality, yoga will return. Yoga will be maintained and thought about by the seers who are concerned with our welfare.

What is relevant are certain principles which we should not, must not and cannot ignore about ourselves and about our interaction with human society. In order to improve the external conditions, we first need to improve the internal conditions. Therefore, there is a need for six principles to be applied in life: practice, attitude, awareness, action, detachment and discrimination. Human nature is composed of basic qualities, three of which are important – creativity, openness and balance. Creativity, openness and balance are the foundation stones on which the building of life is constructed, but these can be attained only through disciplining the self. We have to change the vision, the perspective, by re-educating ourselves, by integrating the concept of self-discipline into education. The educational system has to change because it influences not only how we are going to act, but also creates the necessary samskaras that provide an outlet for our expressions.

Relationship of yamas and niyamas to chakras

The yamas and niyamas represent the achievement of a human being who has gone through the process of self-discovery. The yamas and niyamas have been thought of as external expressions of a balanced mind, but we also need to know that they are expressions of balanced chakras. Chakras represent states of consciousness and states of energy.

Mooladhara chakra represents an earthly state of consciousness and an earthly state of energy. It represents the manifest consciousness, the manifest mind that is being influenced by the senses, by the sense objects, by the environment. When mooladhara is thus being influenced, consciousness at that level experiences attractions and repulsions, which in yogic terminology are known as *raga* and *dwesha*. A magnet has two poles, one that will create attraction and an opposite pole that will create repulsion. In the world of the senses, we continually experience attractions and repulsions. We like or dislike something, we accept or reject something, always the extreme. These attractions and repulsions are represented in this mooladhara consciousness.

People say mooladhara represents sexuality, but sexuality is only a physical, material, gross manifestation of the body and mind which is confined and limited to this world. When we die, our mooladhara consciousness goes with us. In death we do not manifest our sexuality or our sensuality! What happens at that time? How does the mooladhara consciousness manifest when we are not living or existing in the material dimension with a physical body and with a mind?

This is just to give you an indication that the chakras are not only physical, not only psychic, but also exist at the level of consciousness. Their expressions and manifestations can be felt even when we are disembodied. In that disembodied state, mooladhara consciousness is active in the form of samskaras containing information about attraction and repulsion. At that stage, the attractions and repulsions have become part of the nature of consciousness, they are the samskaras of consciousness. These impressions in the field of consciousness determine the next process in our evolution. In brief, the negative side of mooladhara consciousness is insecurity. The positive side is realization of contentment, happiness and joy. So, on one side we have the yamas and niyamas, and on the other we have consciousness manifesting in the chakras.

Five yamas

There are five yamas. The first yama is *ahimsa*, manifestation of a harmonious state that is free from violence and aggression. Ahimsa does not mean that you stop physical violence. Ahimsa means the elimination of violence from the human personality. It means the absence of aggression and disturbance in human nature, representing a state of harmony. Ahimsa is linked with swadhisthana because in its negative form swadhisthana represents fear. When we encounter fearful situations, when we are subject to fear consciousness, then in order to maintain the self-image there will be a reaction. This reaction is aggressive, like thunder.

Aggression is the antidote to fear because it overpowers fear and allows you to project your strength. But that strength is not channelled. When you are able to manage swadhisthana's manifestation, then ahimsa, absence of aggression, manifests itself. When there is absence of aggression, there is absence of fear as well. Is there anything to be afraid of in the world? No. We are fearful of situations and circumstances because of our conditioning, a belief, a way of thinking, a way of living, but fear does not exist beyond that.

People say one of the highest forms of fear is fear of the unknown, the fear of death. Fear of death or fear of the unknown comes because there is a belief that we will not be able to be ourselves when we encounter this particular situation. For us, death means losing our individuality and, therefore, there is fear. The unknown is something that our analytical minds cannot comprehend. We don't know how we are going to confront an unknown situation and, therefore, there is fear. In order to manage fear, aggression is the outcome. When we are able to manage fear and be fearless, aggression finishes and the state of ahimsa dawns.

The second yama is *satya*, manifestation of the truthful nature in human personality.

The third yama is *asteya,* which means 'not stealing'. People associate it with a social lifestyle. What is the real meaning? There is no corresponding word in English, or in

185

any other language. Asteya means accepting the conditions which exist here and now. This relates to manipura chakra, because manipura chakra is power, vitality, dynamism, ongoing motion and activity. We are continually looking forward, trying to get there, and when we get there we are not there, we are looking forward. We are trying to pull the future into the present. Pulling the future into the present is a yogic concept because generally we tend to live in memories of the past: "We had a good time when we were young." "We had a great time when we went on our honeymoon." "We had a great time when we made our first dollar." "We had a great time when we went to the pub . . . "

What is happening in the future? Is anyone aware of it? What is happening in the present? Is anyone aware of it? When we try to superimpose the joys of the past on the present in order to be happy and secure then, according to yogic principles, that is known as stealing – stealing from the past in order to be happy, content and secure in the present. Asteya is recognition of the present: be here now. Therefore, it says: don't steal. Don't steal what? Stealing physical possessions can be a social crime and one may not want to commit a social crime. However, in relation to the individual, asteya means acceptance of the present.

That is a manipura experience because the manipura consciousness seeks fulfilment through power, wisdom, recognition, status, name and fame. We seek these things to create a different kind of self-image, to prove to ourselves that we have the ability, the strength and the will to rise in life. We are not somebody who can be left behind or whom others can treat like dirt. We are equal to other people who have attained a lot, we can be better than many other people who claim to have everything in life. This is manipura consciousness, and asteya belongs here.

The fourth yama is *aparigraha*, non-possessiveness, which is related to anahata chakra. Anahata consciousness is emotional, sentimental. It deals with feelings, expressions of feelings and receiving those feelings as well. We want to possess good things, beautiful things, nice things. Why are we attracted to beautiful objects? Again there is a link with self-image, the ahamkara principle, the ego. It is the ego principle which attaches itself to something beautiful. In the absence of that object, we feel a vacuum; we feel the force of attachment. We can be attached to and desire many things, both material and spiritual.

Paramahamsaji was once asked, "How can we know if we are evolving spiritually? How can we know if we are progressing in life as human beings?" He replied, "Your desires will become less, that is an indication of your progress in life. Your attachments will become less, that is an indication of your mental evolution." Anahata consciousness feeds upon the beauty and the nice things of this world and it attaches itself. Love is attachment, affection is attachment. At present they are not pure, and are confined only to certain aspects.

Five people are travelling in a car and there is an accident. One of the five is your son or daughter or wife or husband or friend. The others are totally unknown to you. They all end up in hospital. What is the first picture that comes to your mind when you hear about it? Who do you go to visit? For whom are you concerned? You are concerned about the person you know, not about the others. You may think about them but your sentiments, your concern and care will go to only one. There will be five people in five beds but you will stand near one bed, glancing occasionally at the other beds, but only worried about one bed.

Therefore, love is conditioned, affection is conditioned, even the feeling of compassion is conditioned, limited and confined because of attachment, because of a sense of possessiveness. Aparigraha is non-possessiveness, the positive outcome of anahata unfolding and opening. Later, the conditioned becomes unconditional. The sun does not shine for one person, or for one country, or for one planet; it shines for everyone who comes within the range of its rays and light. That is unconditional giving, aparigraha, which happens only when the non-possessive nature is experienced in life.

The fifth yama is brahmacharya. Brahmacharya is related to vishuddhi chakra, which represents the transforming centre, where the grossness of the body and materialism is transformed into a spiritual experience. *Brahmacharya* means 'one who becomes established in the real nature of the self'. This person becomes the *drashta*, the seer. Brahmacharya is the last of the yamas, representing a state of harmony, both personal and cosmic. Brahmacharya means to become established in the concept of Brahman, the expanding, the growing, the evolving consciousness.

Five niyamas

The five niyamas are also linked with the five chakras. The first niyama is shaucha, which is related to mooladhara. *Shaucha* means 'purity', 'detoxification'. What is impure? What is disturbed? What is unbalanced? It is the earthly consciousness, the mooladhara consciousness. Transform or eliminate the impurities, detoxify your mooladhara consciousness of the toxins of the world. That is shaucha, purity.

The second niyama is *santosha*, contentment, which relates to swadhisthana. When there are no fears, when you don't miss anything in life, you are content and happy. This is the positive outcome.

The third niyama is *tapas*, which is translated as austerity. It is the process of personal transformation that happens at the level of manipura. It has been stated that a kundalini yogi can awaken the kundalini. If you are not strong enough to make it come up beyond manipura, kundalini can move from mooladhara to swadhisthana to manipura and go back down to swadhisthana, back to mooladhara and back to sleep. It has been stated that kundalini will begin its ascent without danger of falling back down only after it has crossed manipura. Until it reaches manipura, there is always this danger. That is tapas, the process of transformation. When the mind is transformed from the gross nature to the subtle nature there is tapas.

The fourth niyama is *swadhyaya*, self-study, self-analysis, which is related to anahata. We need to observe and analyse

188

anahata and allow it to open up, and then direct the forces of anahata to transform our personality. So, swadhyaya becomes part of the anahata process.

The fifth niyama is Ishwara pranidhana. It is taken to mean belief in God, but that is not what it means. *Ishwara* means 'the undecaying, unchanging, eternal principle', *pranidhana* means 'to become aware of' – to become aware of the unchanging principle of your life. In Sanskrit, changing consciousness is known as *nashwara*. Everyone on this planet is a nashwara being. The unchanging principle, the eternal principle, the continuous principle is Ishwara. Nashwara means consciousness that goes through changes, consciousness that has forgotten its true nature. Ishwara means consciousness that realizes the true nature of omniscience, omnipotence and omnipresence. When we chant 'Om' three times, we are reminding ourselves of these three attributes of consciousness. Chant Om verbally and then say mentally ' . . . nipresent', then again chant Om and then say mentally ' . . . niscient', then again chant Om and say mentally ' . . . nipotent'. That is the idea behind it.

Om has always represented the highest consciousness, the supreme consciousness, the divine consciousness, because it recognizes the all-pervasive nature, the all-pervasive aspect of the cosmos. Om represents the universal consciousness which is visible and invisible, which is manifest and unmanifest. Ishwara pranidhana, the fifth of the niyamas according to raja yoga, is connected with vishuddhi. When you have left all the earthly and worldly attractions, attachments and bondages, you become as all pervasive as the sky. The fifth element, vishuddhi, represents the sky element, ether.

Awakening the yamas and niyamas

So, the chakras and kundalini yoga are connected with the yamas and niyamas. Awakening of the chakras and awakening of kundalini lead to experience of the yamas and niyamas. It is these aspects that you have to hold in your life. If you are able to maintain and sustain them, they become catalysts for you to lead your life in a better, healthier and happier way. Do not think of yamas and niyamas as imposed disciplines. If you try to impose them upon yourself, thinking that they are moral or social disciplines, you will fail, it will never happen.

Why did Patanjali put the yamas and niyamas before asana and pranayama? Why are we unable to practise the yamas and niyamas today and instead need to start with asanas, pranayama, pratyahara, dharana and dhyana? Why, two thousand years after Patanjali, do we say that the yamas and niyamas sound too religious and don't suit our nature or personality? In fact, we are moving back to that religion of humanity through yoga. We are trying to understand what human nature is, what the human qualities are.

Patanjali has explained it as the yamas and niyamas, which are the benefits of having undergone the physical process, the mental process and the psychic process. Patanjali has explained the benefits before describing the practices. Through asana, pranayama, pratyahara, dharana, dhyana and also through samadhi, you come to awaken or to experience the yamas and niyamas. Therefore, samadhi cannot and should not be the end of yoga. Meditation is not and should not be the end of yoga. They are only instruments to till the earth of our personality where seeds, samskaras, are planted. When those samskaras sprout, they are seen as the flowers of the yamas and niyamas. This is the process of yoga.

Real awareness is identification

Whenever you do a practice, an asana or a pranayama, you have to understand that the aim behind these practices is to make you more and more aware. This awareness is not tight, it is a very relaxed, easy, gentle awareness. Awareness does not indicate concentration, it indicates identification. Awareness does not indicate contraction, it indicates identification and appreciation of something that exists with which you have identified.

One example is little children. Another example is so-called 'yogis' trying to meditate. Do you know how 'yogis' try to meditate? They sit down, take hold of their mala, start concentrating on their breath, start repeating the mantra and start moving the mala. Later on, when they find their minds wandering, going here, going there, going to Paris, going to a discotheque, going to parties, they say, "I can't concentrate!" They become so tense and tight because they feel they can't concentrate that the meditation stops. Instead of relaxing and letting go, they become more tight and tense. It happens for a day, for a week, for a month, for a year, for ten years. Ten years down the line, you will still be saying, "I can't concentrate well enough, my mind wavers, my mind wanders. I feel I have reached a point of stagnation in my practice, I feel I am not moving forward any more."

Another example is a mother. When her daughter or son are away studying and are due to come home after a period of time, it is the mother who looks forward to her child's return with anticipation, and thinks, "What nice food can I give my child? Pizza, spaghetti, soup, chocolates . . . " She cooks the best things, keeping in mind what her child likes most. Therefore, we always say, "My mother's food tasted so delicious!" because deep in the back of her mind, you are the important one and it is your memory that makes her bring out the best for you. She does all her other jobs, but at the same time there is identification and anticipation, and she looks forward to your arrival.

That is awareness, identification and recognition, combined with the feeling of affection and love, combined with a feeling of giving you the best. This is real awareness. Awareness is not something to become uptight about. Awareness is a nurturing process. It is a very beautiful process where all your faculties focus and work in harmony with each other to widen the horizons of perception. It is this awareness which eventually leads to the fulfilment of yoga. Therefore, when we say, "Become aware," it is not to make you neurotic about awareness, but in order for you to appreciate the wholeness of being which happens when you are aware.

Bhagavad Gita: Chapter 3
Karma and Karma Yoga (Part 1)

A man named Krishna possibly lived on this planet, and he was a catalyst for many social reforms. When Krishna was born the world was passing through a major crisis, and the only way he felt he could help to re-establish virtue was by creating a war. It was a special war between righteousness and unrighteousness. Krishna became the force behind this war, the greatest in the history of humanity. It was known as the Mahabharata war and took place about five thousand years ago. The heroes of the war were five brothers, the Pandavas, who represented and symbolized righteousness, and who were the epitome of justice. Krishna was very fond of the third brother, the warrior Arjuna, who was considered to be the greatest archer ever. This friendship was so great that during the war, Krishna consented to become Arjuna's charioteer.

When war had been declared and the armies had assembled on the battlefield, Arjuna asked Krishna to take the chariot into the middle of the battlefield so that he could survey both armies. While surveying the armies, Arjuna went into a state of nervous breakdown. This was not because he was afraid of fighting, losing or even dying in the war. He felt that everyone he knew in the world had assembled there, some on the side of virtue and righteousness and some on the side of injustice. An incredible massacre was going to take place in which everyone, friends and foes alike, would be destroyed. So Arjuna went into a state of depression. He said to Krishna, "I can't fight. What is the use of fighting when everyone is going to die and there will be very few survivors?" Then, on the battlefield, Krishna gave Arjuna the message of the *Bhagavad Gita*.

The literal meaning of *Gita* is 'inspired song'. There are eighteen different Gitas and this particular one, the discussion between Krishna and Arjuna, is the most famous. It is known as the *Bhagavad Gita*, the song of the divine, and has eighteen chapters and seven hundred verses. For sannyasins this has been the text to study. For future sannyasins also this is a text to study and reflect upon because it covers a wide range of subjects, practical and philosophical.

The aim of the Gita is to become one with the divine nature and to accept life as it comes, to face life with courage and with faith, knowing that we are part of a plan. The first chapter of the Gita is known as the yoga of depression, the second chapter as the yoga of wisdom and the third chapter as the yoga of action. In this way, the whole book evolves up to the last chapter, which is the yoga of enlightenment. So the Gita begins with depression, frustration, conflict, suffering and anxiety and ends with enlightenment.

Karma yoga
The third chapter is about karma yoga, the yoga of action. In the beginning of the chapter Arjuna, the warrior, asks Krishna the following question: "O Janardana! If it is Thy view that jnana or knowledge of atman is superior to karma or dutiful action, then for what reason does Thou enjoin on me frightful action or karma? It seems as if Thou are causing confusion in my brain by Thy seemingly perplexing words. Pray, decide for me and tell by following which path will I attain prosperity or moksha?"

This question is a relevant one. In chapters one and two, Krishna had been speaking to Arjuna about mind management, about the need to have knowledge and understanding. This need represents the purpose of human life and the culmination of human effort. Krishna had also been speaking about the relationship between the individual and the universe, and about the integration of action with knowledge.

So the question that Arjuna asks at the beginning of the third chapter is: "You have described two paths, two processes. One is the path of jnana yoga, of knowing, and the other is the path of karma yoga. You have said that both are equally important. Now I am confused. How can both paths be equally important?" Because karma yoga, as we know, is confined to the realm of prakriti, whereas wisdom is internal.

Karma is external, wisdom is internal. Karmas are guided by the laws of nature, the three qualities of sattwa, rajas and tamas. Karmas are guided by our motivations and desires, by the sensory experiences and the sensual needs for satisfaction and fulfilment, whereas wisdom is the outcome of knowing the big picture. Wisdom is the outcome of knowing the relationship between the individual nature and the cosmic nature. Karmas represent the outward expression of the self and wisdom represents the inward awareness of the self.

Role of prakriti and purusha

According to the Samkhya system of thought, the entire universe is governed by two principles – purusha and prakriti. Purusha represents consciousness, both finite and infinite. Purusha is the essence of consciousness. Just as water can have different forms, whether it is a rain drop or water in the ocean, a stream, a lake, a well, a glass or a tap, the essence of water is one and the same. In the same way, purusha may be cosmic in nature. Purusha may manifest in a human form, it may manifest in an animal form, as consciousness, somewhere dynamic, somewhere passive, somewhere in a very crude form, somewhere in a very opened and enlightened form. But the essence is the same. So, purusha represents the all-pervasive, omnipotent, omnipresent and omniscient consciousness.

Prakriti, the opposite pole, represents the force behind creation. Whether creation takes place at a very gross physical level or at a subtle, universal, cosmic level, it is the force of creation. Creation is always seen as nature. In creation we find the three gunas: tamas, rajas and sattwa. The nature of sattwa is the state of luminosity, total awareness. The nature of tamas is the state of ignorance, inertia, darkness.

If everything in the world, in creation and existence was luminous, all the fun would be taken out of life. If everything in creation was in a state of inertia, ignorance and darkness, then again there would be no fun, no joy, no happiness in life. One cannot exist alone. In order to recognize that you exist, someone else has to exist. What exists is the state of sattwa and the state of tamas. But again there is a problem. If we consider sattwa to be the positive pole and tamas to be the negative pole, then both poles will cancel each other out and nothing will remain. If sattwa is light and tamas is darkness, they will cancel each other out and there will be no light and no darkness. A third force has to come in between, which is rajas. It is the permutation and combination of the three forces at different levels and in different intensities that becomes the cause of creation. These three forces are inherent in prakriti, the cosmic, impersonal and the manifest, personal nature. Karmas belong to the realm of prakriti, activity leading to result, result leading to cause, cause leading to result, etc. Therefore, karma has also been seen as the law of cause and effect.

Karma is also seen as an ongoing process of activity, happening at all the different levels. Karma is seen as being physical, mental, psychic and spiritual. Karma is seen as being cosmic, global, universal. Karma means interaction between different states of life which give rise to a particular condition, event and experience. Therefore, karmas are guided and motivated at our level by our inclinations, desires, ambitions, senses, needs of the body and needs of the mind. This is what is known as limited karma. There is another aspect of karma which is universal, divine. There are different states of karma. Karma simply means the interactive process connecting one event with another, whether at the individual or the transcendental level. It is a connection between events.

Arjuna was told that as a warrior he had a duty to perform. Everyone, according to their inclination and lifestyle, has a duty to perform. Everyone has an obligation. Parents have certain obligations and duties to their children, citizens have certain obligations and duties to perform in society, business people have certain duties to perform and warriors have certain duties to perform. Krishna was inspiring Arjuna by saying, "Don't run away from your responsibility, perform the action, perform your duty, fulfil your obligations, but at the same time know the reason behind it, so that you are comfortable in the performance of your duties, so that you are not doing it automatically, but with awareness of the outcome of your interaction."

It is here that Arjuna says to Krishna, "Sometimes you say action is important and sometimes you say wisdom is important. Krishna, make up your mind and just tell me what is important? Why does wisdom have to be part of action when they are two different things?" You have to remember that these are the questions of a person who is confused and in a state of depression. Therefore, the question is, "I am confused. Please let me know what I need to do, which path is the right one for me to follow – the path of wisdom or the path of action?"

Jnana yoga and karma yoga

Sri Bhagavan spoke thus: "O sinless Arjuna, earlier in this world, jnana yoga, the path of knowledge, was imparted to the Samkhya yogis, and karma yoga, the path of action, to the karma yogis." Here Krishna tells Arjuna that jnana yoga, or the path of wisdom, is imparted to Samkhya yogis and karma yoga to karma yogis. Two concepts have appeared here. Samkhya yogis follow the Samkhya system. Samkhya is the school of thought that talks about the existence of purusha and prakriti, consciousness and nature. In earlier times, people did not have television sets, aeroplanes and cars; they did not travel around the globe but remained confined to their homes and communities. After fulfilling their duties and responsibilities in the community, what

196

could they do? There were times when they could discuss agriculture. There were times when they could think about the boundaries of the community, or different innovations and inventions to raise the social status of their community. There were times when they could talk about their family and social problems. There were times when they could talk about their thoughts regarding nature, existence, life and God.

Samkhya yogis were the thinkers or philosophers in different communities, just as today we have the tradition of priests, or the tradition of sannyasins, who are concerned with other kinds of welfare, not social but spiritual, who think about different aspects of knowledge, different aspects of the human mind and human consciousness. Today we have psychologists and psychoanalysts who think about what maintains activity in the human mind, nature and personality. Samkhya yogis devoted their time to discovering the nature of the world, human life, God and the universe. So, Krishna tells Arjuna that the pursuit of knowledge is for Samkhya yogis who can find realization, who can see the big picture and experience cosmic and individual unity. Karma yoga, the path of action, is for karma yogis.

In any civilization or society, the number of karma yogis is always greater than the number of jnana yogis. Jnana yogis, the thinkers and philosophers, comprise somewhere between five to ten percent whereas karma yogis or workers, performers, comprise somewhere between eighty-five to ninety percent. In this present day and age, there is also a big mix. Sometimes we are jnana yogis during the day and karma yogis at night; sometimes we are karma yogis during the day and jnana yogis at night. But in earlier times there was a distinct classification and division of work.

For this reason, Krishna is saying that the path of jnana, the process of discovering the truth, is for samkhya yogis, or jnana yogis, who have taken it as their sadhana to discover the higher nature. Participation with greater awareness in the world is for those people who are karma yogis. They are two different paths, but one cannot exist without the other.

Both need to co-exist because it is not possible for anyone to perform a karma without some form of understanding of the karma, and there is no chance of anyone pursuing the path of knowledge by totally ignoring and neglecting karma. Both have to co-exist together.

Bhagavad Gita: Chapter 3
Karma and Karma Yoga (Part 2)

In the third chapter of the *Bhagavad Gita*, Arjuna asked Krishna: "You have said that wisdom, or knowledge of the self, is superior to karma, or dutiful action. Why then are you telling me to perform karma? I am confused by your statements and I would like you to clarify what I should do." To answer this question, Krishna tells Arjuna that jnana yoga, the path of wisdom and knowledge, was imparted to the samkhya yogis, who wanted to know the true nature of the self in relation to everything, microcosmic and macrocosmic. Karma yoga, the path of action, was imparted to the karma yogis, those who are active in doing their duty.

No one is free from karma and it is the aim of everyone to attain wisdom. So it should not be thought that karma, the path of dutiful action, can exist without wisdom, or that wisdom is the outcome of rejecting action. Both go hand in hand because it is only through action that you derive wisdom, and it is only through wisdom that you can guide your action. We have to understand this process through which wisdom or knowledge becomes a medium for balancing, integrating and harmonizing one's actions in life. No one can live without karma.

Krishna clarifies this subject in the following statement: "A person does not achieve a state of being actionless by being inactive, by not doing karma, nor does he achieve deliverance by abandoning action. Verily none remains inactive even for a second, as all persons even dependent (on other circumstances or persons) are compulsorily led to actions by the characteristics of worldly nature, prakriti."

Karma – the door to consciousness

One cannot avoid karmas because they are the foundation stones of life in the realm of prakriti, the cosmic nature. Wisdom, knowledge and understanding are expressions of consciousness that lead to the realization that consciousness is omniscient, omnipresent. At present, there are divisions in the entire field of consciousness which are created because of prakriti. Prakriti is a gravitational force which binds the individual to the world of senses, objects, name, form and idea. It is by living in this world that we have to go full circle in the process of evolution. As long as we live in the world of the cosmic nature, we cannot be free from action.

Action is the process connecting different events, the underlying flow from one to the other. This connection exists in all the different experiences which we can have at the physical level, the subtle level, the cosmic level, in the realm of the body and mind, in the realm of spirit, in the experience of the gross nature and the experience of the divine nature. This entire range of human experience is based on karma, but this karma gives some understanding of the underlying principles of consciousness.

Fire is not seen in wood but fire exists in wood. You have to ignite the wood in order to bring out its nature of fire. Similarly, consciousness exists in its optimum form, in its omniscient, omnipresent, omnipotent form, in every human being, but in a state of dormancy. What we experience now is only one part of the splendour of consciousness. It has been stated in the literature that the light is burning in the room but the doors are closed. From the cracks in the corners, some light filters through the door. It is through the luminosity of this filtered light that we are able to perceive the world. If we were to open the door, the luminosity of the shining light would be bright and brilliant, and we would be unable to see it with the naked eye.

Similarly, consciousness in its optimum form is the state of luminosity, light. The material world is perceived by the light which is filtering through the cracks of the closed door. This is the consciousness we are experiencing today, in a very limited form. So, action becomes the medium; the purpose of action is to open the door and allow the light of consciousness to shine forth. Therefore, from every aspect and angle, one can never be free from action. Some people believe that in order to overcome karma, to become free from karma, one should become inactive. Inaction does not lead to the exhaustion of karma because what we stop is the physical karma, the mental karma continues. If we stop the mental karma, the causal continues.

Effects of karma

If you throw a pebble or a stone into a still body of water, you will see many ripples coming from the source. There is no law that says one stone will mean only one ripple; it does not happen that way. One stone falls into the water, but many ripples come from the source and spread outwards. Similarly, karma can be one but the experience of karma happens in many dimensions. Karmas are static, but the effects of the karmas carry on moving. Take the example of a flower fixed in one place. The smell is contained in the flower, but how far the smell is likely to go depends on the wind. If there is no wind, the smell will remain around the flower, and if there is some wind, the smell will follow its current.

In the same way, karmas are performed only once in the material world, related to the sense objects, related to the ego, the mind, to desires and motivations, and they change from situation to situation, from one environment to another. The results of those karmas are carried forward by the force of the mind, by the involvement and participation of the mind with the karma. An event happens today at five o'clock, creating either happiness or conflict in your environment. Although it has happened today, you will carry the memory

201

for many years because it has affected your mind, feelings, emotions and beliefs. The smell of today's action will be felt over a long distance. It is the impression of karma.

Eliminating or avoiding karma is not important. It is the accumulation of impressions that one should become aware of and try to manage. Therefore, the Gita states that inactivity is not an indication of becoming free from the effects or results of action. Nor will you receive deliverance by abandoning action because action is only one event in the process of life. In this sloka, it is emphasized that the causes of creating karma are the situations and circumstances, personal and also cosmic, in a state of materialistic mentality and also in a state of illuminated, realized mentality.

Even enlightened beings are not free from the karmas. There is the story of Ramakrishna Paramahamsa, who is supposed to be one of the most spiritual figures, one of the luminaries of this century and age. There have been many examples from his life indicating that he had the ability to become free from the karmas affecting the body, the mind and the inner spiritual nature. He was the catalyst for helping a great multitude of people find the source of divinity, strength and peace within. Yet he suffered from cancer of the throat. He had the power to cure it, but did not use that power. When people asked him why, he said, "When I take upon myself the karmas of other people in order to free them, then I have to release them either in a physical form, a mental form or a spiritual form, instead of accumulating them within me."

The effects of the karmas that are physical in nature will manifest physically, those that are mental in nature will manifest mentally, those that are spiritual in nature will manifest spiritually, and they have to be released at all these three levels. If the physical body has to suffer in this process of release, let it suffer, because it is not suffering from holding back, it is suffering because of release. We suffer when we hold back. Yogis suffer when they let go. This is why the concept came about that enlightened beings take

202

upon themselves the suffering, the pain and the karmas of other people.

Another example is Christ. Why do we say he died because of our sins? According to Christian theological belief, he took the sins upon himself. According to spiritual belief, he took on the karmas, the suffering and pain of others. He had to go through that suffering on the cross in order to release it and to revive as a complete whole being. He had to die because of that, but when he had fulfilled and expressed the suffering and pain, he came alive again. Then he was free from suffering.

So there is a process of releasing the suffering. This release can take different forms in different people. The intensity can be physical, mental or spiritual. Therefore, it is said that karmas are circumstantial, guided by circumstances. But it is our ability to understand them, cope with and manage them that is important.

Beyond sensory control

What do we need to do to understand and manage the karmas? It is explained in the following statement. "That person who controls his karmendriyas, his organs of action, but sits thinking of sense objects in his mind is a foolish man, an unenlightened man with a pretence of good conduct." Control of the jnanendriyas, the sensory organs, is often taken by spiritual aspirants as a method of stopping the participation of the senses in the world. However, you may be unable to stop the involvement and identification of the senses with the world if your mind is not pacified, and then such effort leads you nowhere.

Again there is an indication given here that the senses are connected with the mind. The mind is an extension of consciousness and consciousness in whole is spirit. The senses of the body are constantly performing karma: the eyes are continuously observing, the ears are continuously hearing, the nose is continuously smelling, the skin is continuously feeling and the tongue is continuously tasting. These are the basic functions of the different organs. The function of the legs is to walk, the function of the arms is to lift. These functions represent the physical nature. At the same time, the physical function is linked with the mind and it gives birth to a new and different experience which is translated or converted into desire or aversion.

When you see a flower, your eyes watch the flower; that is the physical activity. Something inside tells you, "Oh, it's beautiful, I want to have it." What is that voice? Your eyes are not telling you, the physical senses are not telling you, they are simply saying something is there in the environment. It is the association of the senses with desires, ego and memories which creates a different experience. You may want to possess it or you may want to reject it.

The information of the senses becomes transformed into one form of mental understanding and experience. That mental experience can create the sensation of pleasure, attraction, attachment, or it can create a sense of aversion, rejection, letting it go. When it creates a feeling of attraction, then you want to possess it. Possessiveness comes in and can feed the ego. I may fight to possess something because then I can say, "I have a claim, it's mine." I am the person who possesses something nice and this feeling then feeds my ego. I possess something which other people don't have and it gives me a feeling of superiority. I am superior, not in the sense of body or mind, not in the sense of my intellect or attainment, but because I possess something unique.

Some practitioners say that in order to evolve you have to deny sensorial participation and involvement with the world. You can close your eyes, you can stop seeing the world; you can plug your ears and stop hearing; you can block your nose and stop smelling; but you are only stopping the physical senses. The mind is still active and the mind is also a sense organ, not physical but definitely subtle. If the mind is active, then stopping or trying to control the senses has no meaning. Sensory control in the physical dimension provides no solution. What can provide an answer is explained in the next sloka which we will deal with in the next session.

Bhagavad Gita: Chapter 3
Karma and Karma Yoga (Part 3)

Swami Sivananda used to say, "One ounce of practice is better than ten tons of theory." It has been the experience of yogis that theory or intellectualization of a concept simply creates more confusion. This is because we are dealing with a process which is subtle in nature, beyond the human capacity for analysis and rationalization. It could be one of the reasons why we have not been able to improve ourselves, despite all our knowledge and despite what we have been told by enlightened beings throughout the ages. Whenever we want to improve ourselves, to become better, we always have to look back into the traditions. Therefore, no matter what our thoughts or perceptions may be, we have to find an approach which is practical and suited to our nature and our way of life.

In my study of the many different types of literature and scriptures, I have tried to find a practical way of practising what is written in them. The source of my inspiration has been the *Bhagavad Gita*. In this book I have found the answer to many of the questions which have bothered us again and again, and which have taken us on a futile intellectual journey. It is with this purpose that we are studying the third chapter which deals with human participation in the world and how we can become aware of the interactive process which happens with the senses, with the mind and with consciousness.

This has been the theme of karma yoga. Karma yoga is not the yoga of performing action; karma yoga is not becoming aware of actions. When actions emanate from the head, then they become karma bhoga and we try to derive pleasure from the actions. Pleasure becomes the fruit, the result, the attainment and the achievement of an action. When we are able to convert the karmic process, the active process, into a feeling which emanates from the heart, then it becomes karma yoga, in which unity and harmony is experienced between one's inner feelings and one's actions. So, to understand the concept of karma yoga we have to be very clear and able to differentiate between karma yoga and karma bhoga.

Necessity of action
One can never stay actionless, one can never be without action. Action is a process inherent in creation; it is a sequential process of growth, of interacting with our environment, of interacting with our mind. The body has its own karmas, the mind has its own karmas and the spirit has its own karmas. Karmas are not only performed through the senses but also through speech. I am performing a karma right now. Karmas are also performed through the mind. We are all performing actions through our mind, whether it is in the form of thinking or desiring. Every kind of activity that happens in this dimension is known as karma. We can even say that karma is another name for prakriti or creation.

People believe that in order to become enlightened, to realize the individual nature, it is necessary to overcome the karmas. They think it is necessary to become inactive, passive, to withdraw from active and dynamic participation. Unfortunately, it does not work that way. You can stop your sensory involvement and participation, but what about the natural laws that the body has to follow? Can you stop sleeping? Sleeping is a karma. Can you stop eating and drinking? Eating and drinking are natural karmas. This natural law is necessary for the body to sustain and nurture

206

itself. Can you stop the process, the movement and activity of the mind? No! Is it possible to become desireless? No! Is it possible to become thoughtless? No! However, through conscious effort it is possible to convert the pleasure association of karma into yoga, and that leads to the development of an optimistic and positive attitude. This has been stated in the Gita: "A person does not achieve a state of being actionless by being inactive, by not doing the karma, nor does he get enlightenment and deliverance by abandoning karma."

Sensory awareness and control

At the same time, another concept emerges from Krishna's statement. There is a state of being in which you are able to clean all the thoughts, to purify all the desires. The cleaning and purification is transformation of the earthly nature into a transcendental nature by being aware of the cosmic principle, the cosmic nature, rather than the individual principle, the individual nature. It has been said in many different ways that the cosmic nature is unconditioned, whereas the individual nature is conditioned. The cosmic nature represents creative participation in life rather than selfishly motivated or conditioned, desireful actions. So, conversion of action has to take place.

How can we convert the actions from being conditioned to unconditioned? It has been stated further that there are different methods. One is by controlling the mind: "He is a person par excellence who subjugates the senses by force of mind, and with his limbs (karmendriyas) performs karma or action without attachment to its fruits." This is one way – controlling the senses and controlling the mind. Control of the senses in yogic terminology is known as *indriya nigraha*. The state of indriya nigraha is attained through perfection of pratyahara.

We understand pratyahara to be a meditative process. Later, it becomes an integral part of observing the interactive senses, the senses that interact with the world. It has been said that pratyahara is withdrawal of the senses from the externalized state to the internalized state. However, before you can withdraw your senses, you have to become aware of their reach in the external dimension. It has been said that the state of pratyahara is similar to a turtle withdrawing its limbs into its shell and becoming self-contained. This is an apt description, but it describes the final state of pratyahara.

What is the process? Extension of awareness into the realm of the senses, observing the reach of the senses in the outer dimension, the subtle effect on the mind of the senses interacting with the world and the sense objects. What kind of effect am I experiencing within myself? What kind of experience am I having with the interaction of the senses? What kind of desires am I having? What kind of thoughts am I having? With which dimension of my personality are these thoughts, desires and aspirations linked? With which chakras are they related? The process is going on through observation, by extending the awareness, becoming aware of the sensory interactions and then centring them, focusing them and withdrawing them.

Harmonizing the chitta vrittis

The second process is stilling the mind. The yogic tradition speaks of *chitta vrittis*, modifications of mind, which lead to a different kind of perception. The chitta vrittis can lead to false knowledge, to true knowledge or to conflicting knowledge. They can create imprints which are recognized as memories and which can also blank out the mind – the state known as nidra. These are the activities of the chitta vrittis in relation to the world of the senses and sense objects, in order to recognize a name, a form and an idea. They are nothing more than that.

We all recognize each other by a name, by a form and by the idea that is conveyed in that form and that name. Sometimes the knowledge of name, form and idea can lead to conflict because the knowledge is not precise or clear. Sometimes the knowledge can be false or inaccurate. Sometimes the knowledge or understanding of the

208

environment and the world is compared with past memories, *smriti*. Sometimes there is a total blackout of the mind, it says no more, which is nidra. The *Yoga Sutras* aim at knowing this interactive mind before attempting to go in. When we are able to harmonize this interactive mind, known as the chitta vrittis, then we go deeper into our own nature.

According to the Samkhya system or tradition, manifestation of consciousness passes through four different changes. The first transformation in the omniscient consciousness is known as *ahamkara*, or the ego principle, the 'I' identity, the birth of individuality and recognition of 'me' as an individual. That is the 'I' identity from which come three other states of consciousness: buddhi, chitta and manas.

Buddhi is interactive intelligence, intelligence that is interacting with the material, physical dimension. Buddhi, or intellect, has to be understood in relation to prakriti. *Chitta* is the interactive memory that recognizes the different aspects and nature of creation and retains the information of that experience as an imprint, an image, a symbol, a thought. *Manas* is the interactive thought process, the interactive reflective process. The chitta vrittis are part of manas as well as buddhi and chitta. Subjugation and transformation of the mind happens when we practise dharana, or focusing.

Dharana practices are divided into three groups. The first group is *daharakasha dharana*, harmonization and balancing of the instinctive consciousness. The second group is *hridayakasha dharana*, harmonization and balancing of the feeling consciousness. The third group is *chidakasha dharana*, harmonization and balancing of the thinking consciousness. Perfection of dharana or concentration leads to subjugation and transformation of the mind. So, control of the senses and control of the mind lead to harmonious action. That is one method.

Developing the right attitude
There is another method for those who feel that this path can be too tedious, difficult and involved, which is changing

the attitude. The correct attitude that has been described for karma yoga is awareness of the action to be performed with perfection, without any expectation. Awareness becomes the first item, perfection becomes the second item and having no expectations becomes the third item. This is very difficult!

According to the Gita, for a person who has been able to develop the attitude of a karma yogi, who attains happiness, satisfaction and contentment in the self, there is no karma. This is stated in a cryptic form. Try to understand it. Become aware of action. Extension of awareness into the action makes us perform that action with the idea of perfection. Perfection really does not mean that things have to be in a certain form, because the concept of perfection changes from person to person. The same action can be performed by twenty different people and they will have twenty different concepts of perfection. In relation to karma, or action, perfection is using your full creativity, giving your best.

This is a lesson we can derive from God. God has a factory to manufacture human beings. There are about five billion human beings on this planet. Can you imagine Him or Her having five billion different moulds? No two beings are alike; each face is different. It is incredible. However, when we have to manufacture something, we make one mould and everything comes out exactly the same. That is our idea of perfection; everything has to be identical. Material perfection, social perfection, technological perfection, whatever you want to call it, is one concept of perfection.

Another concept of perfection is the multifarious and also nefarious nature – prakriti. There is so much variety. Each human being is different, each blade of grass, each flower, each animal and bird is different. Would you call that imperfection or would you call it perfection? So, perfection from the yogic perspective, and from God's perspective, means making everything unique and giving your best. Our creativity is seen here and when we are able to express our creativity in action it is known as perfect

210

action. When we become one with the action, and it is not a mechanical process, that is known as perfect action. This is an attitude, an effort, a sadhana. To become perfect is a sadhana, not a concept.

When we follow the path of karma as sadhana, something else happens which is natural and spontaneous – not being attached to the result of the action. Result and action is known as cause and effect. Every cause contains an inherent effect. Every potent cause has a potent effect. Every cause has an effect and every effect has a cause. This is the law. We experience it in our relationships with people; we experience it in the performance of action; we experience it in our daily routine.

Our action and our attitude at present is geared to expecting an outcome from a particular kind of action. Why do we work? What is the expectation? Financial security is the expectation behind work. If you know that the place where you work has gone bankrupt, you will no longer be motivated to go to work. If you know that it is unable to support the workers, you will start looking for another job. You work for a month and at the end you are paid for your work. From the beginning until the end of the month, you are working with the idea that on the second or the third of the month, you will receive a pay cheque.

Parents educate their children with the expectation, deep down, that the child will excel in life. When the child excels, after receiving a proper education, it is you who will feel that joy, happiness and satisfaction. You want to mould the child in a form with which you are comfortable. It is very difficult for parents to say, "I will leave the child to make his or her own destiny." In fact, this idea will not even come into your head. If it does come, it will be later or when the child is established in a set pattern.

Awareness, creativity and perfection in action

Now, there is a solution. You can provide the best for your child and at the same time allow the child to discover his or her own creativity. Some people have incorporated yoga into their children's lives with very good results. One little girl had been given yoga nidra by her mother from an early age. After her first day in kindergarten, the little girl said, "I already know what I will be taught. Now I am ready for primary school." She was four and a half years old! Can you imagine the level of her thought or consciousness? So clear, so sharp, so precise, that she was able to know what she would learn in kindergarten and felt ready for the next stage.

Yoga nidra was being given to that little girl along with some specific sankalpas, or positive resolutions. At a deeper level of consciousness the centres of receptivity were opened up. When the centres of receptivity open up, perfection becomes an integral part of human life. There is no place where perfection can be learned; it becomes a natural part of human life which is expressed according to the pattern of mind. When it is being expressed spontaneously and naturally, the other outcome of perfection comes automatically, which is not being attached to something. This happens because there is the confidence, knowledge and understanding that you are expressing your creativity, your awareness, your feeling of oneness with action.

Expectations become part of action when we think our action is the final one and that we cannot do any better. So it is the change of attitude which leads to perfection, to fulfilment, in karma yoga. When you are able to perform actions with awareness, with creativity, with perfection involved in the action, with an attitude of having no expectation, then you derive inner happiness, satisfaction and contentment. Then you become free from the karmas. This is the statement of the Gita.

Although there are many methods described in the Gita, let us begin with the two I have described. The first is pratyahara, control of the physical senses, and dharana, control of the mind. The second method is awareness of action, combining action with creativity and being detached from the results or effects of the action. One is a passive process, the other is a dynamic process. If you can combine the passive meditative process with the dynamic process, then you will see a very beautiful transformation happen in your life. Right now, we are caterpillars crawling around on and munching our leaves, but there is also the possibility of becoming butterflies and flying.

The Language of Silence

Once God decided to change the language without telling anyone. There was an old man who was very close to God. God said, "I had better warn him so that he doesn't suddenly hear everyone speaking in a different language and feel that everyone has forgotten the language of silence."

God came to the old man in a dream and said, "The day after tomorrow I am going to put something in all the waters of the planet. When people drink the water, they will forget the language of silence and they will speak in many different tongues."

When the man woke up the next day, he was very worried. He said, "If we can't speak the language of silence, then we won't be near God anymore."

What could he do? During the day he filled all the pots that he could find with clear, pure water and put them in his cave.

When everyone woke up the next day, they found that they could not understand each other, because they had drunk the water that had been changed by God and they were all speaking in different languages.

Only the one elderly person who had kept the pure water knew the language that could communicate with God.

He gave a few drops of the water to other people in different communities and tribes so that, while they were

214

speaking their different languages, they would also have an understanding of the language of silence.

Havan is also a language of silence. Nothing has to be said after this. If you have any questions or problems, throw them into the fire right now. Learn to speak the language of silence, for you have been given a few drops of that pure water today.

Round Table Discussion

You said that we must be ourselves. Is the spiritual name myself or is it the quality I must develop in order to approach my true self?

Swamiji: Our nature is recognized by a particular trait of spirit, of consciousness, which is predominant in our being. Identification with the name is identification with the predominant quality of our nature and that becomes the stepping stone to realizing the true self, because the true self is not recognizable by a name. There are two states: one is becoming and the other is being. When we are in the state of being, it is realization of "I am that I am". But when we are in the process of becoming, we have to go through sequential realizations of different aspects and qualities which manifest at different times in the course of our growth and evolution. The spiritual name given at the time of initiation is an intuitive realization of the nature that is predominant in you. By identifying with the name you can go deeper into your being and realize the true self, which has no intellectual name yet contains all names.

Would you please talk about sankalpa and the sankalpas used with children? How can we avoid projecting our own desires onto children and how can we help them to be aware of the difficulties in relationships with parents?

216

Rishi Hridayananda: Sankalpa is one of the greatest things we can do for ourselves. As parents we hold the key to this new generation in our hands and in our hearts. Our children follow everything we do and say, their ears are highly tuned to how we act. When your children are fifty, sixty or seventy years of age they will be acting just like you. How do I know? Because I do it myself.

The best thing you can do for your children is to teach them yoga nidra and use, Swami Niranjan as the greatest example for your inspiration. Turn the yoga nidra cassette on in the evening when you come home from work or school. Let your children hear it and see you practising it. That's the way to teach them. If you can do that, then your children will grow and learn and they will be inspired to practise yoga when they are older, and in time their children will do it as well.

Sankalpa is perhaps the greatest seed that we can place in our inner consciousness. It comes to fruition extremely quickly. If you put your heart and mind to the task, then it becomes easy because it is also enjoyable. Children love it and it helps them to pass their exams.

Swami Yogabhakti: Sankalpa is certainly the absolute weapon against anxiety and fear. When children are preparing for exams, for instance, and also hearing about life as adults present it, about how hopeless the world is today, about unemployment and not being able to find a job even with a degree, then sankalpa is very powerful. Tell the children that if they are truly who they are, they will find their place under the sun, whatever the conditions, whatever the parents. If you tell them to be confident and repeat, "I know I can do it. I know I will succeed," they will succeed. If you give children self-confidence through a sankalpa, then they will find out who they are and what they have to do, and they will manage throughout life.

We have been taught by our guru that a person has to choose their own sankalpa. Therefore, we must explain to school children of eight to eleven years that they have to select their own sankalpa, keeping in mind the fact that they

217

are endowed with inner light. Then they should close their eyes and listen to the tiny little voice telling them the right little sentence, which they will repeat in their heart. Usually when children are told to close their eyes and listen to that key sentence or that strong word, their faces light up because they hear the little voice inside dictating the sankalpa. That is how we deal with sankalpa in the classroom at school.

Dr Rishi Vivekananda: When our youngest son was three or four he was always running onto the road. We had no fence around the house and were very worried about him. So at night, when he was asleep, I would go and whisper in his ear, "Now, Peter, when you come to the edge of the road you must stop and make sure there are no cars coming." I said this three times for about a week. The sankalpa went into his unconscious mind and may have saved his life because he is still alive. After a week he would come running across the footpath and just stop at the side of the road and look down at his feet. He could not work out why his feet had stopped. That is sankalpa!

Swamiji: Swami Sivananda used to say that children are lumps of clay and you can mould them into any way you want them to be. This is true, but unfortunately we have not been moulded properly and we lack the understanding of how to mould others properly. Although Swami Sivananda's statement is correct, we cannot apply it. Instead of working with children, as a first step I would recommend that parents work with themselves. It is the general tendency for parents to become the judge, jury and executioner of their children. The child always sees the parents as authority figures, and the child is always a victim of that authority. No matter how much you may love your child, that image is always there.

The first point yoga suggests is that you should change yourself and try to become a friend to your child. Friendship has a very big influence on the life of a person and the life of a child. Children will listen to and follow what other children say because there is no barrier; they see each other as equals. Even when they are grown up, the concept of equality between friends matures. You remain friends with those

218

who were your friends in childhood and you avoid those people whom you placed on the pedestal of authority. So, the first effort parents have to make is to become friends with their children.

Secondly, after you have become friends with your children you have to encourage them to express their positive nature. As an example, a true story comes to mind about a family who had a small child. Whenever the parents wanted to go to the movies they would tell the child a lie, not that they were going to the movies. But intuitively the child knew that his parents were hiding something from him and he began to rebel against their instructions. It was an intuitive response. Adults function at the level of intellect, but children function at the level of intuition. Therefore, they are able to pick up many things intuitively which adults try to hide from them intellectually. They know when someone is telling them a lie and they know when someone is telling them the truth. They know when someone is trying to control them and they know when someone is trying to let them be free. Their responses are different, their expressions are different, their eyes are different, their smiles are different in every situation.

Once you have become friends with your child, if you are able to encourage them to express their feelings by being truthful with them, then you do not need to have a sankalpa especially modified or made for children, because they learn by example. We all learn by example, but we cannot sustain the example in our lives for long due to our conditioning or our belief or our lifestyle, whatever the reason. But children learn by example and they live by example. So being truthful to your child will automatically bring out the best in them.

Thirdly, if you feel the child is inhibited in some areas of his nature or personality, such as being shy or unable to interact with other children of the same age group; having difficulties relating to people; having some form of insecurity or inhibition; having problems with study, with concentration, retention and memory, then you can begin with simple sankalpas which can encourage positive expression in the child's life. One very broad and basic sankalpa which we generally give to little children is, "I am creative." It is very simple. Give your child this sankalpa and also give your child the opportunity to become creative, because it is no use giving a sankalpa without giving the opportunity. If you give a sankalpa then you also have to give the right opportunity.

So, from my perspective, it is the parents who have to do the hard work, not the children. Children simply have to be encouraged to express themselves.

Can you tell us about vidya and avidya, how to know which knowledge is wrong and which knowledge is right?

Dr Swami Shankardevananda: Vidya is a goddess, a shakti, a universal force containing knowledge. Through meditation we attempt to enter into the vidya. There are many types of vidya. Yoga is one, ayurveda is another. In India there are many of these forms of knowledge. Vidya is a form of knowledge that is attained through meditation, not through intellect, or thinking, or theory, or hypothesis, but through direct experience.

Avidya is ignorance, the cause of all our suffering and anxiety. When we are in avidya, when we are lacking connection to some kind of true power or true knowledge that gives us inner security and certainty, a sense of being sure about life, then we know we are not on the right path.

There are two ways to discern the difference between true knowledge which sustains, gives life and is creative, and the other knowledge, which is dry. The first is through the teachings of an enlightened master or guru, and the second is through the ancient texts, the shastras. I try to steer my life by listening to what Swamiji has been saying and also by the rudder or steering wheel of the shastras. These books contain a lot of the vidyas in a cryptic form, which is then best illuminated through dialogue with someone like Swamiji.

Swamiji: Vidya, or knowledge, realization, is something that supports and nurtures life, and makes one open and creative. Avidya is the opposite, it does not support and nurture

220

creativity or human life. We should not look at these concepts as the presence or absence of knowledge. There is vidya and avidya in every form of knowledge. Vidya and avidya are the outcome of knowing something and either applying it or not applying it. It has been stated in the *Ishavasya Upanishad* that avidya, or ignorance, lack of application of knowledge in life, leads to darkness and suppresses human nature, and that although vidya has the ability to nurture and sustain life, it can also lead one to darkness if it is not applied in the right form.

There is a sutra in Sanskrit which says that if arrogance and ego are the outcome of knowledge, then that is ignorance. When we know a lot, we have the feeling that "I know more than everyone else". That is one of the greatest barriers to vidya, to applied or realized knowledge. The purpose of realized knowledge is to make one help others, not to feed one's ego, not to become arrogant, not to have a superiority complex.

So, please remember that knowledge is one. There is no such thing as right knowledge or wrong knowledge. It is how we apply knowledge in our lives that matters. If we cannot apply it, it is avidya or darkness. If we can apply it, it becomes a path that leads us to luminosity, realization.

We have heard that anxiety, depression, insecurity and fear are related to the activity of the chakras, on the one hand, to past childhood experiences, on the other, and to karma in general. I think all these things play a role in generating those kind of afflictions. How do they interact and combine with each other, thus becoming the cause of psychological illness?

Dr Rishi Vivekananda: You are correct in saying that all these factors are applicable. In the submerged nine-tenths of the iceberg there are millions and billions of impressions that we have taken in over a long period of time. These impressions can be positive or negative. Positive impressions will have built up our sense of security – mooladhara chakra; joy – swadhisthana chakra; power, personal integrity and

221

assertiveness – manipura chakra; love – anahata chakra; an ability to communicate with other people – vishuddhi chakra; and a high self-esteem from our ability to use our heads – ajna chakra. Negative impressions can be memories of times when we have felt very insecure, times when we have felt sad and deeply hurt, times when we have felt unloved or unable to love, times when we have not been able to communicate with other people. All these qualities of the personality have positive or negative impressions attached to them in our unconscious mind. The sum total of how we feel at this time is the balance between all these different qualities and aspects of our nature.

Yoga activates the chakras, which are connected with the memory areas where all these past impressions are held. The practices can allow these memories, samskaras or impressions to come into consciousness so we can deal with them. In my profession as a psychiatrist I deal with people who are already disturbed. In the beginning we give them pleasant things to quieten them down and make them feel more relaxed, to put a little cover over the different aspects where the pain is being felt. But after a while people can use the yogic practices to come to terms with and realize where the conflicts and problems have come from. We can do this by using practices that act upon the chakras by energizing the system, and then by going inside and seeing what is happening there. Yoga is the way to do this, certainly in the early stages.

Modified states of consciousness create mental crisis in which another interpretation of reality is made. What are the reasons and how can it be handled? Can you also speak about the spiritual ego which seems to be the more dangerous ego, and what to do about it?

Dr Swami Shankardevananda: When we are under the sway of either the tamasic force or the rajasic force, then we are unable to see life clearly and we are unable to experience what is happening to us with clarity. This is what Patanjali is talking about. When we are caught up in the vrittis, when we

222

are under the sway of an undisciplined mind, a mind that does not practise stability, that does not develop purity, in the sense of lightness and clarity, then it is possible for the mind to become fractured. It is like looking at a broken mirror: nothing fits together properly. The way through this is to develop greater balance, openness and creativity.

In terms of the spiritual ego, we face many different types of mental problems. We can either have a personality type that is underdeveloped or lacks confidence, or a type of ego that is overconfident. In both of these conditions the shakti is low, the sense of power, the sense of self, is not strong, so we feel that life is stronger than us, that life is able to overpower us, that life is heavy and that we are weak. It is like a child's state. That is the kind of spiritual trap we can fall into if we have a false sense of humility, where we say, "I'm not good enough, I'll be humble." This is one kind of false humility.

The other is when the ego has too much energy and is overinflated. We think, "Yes, I'm doing very well." There are dangers in all these conditions. Managing one's ego is difficult. How to live life in a balanced way is probably one of the most difficult parts of yoga, because the ego is such a subtle component of the mind. This relates back to the question on vidya and avidya. The sources of suffering, Patanjali's kleshas, are firstly avidya, and out of avidya comes the development of the ego. Ego is identification with something that we are not, identifying ourselves with a very limited form through a lot of self-hypnosis. We might be constantly repeating to ourselves a negative sankalpa like, "I'm no good. I can't make it."

Any kind of egoic structure has to be seen with clarity. The way to see yourself is through the development of pratyahara, a journey back into yourself, towards the more subtle aspects of your being. From that position you can feel the tendencies of your personality with greater clarity. We have to try to overcome these mental crises, where we either get too caught up in life, or too immersed in ourselves, or become underconfident, or overconfident. Trying to tread the razor's edge of a truly spiritual life is about developing a balanced awareness of what is going on in the world, in other people and in yourself, so that you are very clear about your own energy, your own desires, your own motivation and where you are coming from.

Most important is to have a teacher or, if possible, a guru. If you cannot find a guru, then find someone who can be your teacher or counsellor, who can reflect back to you what is really going on so that you can start to see yourself. It is hard sometimes to see ourselves, but when we enter into relationships with spiritual practices and spiritual people as in satsang, then we have an opportunity to get a sense of who we are and then hopefully to try and hold onto that in our lives. That is one of the first steps in overcoming this problem.

How should we approach yoga so as to have no conflicts in our lives?
Swamiji: Somebody once asked Paramahamsaji the same question. He answered that the practice of yoga is your personal affair. If there is opposition from your wife or husband or other members of the family, then practise it privately. You do not need a placard saying "I practise yoga." That is the way to manage conflict. Conflict arises due to different opinions and aspirations, one person wanting to pursue an activity which the other person does not support. Once you know the reason for conflict then you adjust and modify your life in such a way that you are able to live and practise yoga without interference from other people.

Paramahamsaji also gave a suggestion. If other members of the family do not support you, then practise yoga in the bathroom. That will solve all the problems. You can practise surya namaskara (salute to the sun) in the bathtub. You can practise the breathing techniques while sitting in a chair in the bathroom. You can practise meditation, pratyahara, sitting there. The only other person who will know is your image in the mirror.

When a thief is planning a robbery, he doesn't tell anyone. He commits the robbery and lives happily ever after. Not a

224

single soul knows he has committed a crime. A thief is secretive. That same feeling doesn't have to exist between yogis or in a yoga practitioner, but there is definitely the possibility of adjusting your personal life so that your aspirations, practices and motivations do not create conflict in other members of the family.

Some people have practised yoga for many years without informing their nearest and dearest. But when the positive changes in the practitioner have been recognized and appreciated then the family has become supportive, because there was a change; there was no fighting or conflict. If you can show them a transformation for the better, you will always have support. If you try to superimpose your ideas because you think they are good, then the other person's ideas may contradict yours.

Will there be a sannyasa training course in Europe? Where can one go in Europe if one wants to become a poorna sannyasin?

Swamiji: At present the environment does not support a sannyasa training course. In order to live sannyasa after training in an ashram, you have to become part of society and live your sannyasa in society.

Sannyasa is also a tradition which at present is not widely known in Europe. People think that sannyasa means monkhood, that it represents a spiritual or religious tradition, but this is not so. The definition of sannyasa is: dedication of one's faculties for the upliftment of humanity. There has to be training in sannyasa, but at present this training is possible only where the cultural environment supports the sannyasa system, although we are trying to make it possible for sannyasa training to become available in different parts of the world. To facilitate the process we have started with jignasu sannyasa and karma sannyasa. Jignasu sannyasa is for the seeker sannyasin or novice. As a spiritual seeker, you have to cultivate certain qualities in life. If you can cultivate those qualities by leading a normal life, they will become more ingrained in your nature, your personality.

I received a note saying, "I have enjoyed the change in my lifestyle during this Festival of Yoga. One week ago it would have been unthinkable for me to sleep in the passage in a sleeping bag on the floor. In my home I am used to sleeping in the comfort and luxury of my bedroom. This has been a new experience. I thank you very much for it and look forward to the next event when I can come back and again sleep in the passageway."

This comment is relevant because we are talking about sannyasa. Sannyasa is adaptability, adapting ourselves to live happily in any situation. If we cannot do this then we cannot become sannyasins. If we become conditioned to living in a certain style and we look for that facility no matter what kind of high-flying ideas we may have, we will never learn to adjust to different situations. Sannyasa at a personal level is knowing how to adjust.

The sannyasa training we received in India in the early days was very tough. For years we did not have a room or a bed that we could call our own. It was not a gypsy or a hippie way of life; we had to learn how to live with the bare minimum. Once three of us went on a padayatra, a walking seminar, in Orissa, a state in India famed for the Konark or Sun temple. We went in different directions. Being the youngest, I had the luxury of using my legs to the maximum. During that month long tour, my only possessions were two dhotis, a notebook, a diary and a pen. There were times when I did not have anything to eat because nobody would give me alms. There were nights when I had to sleep in the rain under a tree with no cover, shivering with cold. There were times when people would set their dogs on me to chase me away from their homes, and there were times when people would invite me into their homes and give me a proper meal, rest and respect. What did we learn from this? How to adjust to and accept different situations and conditions. Now, if you were to attempt to do something similar in Europe, you know where you would end up! So, it is the cultural and social environment which at present does not support the training of adjustment to lifestyle.

Nevertheless there are other aspects of sannyasa which can be cultivated: cultivation of certain qualities in the jignasu sannyasa tradition, cultivation of more qualities in the karma sannyasa tradition and cultivation of even more qualities in the poorna sannyasa tradition. You also have to remember that no one is born perfect. Sannyasa initiation is the establishment of a trust between the guru and the disciple. It is like going to university and getting your degree on the first day without doing a course, with the hope, the belief and the trust that the degree will help, inspire and encourage you to complete your studies. The relationship that exists between guru and disciple is one of trust. The guru initiates you knowing fully well that you are not qualified for initiation, but with the hope that the initiation will provide you with the inspiration to complete the process of sannyasa.

There are some people who, on receiving the initiation, think they have attained everything. Those people are easily identifiable in society. It is not the wearing of a robe that makes one great. There is a saying by Thomas Merton: "If you want to identify me, do not ask me what I like to eat, or what clothes I like to wear, or how I comb my hair, but ask me in detail what it is I am living for and then ask me what is preventing me from fully living that which I am living for." This is the sentiment of sannyasa – how one can live in the best possible manner, combining the best of spiritual and material life, not being associated with or attached to either material life or spiritual life.

Spirituality is a natural expression in the life of a sannyasin. We do not have to become prophets overnight, we have to become aspirants. Apart from the adjustment to different conditions of life, apart from the cultivation of different qualities of life, sannyasa also aspires to deepen the level of trust, to encourage commitment, faith in oneself and willpower. Sannyasa also aspires to encourage universal laughter. We are always sad because of our problems. We are always crying because of difficulties with the family. It is a hopeless situation. Therefore, aspire for universal laughter.

When we stop crying, when we stop seeing the thorns all the time, then we become sannyasins.

Sannyasa is a big subject. In order to facilitate training in poorna sannyasa it is better initially to become perfect as jignasu sannyasins and as karma sannyasins. Swami Sivananda used to sing a song:

> Serenity, regularity, absence of vanity,
> Sincerity, simplicity, veracity,
> Equanimity, fixity, non-irritability,
> Adaptability, humility, tenacity,
> Integrity, nobility, magnanimity,
> Charity, generosity, purity.
>
> Practise daily these eighteen 'ities.
> You will soon attain immortality.
> Brahman is the only real entity.
> Mr So and So is a false non-entity.
> You will abide in eternity and infinity,
> You will behold unity in diversity.

These are the foundations of the sannyasa tradition.

Yoga in Slovenia

Ljubljana, Slovenia, 7–8 May 1997

The Role of Yoga

Greetings from an ancient country known as Bharat. Bharat is the ancient name of modern India, but it does not represent today's India, rather it represents spiritual India. Greetings also from two Indian traditions, those of yoga and sannyasa. Sannyasa is the monastic order to which I belong, and yoga is the science of life that I teach.

We are meeting here today to discuss the role that yoga can play in our lives. We know that yoga means the science of life. Some people believe that yoga is a spiritual science; some believe that yoga deals with the management of the human mind; and others believe that yoga is a physical science that helps to alleviate disease and provide physical harmony and health. All these different definitions of yoga are correct, but the real definition of yoga is a science of living in harmony with nature and with oneself. As human beings, we need to know how to live harmoniously and how to develop a broad vision of life.

When we think of a tree, we think of the trunk, the branches, the leaves, the flowers and the fruit. We see this part of a tree first because it is visible and in our line of sight. But a tree is not only the trunk, branches, leaves, flowers or fruit, a tree is also the roots which are underground. Without the roots a tree has no existence, no life, and will receive no nourishment from the soil. So, just as the roots are important

231

to a tree, similarly, in our lives something else is important. Unfortunately, we tend to look at life as our physical body and mind interacting in the outer world. But there is a deeper aspect of our being which nourishes our body and mind and provides our existence with meaning and purpose. That deeper aspect of our existence is known as spirit.

The experience of spirit

Spirit is the force of existence which keeps our physical body alive and our mind active. This spirit is composed of two separate forces: one is the force of consciousness and the other is the force of energy. Imagine that there are two people: one is blind and cannot see, the other is lame and cannot walk. Both want to attend this meeting, so what kind of arrangement will they make to get here? There are no buses, cars, bicycles or trains; they have to come by their own force. The answer is simple. The blind person, although he can't see, has the use of his limbs, and the lame person, although he can't walk, has the use of his sight, so they both help each other. The lame person sits on the blind person's shoulders and guides and directs him where to walk.

According to the yogic tradition, that is the role of consciousness and energy. Consciousness has eyes but not legs; consciousness is lame. Energy has limbs but not eyes; energy is blind. However, when they both come together they are able to move and to reach their destination. This is a symbolic explanation of the concept of consciousness and energy according to yoga. Consciousness and energy coming together provides the experience of spirit. Spirit is the faculty of consciousness and the faculty of energy combined, living in each one of us. It is this spirit which is the foundation or force behind our existence, motivations and aims. But it is subtle, invisible, it cannot be seen.

We identify with our body because it is physical. We identify with our mind, emotions, feelings and desires because we know they exist. We know that the mind is more subtle than the physical body. We know that the mind exists because we are able to think. We know that

232

emotions exist because we can feel their force and we know that desires exist because they provide us with the motivation to achieve and attain things in life. But the mind, emotions and desires are not physical. We can know of them at the level of experience.

Similarly, we know that the spirit also exists, but we cannot see it physically and we cannot experience it mentally. The spirit exists beyond the range of normal human comprehension and experience. However, when we make an effort to realize our nature and personality, then the spirit also comes into focus and we are able to build a holistic view of our existence, combining body, mind and spirit. The development of this holistic view is known as yoga. Awareness and harmony in this multidimensional existence of body, mind and spirit is known as yoga.

Our journey as human beings begins with life and ends with life. Life means to become alive. We become alive when we take birth, but that birth is physical and the body goes through its own changes and transformations. We also come alive when we develop a holistic vision of our existence. Therefore, the journey begins with life and ends with life. We move from one stage of experience to another stage of experience, which is the transformation of the body and the inner self. This is the aim of every human being. Finding peace can be a desire but not the ultimate aim. Finding happiness can be a desire but not the ultimate aim, and finding fulfilment in life can be a desire but not the ultimate aim of life.

Many people may wonder about this, because we are all searching for peace, happiness and fulfilment. But if you think carefully, you will realize that peace, happiness and fulfilment are the by-products of a realized nature, the attainments of having perfected the process of living. If we search first for peace, happiness or fulfilment, it is a temporary achievement because we have tried to find a source of balance without transforming our personality. If we can transform our personality to become positive and creative, then change will be permanent. The entire process

233

of yoga is based on the gradual transformation of the body and the mind.

Holistic approach of yoga

Many scientists and eminent professionals in the field have investigated the physical aspects of yoga, in India as well as in many countries around the world. We have found that yoga can help many chronic physical conditions. We have seen that a suitable combination of yogic techniques can help manage cancer, diabetes and asthma. We have seen that yogic techniques can help manage hypertension, cardiovascular problems, digestive problems and muscular problems, so much so that slowly yoga is being accepted as a therapy in many parts of the world. We have also seen that yoga provides us with a way to manage mental and emotional problems and conflicts.

However, yoga is a broad subject and it does not limit itself to physical health or mental well-being; rather it provides us with a deeper vision of our participation and interaction in life as human beings. Most of the ancient yogic texts have spoken about disciplining and harmonizing the body, mind and lifestyle. They have spoken about developing awareness of one's interactions and participation in life. They have made an effort to bring about a union between the faculties of head, heart and hands. This is important in order to be responsible members of human society.

If we can use the faculties of our head, heart and hands properly, and if we can use the faculties of our intellect, sentiments and actions creatively and positively, then life begins to open up and one develops what is known as inner vision. This has been defined in the traditional yogic texts. Patanjali's *Yoga Sutras* say that there are eight stages of yoga. The first two stages relate to social and physical relationships, behaviour and attitudes; the third and fourth stages deal with the maintenance of health in the physical body; the fifth and sixth stages deal with the well-being of the mind; and the seventh and eighth stages of yoga deal with the realization of our spiritual roots.

Harmonizing the physical energy

Let us start with the body. The third and fourth stages of yoga are known as asana and pranayama and are related to the physical body. Asanas are the physical postures and pranayamas are the breathing techniques of yoga. We have seen many demonstrations and practices of the physical aspects of yoga. In some parts of the world they are as common as aerobic exercises. What is the aim of the physical practices that we perform in yoga? To harmonize the flow of energies in the body.

In our body there is a vital force flowing, which is known as prana. The same prana has been recognized and given different names in different traditions. In the Taoist tradition this force is known as chi energy. In the yogic tradition it is known as pranic energy and in English it is known as the vital force or energy. Many attempts have been made to ensure that this energy flows without any blockages and, in the course of history, many methods have been devised to stimulate the flow of this vital energy in the body. One such system is acupuncture, which tries to direct and clear the blockages in the energy meridians. But I am not talking here specifically about these pranic energies, rather in the body there are many currents and flows of pranic force that create disease when they are not flowing harmoniously.

Every human being has a weak side to their body. In situations of conflict, stress or tension that weak aspect will suffer the most. We will feel a weakness in different organs or parts of the body. We will feel that our body has a constitutional weakness. In some people the respiratory system may be weak and in a stressful environment they will be more prone to respiratory problems. In others the digestive system is weak and they are prone to digestive disorders in stressful conditions. In some the cardiovascular system is weak and they are prone to cardiovascular problems in stressful situations. It goes on and on like this. In each individual a different part of the body will be weak.

Vitality, comfort and stability

However, it is possible to strengthen the body by stimulating the flow of this vital force. In order to strengthen and stimulate this flow, certain postures are performed. When the postures are performed, the movements influence the internal organs such as the endocrinal gland system and the hormonal system, and everything is altered.

The first effect that we experience with the performance of physical postures is an increase in vitality. This is the experience of doctors and scientists who have conducted research into yoga. Many of you will have heard of the concept of mind over matter, but yoga has another concept. It speaks of energy over mind and matter, because it is energy that controls the mind and the body. Once we are able to increase the vital force with the practice of postures, all the defects of the body are rectified and we experience physical health and well-being.

According to Patanjali, the definition of asana or posture is a physical condition that provides stability and comfort to the body. Stability here represents a body which is at total ease with itself. Tensions are released, there is no tightness in the muscles and the body is in tune with itself. Comfort means harmony between mind and body. If you are mentally agitated, then physically you cannot sit quietly. You will shift or change your position and be in a state of nervous tension. Similarly, if your mind is at peace but your body is under stress, you will feel discomfort. So, comfort represents the state of harmony between body and mind, and stability represents the state of harmony between the different systems of the body. By achieving comfort and stability, you experience physical health.

The fourth aspect, which is also physical, is known as pranayama, the breathing techniques. Pranayama begins as a system of regulating the breathing process, but ends with the awakening of the vital force within the body. According to the system of Patanjali, asana and pranayama are the physical practices of yoga.

Pratyahara and dharana

With the fifth and sixth steps of yoga, pratyahara and dharana, we deal with our mental nature and we learn mind management. How can we focus our attention and develop concentration? One of the greatest lessons of the mental practices of yoga is to be yourself. We are either overconfident or underconfident. When we are at one extreme, there is a lack of concentration due to happiness, joy and dissipation of the mental attention. When we are at the other extreme, there is withdrawal and we hold back our creativity, attention and focus because we are unsure and uncertain of ourselves.

These states are also recognized as high anxiety and depression. We move through these extremes in our interactions, and we put on a different image, nature and personality in order to project ourselves as a different being. We are never who we truly are. We hide behind an image or a mask and we never recognize our true nature. Our mind hides behind its own creations. We can never open up because we are afraid and fearful of what others are going to say. We lack self-confidence and willpower. We are easily influenced by attractions and deceptions, or by positivity and negativity, and we lack the ability to make our own decisions because we have not come to terms with our mind.

Pratyahara and dharana teach us methods of relaxation and concentration, so that we can relax the tensions that are built-up in our continuous projection of a different image. We can learn how to focus the dissipation of our mind and become centred in the harmony that exists within. The mind is like a light. When the light is on there is illumination, but if, by some process, we are able to concentrate all the light at one point, it becomes a laser beam. A laser beam is focused light. It is a very powerful beam of light that can cut through steel and perform minute, sensitive operations without damaging other parts of the body.

Relaxation and concentration

Our mind is like the light, but right now the energies of the mind are being dissipated in all directions. When we learn how to relax and how to focus, then we can concentrate the forces of the mind. A focused state of mind is known as willpower, and willpower is a quality of mind. Willpower means a force which can transform the personality. Willpower is a sensitive state of mind, not a rude, arrogant state.

We undertake training in relaxation to experience pratyahara and dharana. Relaxation is an art; it is not a state where you lose body consciousness. It is an art of releasing tensions and stresses at different levels of the personality. You learn how to focus and how to concentrate. Concentration, the process of focusing, is also an art. You do not have to isolate yourself in order to focus or concentrate. You do not have to block your eyes and ears in order to concentrate. You have to gradually bring together the dissipated and fluctuating states of the mind by knowing how emotions can transform the individual nature. It is the understanding and realization of these different areas of human nature that leads to concentration.

Concentration is the product of a sensitive mental awareness and a developed mind. It is not forcing oneself to become one-pointed. It is a very simple yet joyous process of personal discovery. Through it we gain the ability and the understanding to realize our personality. When this happens the negative nature is transformed into a positive one. The negative nature represents our insecurity, our fears, aggression, anxieties and inhibitions. However, when we go through the process of discovering the mind, the negativity changes into positivity. Love, compassion and creativity manifest and the mind becomes sensitive to an understanding of our needs, ambitions, strengths and weaknesses. Behaviour, attitudes and perceptions change naturally and spontaneously.

Realizing our spiritual roots
The creative expressions of human nature are recognized as the yamas and niyamas, which in the yogic tradition are described as the first and second stages of yoga. The ability to express oneself truthfully, the absence of aggression, the

238

sense of righteousness and virtuous living are the components of human nature that manifest when the mind is in harmony. One then moves automatically into a meditative state. That state is known as dhyana, which later moves into the experience of samadhi. Samadhi means developing the whole picture of existence and living in harmony with nature and with oneself. In this context, samadhi also means realization and freeing oneself from self-imposed isolation, restrictions and limitations. This is what we mentioned before as coming into new life. Meditation leads to the experience of being holistic and complete.

The movement of yoga is from a limited life to an unlimited experience in life; from a limited expression to a creative expression. Later, when you live in harmony and in tune with yourself, your nature and the environment around you, then you perceive the radiance of the divine nature in every aspect of creation. It is the appreciation of the beauty around you, the expression of your compassionate sentiments towards the people around you and the harmonious interaction between yourself and other people that is the aim of yoga.

Remember that a journey of a thousand miles always begins with the first step. It is the first step which is important and which represents your new beginning. Therefore, you can begin yoga at any stage, whenever you feel ready and whenever you feel inspired. It is a transformative process in you which will make yoga come alive in your life. Yoga is a science of life. It is a physical science which can help us attain health. It is a mental science and a way of thought which can provide us with an understanding of our human nature and personality. It is also a spiritual experience because it gives us a holistic picture of ourselves. Therefore, my request to all of you is to give yoga a chance in your lives.

Jnana Yoga, Bhakti Yoga and Karma Yoga

Of all the yogas, bhakti yoga, jnana yoga and karma yoga are more mental than physical. We know of hatha yoga as a series of physical practices. We know that raja yoga involves a series of practices to understand one's personality. We know of kriya yoga as a series of techniques that can awaken the dormant potential in each person and we know that kundalini yoga is a group of practices that can awaken the primal energy. But it is difficult to develop a concept of jnana yoga, bhakti yoga or karma yoga because they are non-physical and do not involve a group of practices like asana and pranayama.

However, these three yogas deal more deeply with the awakening of the human personality. As human beings we need to integrate and utilize properly the qualities of head, heart and hands. These three yogas deal with our head, our heart and our hands. The head represents the human intellect, the faculty of knowing, observing, analyzing and thinking. The heart represents human sentiments and feelings. The hands represent the ability to perform an action and to interact with the environment and with life.

There are two dimensions of yoga: one is physical and the other is mental. In the physical aspect of yoga, there are physical practices: postures, breathing techniques and cleansing techniques, including certain forms of meditation.

In the mental or non-physical aspect of yoga, there are techniques of awareness which give us a deeper insight into our personality, our nature and our behaviour.

The human intellect has a nature, a recognizable pattern. We think in a certain way, we believe in a certain way and we observe and analyze in a set way. Our intellect is subject to the conditioning of society, culture, religion and lifestyle. Society decides how our head is going to act; our culture decides how our intellect is going to function; and our religious beliefs decide what we are going to accept as true intellectually. All these represent impressions in the mind at the level of intellect. They are also known as conditioning. We are conditioned by society, by our lifestyle, by our culture and by our environment. Our intellect is a process of expressing this conditioning.

Jnana yoga

Jnana literally means 'knowledge', and knowledge is two-dimensional. One dimension is intellectual knowledge. Our understanding is derived from books. That knowledge and understanding helps us to excel in our material, social life and behaviour. The process of cramming our heads with information is one dimension of knowledge, it is intellectual knowledge. The other form of knowledge is experiential, it is applied understanding. You apply what you know and you understand through experience what you have understood and realized. These are the two dimensions of knowledge: one is filling the head with information but never applying it, and the other is the application of knowledge and understanding.

Why is jnana yoga a part of the yogic structure? Why is jnana or knowledge important in the yogic system? Many teachers have said that it is important to know oneself. Socrates said, "Know thyself." "Who am I?" is a very ambiguous concept. People have tried to analyze it from a religious viewpoint, a spiritual viewpoint and a personal viewpoint. Despite all the thought that has gone into the question, an answer has never been found because there has

241

never been an experience of 'who I am'. Philosophically some people may say, "I am consciousness, I am the soul, I am the body and I am the mind," but it is not an experiential process and we become caught in the mental web of intellectualization.

Once I met a person who said that he was a follower of the teachings of Ramana Maharshi. In the course of our discussion I asked him what he practised. He said, "I practise self-inquiry." I asked him, "Do you know what self-inquiry is?" He replied, "Yes, of course I know what self-inquiry is! It is asking oneself the question 'Who am I?' and trying to know who I am." So I asked him, "How do you practise this self-inquiry or jnana yoga?" He replied, "Every morning when I have my breakfast I ask myself the question 'Who am I?' and allow answers to come into my head. That is how I practise jnana yoga."

The majority of people who do not know yoga practise jnana yoga in this manner. However, there is a process of knowing the intricacies of our intellect. That intellect which is at present manifesting in our life is being conditioned by the different things around us. We have to become aware of those influences which have shaped our intellect, which have made us what we are today, which make us think, analyze and rationalize things in a certain way and which have given us a sense of what is right and wrong, positive and negative, just and unjust. So, jnana yoga is not a process of inquiry into the subtle nature of an individual, but a process of gradually discovering the nature of our personality, which is guided by our intellect.

Review of the day

What are the practices of jnana yoga? There is a very simple practice that you can do when you go to bed at night, while you are getting ready to sleep. Instead of thinking about many different things, just think of one thing: what you did during the whole day from the time you woke up till the time you went to bed. It is a process of reflecting on your activities during the day. Say to yourself, "In the morning I

242

woke up at such and such a time and then I went to the bathroom, washed and dressed myself. When I woke up I had a horrible hangover, I had a headache and my eyes were swollen. The first person I saw was such and such; then I had my breakfast; this is what we spoke about; and this is what I had for breakfast." See yourself as if someone else is looking at you and observing you from morning till night.

Live every moment of the day and try to picture the whole day like a movie. See who you spoke to, where you went, how you went there, what your mood was, what your thoughts were, how you interacted with people, what your feelings were and what your understanding was of the different interactions that you had during the day. In this way, relive the whole day from morning till night.

After you have seen the whole day unfold before you, then try to know if there was some mistake in your action, behaviour or attitude. What was the fault? Whose fault was it – yours or the other person's? We always tend to react to different situations and we don't have to feel guilty about it, we just need to know our reactions. If you were angry, it doesn't matter; if you were depressed, it doesn't matter; if you were happy, it doesn't matter. Recognize whatever state you were in, and after that have just one thought: "If I face a similar situation again, how will I react?" Make a positive resolution: "If I face a similar situation, I will be more balanced." Then go to sleep.

When you wake up the next day, go through the routine again. At night, before you go to sleep again relive the entire day, moment to moment. Observe your actions; analyze your actions, your speech, your attitude and your behaviour. Think again, "If I encounter the same situation, how can I react in a more controlled, balanced and harmonious way?" Then go to sleep. On the third day again live your life normally and at night do the same practice. Within a month you will find that your responses to the situations and conditions around you will change drastically.

This is just one practice of jnana yoga, the process of knowing how you interact with your environment. It will

243

give you a deeper understanding of yourself and allow the harmony of the intellect to arise. This will allow you to be broad-minded, to understand your thoughts and feelings in a positive way and to accept yourself in a positive way. Jnana yoga begins from here. It does not begin by thinking, "I am a spirit" or "I am an extension of God." Jnana yoga is learning to recognize and accept the realities of life, it is learning to recognize our responses to the realities of life, it is learning to apply the understanding and knowledge practically in life.

Bhakti yoga

The second area is the heart, which includes the sentiments, feelings and emotions. The yoga for harmony of feelings, emotions and sentiments is known as bhakti yoga. Right now we continuously express our feelings. Our feelings are also two-dimensional. At one level we become attracted to something because of a feeling, or we reject something because of a feeling.

One example is when you look at a flower. There is an impression of beauty and you are attracted to that feeling of beauty. That is known as attraction. Another example is money. If somebody places a box full of money in front of you, you look at it and want to possess it. There is also a feeling for the money, which is recognized as greed.

A feeling exists between lovers. When you look at somebody you like the feeling generated is known as passion. When you look at a baby the feeling generated is known as affection. When you look at a person you consider to be your competitor, the feeling associated with that person is jealousy. You will have a feeling of respect for a person who is above you, a figure or an image of what you want to be. For a person whom you consider to be your enemy, the feeling generated is animosity. With a flower you see the beauty and the feeling generated is an appreciation of that beauty. Or you smell something rotting, such as meat which has been in a refrigerator without electricity for a month, and the feeling generated is aversion.

244

In this way, all feelings can be classified either as attraction or repulsion. Normally when we are attracted towards something, it is for seeking fulfilment and pleasure, and if we find that something does not provide us with fulfilment and pleasure, it is put aside. During our entire life we simply try to find satisfaction and pleasure in the different things that we do. Bhakti yoga is the channelling of that feeling to experience harmony inside. People say that bhakti yoga means the yoga of devotion but in reality it is not the yoga of devotion. Real bhakti yoga is harmony of feelings and recognition of the feelings that are generated in life.

Mantra

How do we practise bhakti yoga? How do we direct the feelings which can help us evolve? How can we direct our emotions inwards? How can we find a state of balance between attractions and repulsions? That method is explained in bhakti yoga. In fact there are nine forms of bhakti yoga and nine techniques in bhakti yoga.

One technique is mantra. Mantra is a sound vibration. Before the beginning of satsang we chanted shanti path, which is a collection of mantras. Mantras are universal and mantras are personal sound vibrations which can alter the frequency of the brain and take one to a state of deep concentration, relaxation and harmony. Mantras are not religious chants. In different traditions there are different mantras. In different traditions some mantras are associated with religion and some mantras are related to the process of going deep inside the dimension of feelings. In yoga, the concept of mantra is a process by which we can alter the nature of feelings and emotions; a process by which we can harmonize the attractions and repulsions which are everyday events in our life.

The word *mantra* literally means a force which can liberate the mind from being confined to the material dimension; a force which can free the sentiments and feelings from the search for pleasure and enjoyment; a force which can make you come in tune and in harmony with your inner sentiment.

There is a whole subject of mantra which is also known as mantra yoga. The repetition or chanting of mantra creates a specific frequency and rhythm in your personality. If you are a musician, you can try an experiment. Put some very fine sand on a piece of paper. Place it on top of a guitar. Just play one guitar string and you will see the sand form a shape. That is a physical manifestation of the vibrations altering a physical object. Another example is an army that is marching in step. They create a very powerful vibration and if they have to cross a bridge, they will have to break step. If not, the bridge can collapse because of the vibration.

Scientists today tell us that every sound has a pitch, a frequency and a wave, and these affect our emotions. Music is a good example. If you go into a room where heavy metal is being played, you will know what I mean. Or you can go into a room where gentle, soothing classical music is playing and you will know what I mean. Music can affect harmony. There are sound vibrations which can stimulate a particular hormone to flow. Music can make the adrenalin or melatonin flow in abundance. There is some music which you listen to and simply drift off into a deep relaxed sleep; and there are some music vibrations which can wake up even the sleepiest person.

This is the background to mantra. Mantras are sound vibrations which affect and alter our internal personality. These mantras are also related to the psychic centres in the body. When we repeat or chant a mantra, verbally or mentally, we create a corresponding change in our feelings, in our brain at the level of brain waves, in our nervous system and also at the level of our subtle psychic centres. It allows us to be more in control of the feelings that are emanating from the individual to the outside.

So, bhakti yoga is the balancing of manifesting emotions, and one of the practices of bhakti yoga is mantra. Mantra takes a meditative form. It makes you go deeper into your being; it makes you observe how you are responding at the level of emotions. Once you are able to harmonize the feelings and emotions, when they are in balance, then you

246

have the experience of peace and tranquillity, which brings you closer to the source of inner strength. It develops a balanced awareness of yourself, and that is known as bhakti yoga.

Karma yoga

The third yoga is karma yoga. Karma means 'action'. We are all performing actions. Our senses, our brain, our bodily organs and our mind are all performing actions and our environment is in a state of action. Our whole life is a process of action. Why has the word 'yoga' been added to the process of action? It indicates harmony in action. Harmony in action is known as karma yoga.

When we are performing action there is always some form of expectation associated with it, and when it is fulfilled, that expectation gives birth to another expectation and another action. When that expectation is not fulfilled, it gives birth to another expectation and action. Expectations and actions are integrated parts of the same thing; it is very difficult to separate an action from an expectation. Why do you work, for example? Because at the end of the month you expect a pay cheque. You expect the result of your action in the form of a cheque. Why do you practise yoga, for example? Because there is an expectation that something good and wonderful will happen. You become involved with different things always because of an expectation.

Life without expectation is something that most people cannot understand. Yoga has a philosophy which says that if you can perform an action without any expectation, and with utmost perfection, then you are a yogi. This definition of yoga is the most important one for us in this life. Meditation is not yoga, meditation is isolation. Meditation is not the aim of yoga because in meditation you isolate yourself from the environment. But, if you recognize the role of action without expectation, and if it is done with perfection, then it leads to a more creative participation in life.

Karma yoga is also associated with an awareness of action. You should be aware of your action and the corresponding expectation; you should be able to understand that you may or may not attain the goal, and you should be able to detach yourself from the expectation. It does not mean that you reject an expectation. We are not talking about rejecting anything; we are talking about recognizing the expectation and being detached from that involvement in expectation. Then you will find your creativity becoming more dynamic. Maybe you will be known as a genius. Expectations do not allow our genius nature to manifest. When you are giving your best shot, without holding yourself back, then that is karma yoga.

Karma yoga is recognition of action and the corresponding expectation, being detached from the influence and attraction of expectation, allowing the creativity to manifest in the performance of an action, and offering that as service to humanity and to divinity. You will be surprised to know that you gain more by not having any expectations. This is known as karma yoga.

Integration of head, heart and hands

Jnana, bhakti and karma yoga are the three non-physical yogas. They do not involve the practice of postures or breathing techniques, and they do not involve meditative concentration. They are based on the principle of awareness and management of the human faculties, trying to improve these faculties and making them more creative. It is the integration of the faculties of head, heart and hands, and it becomes part of the transformative process that we experience in our lives. They are the most important yogas. It is not necessary to practise hatha yoga and raja yoga in order to become a better human being, but it is necessary to practise these three yogas to become a creative human being. The other yogas simply help the process of these three yogas. Postures keep the body fit and healthy, breathing techniques vitalize the personality, and the cleansing techniques detoxify the body and personality. They are aids to the perfection of the three yogas.

Is yoga a process or a part of coming out of samskara?

Yoga philosophy is based on overcoming the limitations and suffering of life. In one aspect, when you overcome the limitations you become more creative, and this creativity leads to greater understanding of the influences of samskaras. The other aspect is overcoming suffering by knowing its cause, knowing how you respond to suffering and overcoming the suffering so that you become free. That is known as the final liberation, moksha, nirvana.

Is prayer different from bhakti yoga?

No, prayer is one aspect of bhakti yoga. There are nine stages of bhakti yoga. Bhakti begins with mantra and harmonization of the feelings and emotions. Then it slowly evolves into a recognition of our connection with a higher nature. In yoga we don't have a concept of God; we only have a concept of Ishwara, which means the unchanging reality.

If someone receives languages inside that she is not able to understand, what does it mean? Some kind of hieroglyphs, mudras or asanas manifest which she has never learned before.

Has she done yoga before? Meditation or any other techniques?

Yes. She attended a sahaji yoga seminar and then she was rejected because it started to happen.

She has a sensitive personality and whatever she practised with the hope of awakening the kundalini might have aggravated the process, which is the reason she is having these experiences. Sahaji yoga is a process that aims to awaken the kundalini very fast. We don't subscribe to that philosophy because kundalini is not something that can be experimented with by everybody at this stage in life. Before you can enter university, you have to go through a proper system of education. Similarly, before you attempt the higher practices of yoga, you have to undergo proper preparation and purification, otherwise such things can happen. My recommendation would be to actually make a note of the experiences and to start practising yoga nidra and a series of techniques known as pawanmuktasana to realign the forces and energies in the body and mind. Go step by step, rather than taking a big jump. Then, in the course of time, you will understand what you have received as symbols, which have come up from consciousness, and you will be able to know what they represent in terms of your spiritual progress.

How can one treat juvenile type diabetes with yoga, for young persons of thirteen or fourteen years who are on insulin therapy already?

The diet has to be managed. Carbohydrates should be avoided. More fibre and greens should be eaten. Laghoo shankhaprakshalana, the practise of cleansing the entire digestive tract, should be done for forty days continuously. During that period there should be no meat intake and the diet should be vegetarian as far as possible. The practice of surya namaskara and two other asanas, ardha matsyendrasana and gomukhasana, should be undertaken.

How can one practise karma yoga? What are the techniques?

First detach the expectations from the actions by recognizing that this is the expectation from this action, and by accepting the fact that if you attain it, that is fine, and if you don't attain it, that is also fine. Involve yourself in more social work, doing work for others without any expectations. There are two kinds of work: what you do for yourself and what you do for others. If you can do fifty-fifty, you will be well on the path of karma yoga.

Can you tell me briefly about the sound vibration of Om?

The physical, mental and spiritual aspects involved in the chanting of Om are all important. Physically, the chanting of Om balances the activities of the sympathetic and para-sympathetic nervous systems. It induces a deeper alpha state and reduces the beta activity, and if you continue for a longer period, you can go into delta and theta states. As you move from alpha to deeper states, you have more concentration, more physical and mental relaxation, and you come in tune with your vibratory field, which then realigns the energies of the body. Once the energies within the human personality are realigned with the chanting of Om, then you experience peace, tranquillity, joy and harmony. So, the physical, mental and spiritual experiences are all interrelated.

How much is karma affecting our present life? How much is karma from previous lives affecting us?

That would be a lecture! Karma is a sequence of cause and effect. There are natural karmas of the body and mind, and there are imposed karmas on the body and mind. Natural karmas are not carried over. Imposed karmas, which are motivated and to which there is an emotional attachment, are the ones that carry over. If you can become aware of the karmas now, if you can become positive, balanced and creative now, if you can bring awareness into the action now and if you can become aware of the influence of the karmas on you now, then you will reduce the intensity of their grip on your nature. Karmas are powerful when we are not aware of them. But when we are aware of them and we have the ability to guide our actions and are not swayed or influenced by cause and effect, then the force of the karmas is greatly reduced and can be exhausted in one lifetime. It is possible to do that through meditative reflection.

Interviews

INTERVIEW WITH AURA MAGAZINE

Yoga, especially hatha and bhakti yoga, is very popular today in the West. In spite of this some people feel that it would be better for westerners to lean on the European spiritual tradition for their spiritual evolution and not on an eastern one, as it is not compatible with the western lifestyle. Do you think that yoga is useful for everyone, no matter what their culture and history?

Yoga is an ancient system of balancing. It is a twofold process of balancing the forces within the individual and balancing the forces between the individual and his natural and social environment. As such, yoga is suitable for everyone. There is no need to be born in the East in order to live according to yogic principles and to use yoga as an aid in everyday life and self-realization. Yoga can help you to cope with daily tension and stress. It offers the way to physical health and a lot more. Research carried out by western scientists has also confirmed that yoga can be useful for everyone.

But westerners probably face difficulties when trying to follow some of the yogic principles. For example, some laws are contrary to the yamas and niyamas. How can a practitioner solve this dilemma?

The yamas and niyamas are only two aspects of yoga. Although many claim that the yamas and niyamas should be practised before other branches of yoga, the Bihar School of Yoga, disagrees with this statement. Our school suggests that we should begin with those branches of yoga which will help us to control our physical body and our mind more easily. People today need this far more. Only later, when we have mastered them, do we devote ourselves to other aspects of yoga. So, the beginner starts with asana, the mastering of certain physical postures, and pranayama, the mastering of breathing techniques. At the same time the beginner learns meditation and relaxation techniques. Gradually he also deepens his study and experiences in pratyahara and dharana. The last two branches, dhyana and samadhi, and the first two principles, yama and niyama, are only for those who truly wish to live a yogic lifestyle.

Although there are yoga courses in Slovenia where students can learn asana and pranayama techniques under the guidance of a teacher, many students still study by themselves, from books. Their only support are texts and illustrations. How can we check if we are performing certain asanas and pranayamas correctly, or if we have mastered a technique sufficiently to proceed to a more difficult one?

When we practise an asana, we should take care of two physical aspects of the body – comfort and stability. We stop the asana at the moment when comfort changes to discomfort or when stability and calmness change to movement. We go only according to the limits of our body's capacity. Gradually, with regular practice, we will be able to hold a certain posture for a longer period of time. It is unwise to hurry because this will not give us any benefit. On the contrary, we should not force our body into a certain position for longer than is comfortable. It is the same with pranayama. Lung capacity and flexibility of the muscles used in breathing should be developed gradually. During pranayama, it should never happen that we are left without air. Again we have to pay attention to what is happening in our body, how it reacts to certain breathing techniques, so as to estimate its momentary limits.

The purpose of all physical yogic techniques is to create balance and harmony in the body. For beginners it would probably be most appropriate to spend at least one week on each individual asana and breathing technique before going on with the next. Notwithstanding all this advice, I would recommend to the readers of this magazine not to learn yoga only from books, but to find a teacher who can give them expert guidance and assistance.

Is it possible to prove that someone has attained the state of dhyana or samadhi?

No. In my thirty years experience in yoga I might have met three or four people who have reached dhyana. Dhyana is a commonly used word, but this causes more misunderstandings than solutions. We do not practise dhyana, we practise pratyahara. Dhyana is a state which appears as a natural consequence of the perfection of pratyahara and dharana. Dhyana and samadhi are states which are the consequences of certain changes in the meditator. They are not something that you can learn, but something that comes by itself.

You said that you have met some people who had attained the state of dhyana. How do you know that they had?

By observation of the functioning of their mind and their life in general.

Since the lifestyle in the West demands a great deal of concentration of mind, is it easier for westerners to practise concentration?

Concentration does not depend on the ability to direct and focus the mind. Concentration is a natural result of a relaxed and conscious mind. It does not include the mind's effort to focus on only one object.

Would you say that a person who wants to practise yoga correctly and completely has to clean his karma first?

No. Understanding and experiences become deeper with the growth of the practitioner. There are a few million

254

people in the world who practise yoga. Does this mean that their karmas are cleansed? No. If we have a motivation and a purpose to attain spiritual awareness and inner balance, certain yogic practices can contribute to our coping more easily with karmic challenges.

Is it enough for westerners to take care of the body with a balanced vegetarian diet and normal hygiene? Are kriyas therefore not necessary?

Many people project the idea of what healthy food is on to yoga. Nowhere in the yogic tradition can you find an instruction that says we have to be vegetarians if we wish to practise yoga. In the past yogis were mostly vegetarians, but that was not an order. Yoga teaches that our food should be healthy, should give enough strength and vitality to the body and should be easily digestible. Yoga also teaches that we absorb more vitality, strength, shakti, if we eat fruit and vegetables. By eating meat we also consume many hormones and chemicals that create a different state of energy in the body. It is up to each individual to decide what he/she should eat. Yoga does not command that we should eat only vegetarian food. Yoga is never conditioned by vegetarian principles.

Kriyas are recommended but not necessary. Neti kriya, for example, helps to cleanse blocked sinus cavities, but the decision to do it would be made by a person who found that it was useful or necessary for them. Some of the body cleansing techniques may seem rather strange and even painful to some westerners, but yoga only follows the natural processes of cleansing the body. Therefore, this means that kriyas, if performed correctly, cannot injure you or cause any damage.

Can the use of bandhas and mudras be dangerous if undertaken without a teacher's advice and guidance?

It is dangerous to sit behind the wheel of a car if you haven't learnt to drive. It is dangerous to walk if you haven't learnt how and where to walk. It is dangerous to eat food if you don't really know what you are eating. There is danger in everything we have not been taught. If we are careful in other things, why shouldn't we be careful when practising yoga? Some yogic practices require study. They require a qualified teacher who can guide the student.

Is there anything you would like to tell the readers of Aura?

People who read *Aura* probably have a different view of the world, one that encourages them to search for answers. If there was no motivation to look for answers, they probably would not read *Aura*. I would recommend that they recognize yoga as a science, a philosophy and a lifestyle that is not contrary to their everyday lifestyle. Yoga can enrich and refine them.

INTERVIEW WITH JANA MAGAZINE

You have dedicated your whole life to yoga and you inspire students all over the world. What does yoga mean to you?

Some people see yoga as a spiritual science. Others believe that it helps to improve health and manage disease. A third group believes that yoga directs human life. All these different definitions are correct, but the most correct is that yoga is a science of how to live in harmony with nature and with oneself. Just as a tree consists of not only a trunk, branches, leaves and fruit, which can be seen above the ground, but also of roots, which are underground, in the same way we cannot see our life as a physical phenomenon and mind only. There is a deeper aspect of our being, known as spirit. The union of body, mind and spirit is the evolution of a holistic dimension of life, known as yoga.

That is why yoga has been an increasingly recognized method of treatment in the West.

It has been discovered that yoga can help with many problems for which there are no other therapies. In modern medicine yoga is used in the management of cancer, cardiovascular illnesses, respiratory diseases, digestive problems, etc. But yoga is not only limited to physical health and well-being. It tries to help us to gradually transform our body and mind.

What happens in the body during the practices?

There is an energy flowing in our body called prana. In the Taoist tradition this energy is known as chi, in English it is known as vital energy. These energies are stimulated by yoga. But every human body has a weak point which manifests in situations of conflict and stress. We feel this as a disease. We feel that our body is weak. Some people have breathing problems or digestive problems in stressful situations. We can strengthen our body by encouraging the flow of our vital energy through yoga practices. By doing asanas we raise our vital energy. By enhancing it, we eliminate all the deficiencies in the body. A person feels physically well. There is no tension in the body any more and the body is in harmony with itself.

What is the percentage of men and women practising yoga in the world today?

Sixty percent women and forty percent men.

What is the role of women in today's society? What makes a woman different from a man?

Women give children sensibility, openness, feelings. These are the qualities that our society lacks most. Women can do a lot to promote these qualities in society.

Men still prevail in all fields . . .

This is a sociological question and society should find an escape from it. From the point of view of the spiritual traditions, women have an inherent sensibility and act more from their feelings. This is why they are more understanding and capable of leading the human race in the future.

What is the symbolic meaning of the orange coloured clothing which the sannyasins of Bihar School of Yoga are wearing?

It is the colour of the rising sun.

INTERVIEW WITH HORUS MAGAZINE

Yoga is a science similar to medicine. There is a general yoga that can be practised by anyone, which can be compared to a general medical practice. Then there is a specialized yoga, dealing with therapy and healing. It includes different techniques of which amaroli is one. We also have a special yoga for developing the dormant potential of the mind, then kriya yoga, kundalini yoga, mantra yoga and laya yoga. There is also a special yoga for spiritual development. All these techniques have been tested for thousands of years and offer certain solutions to certain questions, based on the experiences of many generations of thinkers.

Yoga is therefore a complete system. Do you believe that because of its numerous advantages it is better than other techniques of spiritual evolution such as Reiki and Tai Chi and other holistic methods?

Reiki is not spiritual, it is pranic. Tai Chi is not spiritual, it means the coordination of energy flows in the body.

What is the relationship between tantra and yoga?

Yoga is a son of tantra, tantra is a father to yoga. Tantra is knowledge of consciousness and energy. There is a combination of actions, techniques and lifestyle which encourages the evolution of man's consciousness and the freeing of his energy. Tantra, as it is understood in the West today, is not the original tantra. Tantra today is understood as sexual activity. This is not tantra. It is very clear that these are the feelings of people who want to hide their guilt under the cover of spiritual practice. Tantra is a practice, a system, that does not exist in either western culture or eastern culture. Very few people in India know what real tantra is and in the West maybe one or two persons know.

Yoga is a branch of tantra and, therefore, it represents a holistic approach towards life. This holistic approach includes body, mind and spirit. These three dimensions together on a personal level deal with society, lifestyle, environment and social status. What in the West is understood as a spiritual science is a concept that should be refined and re-evaluated. What is a spiritual science? If you think that belief in God is spiritual, I would say no. If you think that one has to become a member of a spiritual organization to evolve, I would disagree. I represent two traditions. One is the monastic tradition of sannyasa and the other is the tradition of yoga and tantra. Yoga and tantra are based on a recognition of life's conditions, the acceptance of these conditions and their modification if needed.

Anyone has the potential to recognize their strengths, weaknesses, needs and ambitions. We all function because of our strengths. These strengths are either physical, mental or spiritual. We all have our weaknesses, which can be physical, mental or spiritual. We have our needs, which are physical, social, cultural, religious and spiritual. We have our ambitions, which may be personal, in relation to the family, society, name, glory and status. These things are the foundation stones of life for each one of us.

In English this is called the SWAN principle – Strength, Weakness, Ambition, Need. If we do not take care of our strengths, weaknesses, ambitions and needs, then moral, spiritual, mental and emotional deviation and physical imbalances and illnesses appear. Recognition and control of these four principles allows the evolution of consciousness and the awakening of energy. This is called tantra and yoga.

Do you believe that with the coming of the new age of Aquarius, people in the world are coming closer to the knowledge and practice of yoga, not only in the East, but also more and more in the West? Does it appear to you that interest in yoga has greatly increased?

259

The era of Aquarius plays a certain role, but primarily people's personal aspiration is the important part. Cosmic and individual compatibility have created conditions for the awakening, which has led to certain questions being asked such as how to find peace and happiness, and a looking into the different traditions and systems that represent the real inheritance of all humankind. Let us hope that this searching will result in the creation of a deeper understanding of relationships with the human race and the universe, beyond prejudice.

Glossary

Ahamkara – ego; awareness of the existence of 'I'

Ahara – third basic instinct; food; nourishment for the body-mind

Ahimsa – non-violence; abstaining from giving pain to others in thought, word or deed

Ajna chakra – psychic command centre situated in the midbrain; seat of intuition

Akasha – element of ether, space; the three internal spaces most often used in meditation are chidakasha, daharakasha and hridayakasha

Anahata chakra – psychic centre situated in the region of the heart and cardiac plexus; emotional centre

Anandamaya kosha – body of bliss

Annamaya kosha – material or food body

Antar darshan – inner vision

Antar mouna – inner silence; meditative technique of pratyahara, consisting of six stages

Anushasana – instruction; command; advice, laying down rules or precepts; subtle management

Aparigraha – abstention from greed, non-possessiveness

Artha – material need, prosperity

Asana – physical posture in which one is at ease and in harmony with oneself

Ashram – place of spiritual retreat and inner growth through internal and external labour

261

Ashrama – stage or period of life, of which there are four according to vedic tradition: brahmacharya, grihastha, vanaprastha and sannyasa

Asteya – honesty, not stealing

Atma – pure consciousness which pervades everything; undying; self; spirit; soul

Avidya – ignorance of true reality

Bandha – psychic lock that concentrates the flow of energy in the body at one point or plexus

Bhagavad Gita – literally 'Song of God'; discourse on yoga between Sri Krishna and Arjuna on the battlefield at the onset of the Mahabharata war

Bhakti – intense inner devotion or love; channelling of the intellect, emotions and self towards a higher purpose

Bhava – intense inner attitude or subtle emotion; state of being

Bindu – point of potential energy; psychic centre situated at the top back of the head

Brahmacharya – redirection of sexual energy towards spiritual and meditative experience; living in constant awareness of higher consciousness

Brahmacharya ashrama – first stage of life to twenty-five years of age, devoted to study and learning

Brahman – ever-expanding consciousness, absolute reality

Buddhi – higher intelligence, discrimination; intuitive aspect of consciousness

Chakra – literally, 'wheel or vortex'; major psychic centre in the subtle body responsible for specific physical and psychic functions

Chidakasha – vast space of individual consciousness where infinite psychic events can be visualized in front of the closed eyes during meditation; mental screen

Chitta – individual consciousness which includes the conscious, subconscious and unconscious dimensions of the mind; aspect of mind which receives impressions of experiences and stores them for future use in the form of samskaras

Chitta vritti – mental fluctuation, movement or modification

Daharakasha – lower or deep space, encompassing mooladhara, swadhisthana and manipura chakras

Darshan – a glimpse; sight, vision; knowing, understanding

Devi – luminous nature of spirit in its female aspect; goddess; divine mother

Dharana – concentration or complete attention; holding or binding the mind to one point

Dharma – natural role one has to play in life; duty; right conduct

Dhyana – spontaneous state of meditation which arises out of the perfection of dharana, constant total awareness

Drashta -- witness, uninvolved observer; the seer

Grihastha ashrama – second stage of life from twenty-five to fifty years; married householder life

Guna – attribute, quality or nature of the manifest world or prakriti viz. tamas, rajas and sattwa

Guru – 'dispeller of darkness'; spiritual master; realized person who by the light of his own soul, or atma, can dispel ignorance and delusion from the disciple's mind

Hari Om Tat Sat – an invocation of divine blessing

Hatha yoga – yoga of attaining physical and mental purity, and channelling of the pranas in the body

Hridayakasha – heart space, experienced between manipura and vishuddhi chakras

Ishwara – higher reality; supreme being or God; state of unchanging transcendental reality

Ishwara pranidhana – cultivation of faith in the higher reality

Japa – repetition of a mantra or a name of God

Jignasu sannyasa – aspirant; spiritual seeker; preliminary stage of sannyasa

Jivatma – individual soul or consciousness

Jnana – higher knowledge, cognition or wisdom

Jnana yoga – yoga of knowledge and wisdom attained through spontaneous self-analysis and investigation of abstract or speculative ideas

Jnanendriyas – five organs of sense perception and knowledge, viz., ears, eyes, nose, tongue and skin

263

Kailash – name of a mountain peak in the Himalayas; residence of Shiva

Kama – emotional need or fulfilment

Karma – action in the manifest and unmanifest dimension; law of cause and effect which shapes the destiny of each individual

Karma sannyasa – householder sannyasa; renunciation combined with duty; second stage of sannyasa initiation

Karma yoga – yoga of action; action performed with meditative awareness; yoga of dynamic meditation; yogic path of selfless service

Karmendriyas – five organs of action: hands, feet, vocal cords, tongue, excretory and reproductive organs

Kleshas – fivefold afflictions or sources of all suffering accompanying human birth

Kosha – sheath or body; dimension of experience or existence

Krishna – eighth incarnation of Lord Vishnu; guru of Arjuna in the Bhagavad Gita

Kundalini – spiritual energy; evolutionary force referred to as serpent power; latent energy in mooladhara chakra

Kundalini yoga – path of yoga which awakens the dormant spiritual force

Laya yoga – yoga of conscious dissolution of individuality

Mahabharata – epic of ancient India involving the great battle between the Kaurava and Pandava princes

Mahat – cosmic intelligence; higher individual consciousness; greater mind

Manipura chakra – literally, 'city of jewels'; psychic centre situated behind the navel, associated with vitality and energy

Manomaya kosha – mental sheath or body

Manas – rational aspect of mind which creates thought/counter thought; lower or empirical mind

Mandala – diagram within a circumference symbolizing the deeper aspects of the psyche

Mantra – subtle sound vibration which liberates energy from the limitations of mundane awareness and expands the consciousness

Maya – illusory nature of the manifest world; ignorance of reality

264

Moksha – liberation from the cycles of birth, death and rebirth

Mooladhara chakra – lowest psychic centre in human body from where kundalini shakti emerges; situated in the perineum in men and the cervix in women

Mudra – gesture or attitude utilized to express or channel pranic energy within the mind/body as an aid to concentration

Nada yoga – yoga of tracing subtle internal sound back to its source

Nadi – flow; pranic channel which conducts the flow of energy in the body; 72,000 in number

Nidra – deep sleep; isolation from mind and senses; unconscious state

Niyama – five observances or conduct and character; inner disciplines

Om – bija mantra of ajna chakra; the universal cosmic mantra representing the four states of consciousness

Patanjali – sage or rishi who codified the Yoga Sutras; propounder of the eightfold system of raja yoga

Poorna sannyasa – third stage of sannyasa initiation; complete renunciation

Prakriti – active principle of the manifest world and energy; individual nature

Prana – principle of energy that sets life in motion; vital air or energy force, sustaining life and creation

Pranamaya kosha – energy sheath or body

Pranayama – yogic practices involving control of inhalation, exhalation and retention of breath; technique for expanding the dimensions of prana or vital energy

Prana shakti – dynamic solar force governing the dimension of matter

Pratyahara – process of withdrawing the senses from external objects; an important prerequisite for dharana and higher stages of meditation

Pratyaya – seeds or impressions in the field of consciousness

Purusha – pure consciousness undefiled and unlimited by contact with prakriti or matter

Purushartha – personal effort; four goals to be fulfilled in life: artha, kama, dharma and moksha

Raga – liking; attachment; attraction

Raja yoga – eightfold path classified by Patanjali in the Yoga Sutras; yoga of awakening the psychic awareness and faculties through meditation

Rajas – one of the three gunas representing the dynamic, active state of mind and nature

Sadhana – spiritual practice done regularly for attainment of inner experience and self-realization

Sahasrara chakra – 'thousand-petalled lotus'; spiritual centre situated at crown of head; represents state of enlightenment; abode of Shiva; transcendental consciousness

Sakshi – eternal witness; seer; that which passively observes the actions of the body and the senses; drashta aspect

Samadhi – culmination of meditation; state of union of mind with the object of meditation; merging with divine consciousness; final step of raja yoga

Samkhya – one of the six systems of Indian philosophy; basis of the system of yoga

Samskara – mental impression stored in the subtle body as an archetype; unconscious memory or impression which sets up impulses and trains of thought and which governs our personality and performance

Sankalpa – spiritual resolve; positive affirmation; willpower; important tool used in the practice of yoga nidra

Sannyasa – dedication; renunciation of the world, possessions and attachments

Sannyasa ashrama – fourth stage of life from seventy-five years onwards; total renunciation

Santosha – contentment, satisfaction

Sanyam – harmonious control; balanced restraint; concentration, meditation and samadhi practised at one and the same time

Satsang – gathering of spiritually-minded people in which the ideals and principles of truth are discussed

Sattwa – one of the three gunas representing steadiness, purity,

266

harmony and light; harmonious expression of inner self experienced when tamas and rajas are balanced

Satya – absolute truth; reality

Shakti – vital energy; creative potential force; feminine aspect of creation and divinity

Shatkarmas – six purificatory techniques of hatha yoga

Shaucha – cleanliness, purity, internal and external

Shiva – destroyer of ego and duality; Lord of yogis, who is said to dwell on Mount Kailash; symbol of cosmic consciousness

Siddhi – psychic power associated with awakening of chakras

Sthira – stability

Swadhisthana chakra –psychic centre situated at the base of the spinal column, associated with the sacral plexus; storehouse of subconscious impressions

Swadhyaya – self-study, self-enquiry; continuous conscious awareness of what one is doing

Swami – literally 'master of the mind'

Tamas – one of the three gunas representing stability; responsible for inertia, laziness, procrastination, dullness, darkness and fear of change

Tantra – process of expansion of mind and liberation of energy and consciousness from matter; ancient universal science, philosophy and culture dealing with transcendence of gross human nature from the present level of evolution to the highest state of human attainment; one of the classical Indian philosophies

Tapas – austerity; effort involving purification and self-discipline; a process in which the inner dirt covering the inner personality is completely eliminated

Tattwa – essential element or principle, five in number: earth, water, fire, air and ether

Turiya – fourth dimension of consciousness transcending the waking, dreaming and deep sleep states, and linking these states; superconsciousness

Vairagya – dispassion; non-attachment; state in which one remains internally calm and balanced under all circumstances

Vanaprastha ashrama – third stage of life from fifty to seventy-five years of age; retirement from worldly life in order to practise sadhana in relative seclusion

Vedanta – one of the six systems of vedic philosophy, which deals with the transcendental and manifest nature of consciousness; philosophy of realization of Brahman

Vidya – inner knowledge

Vijnanamaya kosha – higher mental sheath or body

Vishuddhi chakra – psychic centre located at the level of the throat pit or the thyroid gland, connected with communication

Viveka – the power to discriminate correctly; right knowledge or understanding

Vritti – mental fluctuation, modification, wave or pattern

Yama – five self-restraints or rules of conduct pertaining to ethical perfection

Yantra – geometrical form of mantra used for concentration

Yoga – literally, 'union' or 'yoke'; systematic science of body/mind leading to union of individual consciousness with cosmic consciousness; process of uniting opposing forces in the body/mind to realize the spiritual essence; one of the six classical Indian philosophies

Yantra – geometric symbol designed for concentration in order to unleash the hidden potential within the consciousness

Yoga Sutras – classical yoga text codified by Sage Patanjali, which delineates the system of ashtanga yoga or eightfold path of raja yoga: yama, niyama, asana, pranayama, pratyahara, dharana, dhyana and samadhi

Index

271

SYNOPSIS OF THE LIFE OF
SWAMI SATYANANDA SARASWATI

Swami Satyananda Saraswati was born in 1923 at Almora (Uttaranchal) into a family of farmers. His ancestors were warriors and many of his kith and kin down the line, including his father, served in the army and police force.

However, it became evident that Sri Swamiji had a different bent of mind, as he began to have spiritual experiences at the age of six, when his awareness spontaneously left the body and he saw himself lying motionless on the floor. Many saints and sadhus blessed him and reassured his parents that he had a very developed awareness. This experience of disembodied awareness continued, which led him to many saints of that time such as Anandamayi Ma. Sri Swamiji also met a tantric bhairavi, Sukhman Giri, who gave him shaktipat and directed him to find a guru in order to stabilize his spiritual experiences.

In 1943, at the age of 20, he renounced his home and went in search of a guru. This search ultimately led him to Swami Sivananda Saraswati at Rishikesh, who initiated him into the Dashnam Order of Sannyasa on 12th September 1947 on the banks of the Ganges and gave him the name Swami Satyananda Saraswati.

In those early years at Rishikesh, Sri Swamiji immersed himself in guru seva. At that time the ashram was still in its infancy and even the basic amenities such as buildings and toilets were absent. The forests surrounding the small ashram were infested with snakes, scorpions, mosquitoes, monkeys and even tigers. The ashram work too was heavy and hard, requiring Sri Swamiji to toil like a labourer carrying bucket loads of water from the Ganga up to the ashram and digging canals from the high mountain streams down to the ashram many kilometres away in order to store water for constructing the ashram.

Rishikesh was then a small town and all the ashram requirements had to be brought by foot from far away. In addition there were varied duties, including the daily pooja at Vishwanath

Mandir, for which Sri Swamiji would go into the dense forests to collect bael leaves. If anyone fell sick there was no medical care and no one to attend to them. All the sannyasins had to go out for bhiksha or alms as the ashram did not have a mess or kitchen.

Of that glorious time when he lived and served his guru, Sri Swamiji says that it was a period of total communion and surrender to the guru tattwa, whereby he felt that just to hear, speak or see Swami Sivananda was yoga. But most of all his guru's words rang true, for through this dedication and spirit of nishkama seva he gained an enlightened understanding of the secrets of spiritual life and became an authority on Yoga, Tantra, Vedanta, Samkhya and kundalini yoga. Swami Sivananda said of Swami Satyananda, "Few would exhibit such intense vairagya at such an early age. Swami Satyananda is full of Nachiketa vairagya."

Although he had a photographic memory and a keen intellect, and his guru described him as a versatile genius, Swami Satyananda's learning did not come from books and study in the ashram. His knowledge unfolded from within through his untiring seva as well as his abiding faith and love for Swami Sivananda, who told him,"Work hard and you will be purified. You do not have to search for the light, the light will unfold from within you."

In 1956, after spending twelve years in guru seva, Swami Satyananda set out as a wanderer (parivrajaka). Before his departure Swami Sivananda taught him kriya yoga and gave him the mission to "spread yoga from door to door and shore to shore".

As a wandering sannyasin, Swami Satyananda travelled extensively by foot, car, train and sometimes even by camel throughout India, Afghanistan, Burma, Nepal, Tibet, Ceylon and the entire Asian subcontinent. During his sojourns, he met people from all stratas of society and began formulating his ideas on how to spread the yogic techniques. Although his formal education and spiritual tradition was that of Vedanta, the task of disseminating yoga became his movement.

His mission unfolded before him in 1956 when he founded the International Yoga Fellowship Movement with the aim of creating a global fraternity of yoga. Because his mission was revealed to him at Munger, Bihar, he established the Bihar School of Yoga in Munger. Before long his teachings were rapidly spreading throughout the world. From 1963 to 1983, Swami Satyananda took yoga to each and every corner of the world, to people of every caste, creed, religion and nationality. He guided millions of seekers in all continents and established centres and ashrams in different countries.

His frequent travels took him to Australia, New Zealand, Japan, China, the Philippines, Hong Kong, Malaysia, Thailand, Singapore, USA, England, Ireland, France, Italy, Germany, Switzerland, Denmark, Sweden, Yugoslavia, Poland, Hungary, Bulgaria, Slovenia, Russia, Czechoslovakia, Greece, Saudi Arabia, Kuwait, Bahrain, Dubai, Iraq, Iran, Pakistan, Afghanistan, Colombia, Brazil, Uruguay, Chile, Argentina, Santo Domingo, Puerto Rico, Sudan, Egypt, Nairobi, Ghana, Mauritius, Alaska and Iceland. One can easily say that Sri Swamiji hoisted the flag of yoga in every nook and cranny of the world.

Nowhere did he face opposition, resistance or criticism. His way was unique. Well-versed in all religions and scriptures, he incorporated their wisdom with such a natural flair that people of all faiths were drawn to him. His teaching was not just confined to yoga but covered the wisdom of many millenniums.

Sri Swamiji brought to light the knowledge of Tantra, the mother of all philosophies, the sublime truths of Vedanta, the Upanishads and Puranas, Buddhism, Jainism, Sikhism, Zoroastrianism, Islam and Christianity, including modern scientific analysis of matter and creation. He interpreted, explained and gave precise, accurate and systematic explanations of the ancient systems of Tantra and Yoga, revealing practices hitherto unknown.

It can be said that Sri Swamiji was a pioneer in the field of yoga because his presentation had a novelty and freshness. Ajapa japa, antar mouna, pawanmuktasana, kriya yoga and prana vidya are just some of the practices which he introduced in such a methodical and simple manner that it became possible for everyone to delve into this valuable and hitherto inaccessible science for their physical, mental, emotional and spiritual development.

Yoga nidra was Sri Swamiji's interpretation of the tantric system of nyasa. With his deep insight into this knowledge, he was able to realize the potential of this practice of nyasa in a manner which gave it a practical utility for each and every individual, rather than just remaining a prerequisite for worship. Yoga nidra is but one example of his acumen and penetrating insight into the ancient systems.

Sri Swamiji's outlook was inspiring, uplifting as well as in-depth and penetrating. Yet his language and explanations were always simple and easy to comprehend. During this period he authored over eighty books on yoga and tantra which, due to their authenticity, are accepted as textbooks in schools and universities throughout the world. These books have been translated into Italian, German, Spanish, Russian, Yugoslavian, Chinese, French, Greek, Iranian and most other prominent languages of the world.

People took to his ideas and spiritual seekers of all faiths and nationalities flocked to him. He initiated thousands into mantra and sannyasa, sowing in them the seed to live the divine life. He exhibited tremendous zeal and energy in spreading the light of yoga, and in the short span of twenty years Sri Swamiji fulfilled the mandate of his guru.

By 1983, Bihar School of Yoga was well established and recognized throughout the world as a reputed and authentic centre for learning yoga and the spiritual sciences. More than that, yoga had moved out of the caves of hermits and ascetics into the mainstream of society. Whether in hospitals, jails, schools, colleges, business houses, the sporting and fashion arenas, the army or navy, yoga was in demand. Professionals such as lawyers, engineers, doctors, business magnates and professors were incorporating yoga into their lives. So too were the masses. Yoga had become a household word.

Now, at the peak of his accomplishment, having fulfilled his guru's wish, Swami Satyananda renounced all that he created and appointed his successor, Swami Niranjanananda, to continue the work.

In 1988 Sri Swamiji renounced disciples, establishments and institutions, and departed from Munger, never to return again, on a pilgrimage through the siddha teerthas of India, as a mendicant, without any personal belongings or assistance from the ashrams or institutions he had founded.

At Trayambakeshwar, the jyotir linga of Lord Mrityunjaya, his ishta devata, he renounced his garb and lived as an avadhoota, during which time his future place of abode and sadhana were revealed to him.

According to the mandate of his ishta devata, which was revealed to him at the source of the Godavari river near Neel Parbat at Trayambakeshwar (Maharashtra), Swami Satyananda came to the cremation ground of Sati in 1989, and took up residence in Rikhia, on the outskirts of Baba Baidyanath Dham in Deoghar (Jharkhand).

Swami Satyananda has been residing at Rikhia since September 1989. During this period he has undertaken long and arduous sadhanas such as Panchagni and Ashtottar-shat-laksh (108 lakh) mantra purascharana. Here he entered the lifestyle of the Paramahamsas who do not work for their flock and mission alone but have a universal vision. He does not associate with any institutions, nor does he give diksha, upadesh or receive dakshina, but remains in seclusion and sadhana, only on rare occasions coming out to give darshan to devotees who are always yearning for a glimpse of him.

INTERNATIONAL YOGA FELLOWSHIP MOVEMENT (IYFM)

The IYFM is a charitable and philosophical movement founded by Swami Satyananda at Rajnandgaon in 1956 to disseminate the yogic tradition throughout the world. It forms the medium to convey the teachings of Swami Satyananda through its affiliated centres around the world. Swami Niranjanananda is the first Paramacharya of the International Yoga Fellowship Movement.

The IYFM provides guidance, systematized yoga training programs and sets teaching standards for all the affiliated yoga teachers, centres and ashrams. A Yoga Charter to consolidate and unify the humanitarian efforts of all sannyasin disciples, yoga teachers, spiritual seekers and well-wishers was introduced during the World Yoga Convention in 1993. Affiliation to this Yoga Charter enables the person to become a messenger of goodwill and peace in the world, through active involvement in various far-reaching yoga-related projects.

BIHAR SCHOOL OF YOGA (BSY)

The Bihar School of Yoga is a charitable and educational institution founded by Swami Satyananda at Munger in 1963, with the aim of imparting yogic training to all nationalities and to provide a focal point for a mass return to the ancient science of yoga. The Chief Patron of Bihar School of Yoga is Swami Niranjanananda. The original school, Sivanandashram, is the centre for the Munger locality. Ganga Darshan, the new school established in 1981, is situated on a historic hill with panoramic views of the river Ganges.

Yoga Health Management, Teacher Training, Sadhana, Kriya Yoga and other specialized courses are held throughout the year. BSY is also renowned for its sannyasa training and the initiation of female and foreign sannyasins.

BSY provides trained sannyasins and teachers for conducting yoga conventions, seminars and lectures tours around the world. It also contains a comprehensive research library and scientific research centre.

SIVANANDA MATH (SM)

Sivananda Math is a social and charitable institution founded by Swami Satyananda at Munger in 1984, in memory of his guru, Swami Sivananda Saraswati of Rishikesh. The Head Office is now situated at Rikhia in Deoghar district, Jharkhand. Swami Niranjana-nanda is the Chief Patron.

Sivananda Math aims to facilitate the growth of the weaker and underprivileged sections of society, especially rural communities. Its activities include: distribution of free scholarships, clothing, farm animals and food, the digging of tube-wells and construction of houses for the needy, assistance to farmers in ploughing and watering their fields. The Rikhia complex also houses a satellite dish system for providing global information to the villagers.

A medical clinic has been established for the provision of medical treatment, advice and education. Veterinary services are also provided. All services are provided free and universally to everyone, regardless of caste and creed.

YOGA RESEARCH FOUNDATION (YRF)

The Yoga Research Foundation is a scientific, research-oriented institution founded by Swami Satyananda at Munger in 1984. Swami Niranjanananda is the Chief Patron of the foundation.

YRF aims to provide an accurate assessment of the practices of different branches of yoga within a scientific framework, and to establish yoga as an essential science for the development of mankind. At present the foundation is working on projects in the areas of fundamental research and clinical research. It is also studying the effects of yoga on proficiency improvement in various social projects, e.g. army, prisoners, children. These projects are being carried out in affiliated centres worldwide.

YRF's future plans include literary, scriptural, medical and scientific investigations into other little-known aspects of yoga for physical health, mental well-being and spiritual upliftment.

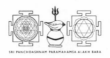

SRI PANCHDASHNAM PARAMAHAMSA ALAKH BARA
(PPAB)

Sri Panchdashnam Paramahamsa Alakh Bara was established in 1990 by Swami Satyananda at Rikhia, Deoghar, Jharkhand. It is a charitable, educational and non-profit making institution aiming to uphold and propagate the highest tradition of sannyasa, namely vairagya (dispassion), tyaga (renunciation) and tapasya (austerity). It propounds the tapovan style of living adopted by the rishis and munis of the vedic era and is intended only for sannyasins, renunciates, ascetics, tapasvis and paramahamsas. The Alakh Bara does not conduct any activities such as yoga teaching or preaching of any religion or religious concepts. The guidelines set down for the Alakh Bara are based on the classical vedic tradition of sadhana, tapasya and swadhyaya, or atma chintan.

Swami Satyananda, who resides permanently at the Alakh Bara, has performed the Panchagni Vidya and other vedic sadhanas, thus paving the way for future paramahamsas to uphold their tradition.

BIHAR YOGA BHARATI (BYB)

Bihar Yoga Bharati was founded by Swami Niranjanananda in 1994 as an educational and charitable institution for advanced studies in yogic sciences. It is the culmination of the vision of Swami Sivananda and Swami Satyananda. BYB is the world's first accredited institution wholly devoted to teaching yoga. A comprehensive yogic education is imparted with provision to grant certificates, diplomas and degrees in yogic studies. BYB offers a complete scientific and yogic education according to the needs of today, through the areas of Yoga Philosophy, Yoga Psychology, Applied Yogic Science and Yogic Ecology.

At present, residential courses of four months are conducted in a gurukul environment, so that along with yoga education, the spirit of seva (selfless service), samarpan (dedication) and karuna (compassion) for humankind is also imbibed by the students.

YOGA PUBLICATIONS TRUST (YPT)

Yoga Publications Trust (YPT) was established by Swami Niranjan-ananda in 2000. It is an organization devoted to the dissemination and promotion of yogic and allied knowledge – psychology (ancient and modern), ecology, medicine, vedic, upanishadic, tantric darshanas, philosophies (Eastern and Western), mysticism and spirituality – nationally and internationally through the distribution of books, magazines, audio and video cassettes and multimedia.

YPT is primarily concerned with publishing textbooks in the areas of yoga philosophy, psychology and applied yogic science, research materials, practice texts and the inspiring talks of eminent spiritual personalities and authors aimed at the upliftment of humanity by means of the eternal yogic knowledge, lifestyle and practice.